MW00993851

THE SCENARIO-PLANNING HANDBOOK

A PRACTITIONER'S GUIDE TO DEVELOPING AND USING SCENARIOS TO DIRECT STRATEGY IN TODAY'S UNCERTAIN TIMES

**Bill Ralston and
Ian Wilson**

THOMSON
™
SOUTH-WESTERN

Australia · Brazil · Canada · Mexico · Singapore · Spain · United Kingdom · United States

THOMSON
SOUTH-WESTERN

The Scenario-Planning Handbook:
A Practitioner's Guide to Developing and Using Scenarios
to Direct Strategy in Today's Uncertain Times

Bill Ralston and Ian Wilson

COPYRIGHT © 2006 by Texere, an imprint of Thomson/South-Western, a part of The Thomson Corporation. Thomson and the Star logo are trademarks used herein under license.

Composed by: Interactive Composition Corporation

Printed in the United States of America by RR Donnelley Crawfordsville, Indiana

2 3 4 5 09 08 07 06
This book is printed on acid-free paper.

ISBN-13: 978-0-324-31285-0
ISBN-10:   0-324-31285-7

Library of Congress Cataloging in Publication Number is available. See page 264 for details.

For more information about our products, contact us at:

Thomson Learning
Academic Resource
Center 1-800-423-0563

Thomson Higher Education
5191 Natorp Boulevard
Mason, Ohio 45040
USA

ABOUT THE AUTHORS

BILL RALSTON   **IAN WILSON**

Two scenario-planning experts—both former SRI International scenario-planning practice leaders—lay out comprehensively, for the first time, their methodology, techniques, and experience for using scenario planning to make important strategic decisions in the face of an uncertain future.

DEDICATION

Every book owes its existence and quality to more than the efforts of its authors. This book is no exception. We gratefully acknowledge the debt we owe to:

- Pierre Wack of Royal Dutch Shell and Tom Mandel of SRI International, who served as our gurus and led the way
- The many clients and colleagues who shared their knowledge and ideas with us, turning our projects into learning experiences
- Our wives, Barbara and Adrianne, who have offered encouragement and support throughout the long gestation period of this book

PREFACE

In an age of uncertainty, many executives and planners in both the private and public sectors have begun to see the need to conduct strategy development, planning, and decision making with a focus on the external environment and its attendant uncertainties. They are attracted to the promise and possibilities that lie in the scenario-planning approach but are deterred by what they see as its complexity and demands. They understand that scenarios are a lot more than just another planning tool. Scenarios challenge our traditional ways of thinking about the future and the threats and opportunities it presents. Scenarios demand a greater tolerance for ambiguity. And they require a radical change in strategic management and culture.

A number of excellent books and articles have been written about scenarios and their role in strategic planning and decision making, starting with Pierre Wack's two *Harvard Business Review* articles published in the 1980s about Royal Dutch Shell's use of scenarios, and Peter Schwartz's book *The Art of the Long View,* published in 1991. More recently, scenarios have received excellent treatment in Arie de Geus's book, *The Living Company;* in Gill Ringland's *Scenario Planning: Managing for the Future;* in Kees van der Heijden's *Scenarios: The Art of Strategic Conversation;* and in Liam Fahey's and Robert Randall's book of collected essays *Learning from the Future: Competitive Foresight Scenarios.* All of these focus on the need for scenarios in decision making, explain what scenarios are and are not, and discuss where they are used to the greatest benefit.

In contrast, our book is for managers who want to use scenarios more effectively to help their organizations realize the benefits they offer. It is for managers who face an array of problems in developing and using scenarios in their organizations and who want to know, "How should I go about doing things?" Our book takes its shape and meaning from the experience not only of the authors but also of all the managers who have struggled with developing decision-focused scenarios for their organizations.

Over the years we have interacted with hundreds of managers who were convinced of the importance of using scenarios to help them make strategic decisions. But most of them, after reading many of the books and articles like the ones mentioned above, were still not certain how to put the concepts into practice. They said, "Scenarios are definitely what we need to support our strategic decision making, but how exactly do we go about developing them—with senior management involved—so they meet our needs? What steps should we take to instill the practice of using scenarios in the organization? How can we integrate the results in such areas as strategic planning, capital budgeting, and marketing? How do we work our way round the many barriers to scenario thinking? What does it take to get started?"

Because applying scenarios is so complicated, the managers responsible for creating them will want to learn about others' attempts, experiences, and lessons. The more detailed and clear we can be about how to develop scenarios effectively, the lower the barrier will be for organizations to apply scenarios to major decisions or to use them for the first time. Our goal is to develop scenario practitioners so that they can bring challenging scenarios of the future to life; manage the critical collaboration of experts, thinkers, and decision makers; and reveal the important issues that need to be addressed.

Our aim in writing this book, therefore, is to reach out to these individuals and provide them with a road map for creating effective scenarios. We aim to guide them through the intricacies of introducing scenarios into the strategy-development, planning, and decision-making systems, and, most particularly, to help them understand what changes are required in an organization's strategic-planning system and culture if the full benefit of scenarios is to be obtained.

As we have noted, the foundation of this book is the insight and experience we have gained from helping corporations and other organizations in many fields around the world make major strategic decisions using scenarios. For more than 25 years, we have specialized in developing and applying scenario-planning approaches and techniques through our overlapping careers at SRI International (formerly Stanford Research Institute) and related SRI subsidiaries and spin-offs, and in that time we have experienced all the common and many of the uncommon issues related to the use of scenario planning.

We describe in detail the step-by-step approach that has worked for us in hundreds of assignments. The approach we have evolved provides the means for managers to address the complexities of their external environments in their strategy development and execution, to take into account the important trends and emerging issues of concern, to explore the spectrum of new strategic opportunities, to see the strategic choices for the business in clear terms, and to accomplish all this in doable steps and in a reasonable time frame. Equally important, we believe that our step-by-step approach to scenario planning can and will lead to those special moments of understanding, insight, and conviction that are so needed for strategies to be adopted, communicated, and well executed by management teams in just about any environment of uncertainty.

TABLE OF CONTENTS

PART 1

THE ROLE OF SCENARIOS

This is principally a "how-to" book, a handbook on how to develop and use scenarios to guide strategic decision making in uncertain times. However, before describing a step-by-step approach to this methodology, Part 1 seeks to establish the conceptual and practical foundations on which the methodology is based.

Thus, Chapter 1 grounds the need for scenarios on the pervasive uncertainty that marks our times. It argues that while traditional responses—improved forecasting capability, better monitoring, greater flexibility—are needed and commendable, they are inadequate to meet the full extent of this challenge. What is needed is a system geared to speculate not only about "the future," but about a range of possible futures.

Chapter 2 then takes this argument a step further by defining more specifically what scenarios are, and are not, for senior managers. Well-developed scenarios make their main contribution to future success by enabling managers to gain some level of control over their situation, to transform uncertainty from a threat to a source of competitive advantage. The scenarios force the managers to get their arms around the issues, to engage in "rehearsals of the future," and so be better prepared for whatever the future may bring.

There is considerable variety in approaches to the development and use of scenarios, including the so-called "objective/normative" and "subjective/intuitive" models. However, the model that we use here is the Stanford Research Institute (SRI) "intuitive-logic" approach that combines many of the features of both of the other models. It is this composite approach, involving 18 discrete steps, that forms the structure for the central portion of this book.

Finally, in Chapter 4, we present a case study that outlines in detail the development and use of scenarios by the Finnish mobile communications company, Nokia, to deal with the problem of business growth. The detail that such a case study makes possible will, we hope, give the reader a better sense of the planning and flow of the overall scenario-planning process.

CHAPTER 1

INTRODUCTION

Grappling with Uncertainty in Developing Strategy

"However good our futures research may be, we shall never be able to escape from the ultimate dilemma that all our knowledge is about the past, and all our decisions are about the future."

When one of the authors of this book first expressed this fact publicly—at the 1975 annual meeting of the American Association for the Advancement of Science (AAAS)[1]—he thought that this statement was indeed an obvious and accepted fact, not just an opinion. For the preceding eight years, he had been working in what we would now call the "futures research" field and had become convinced that our evident inability to forecast the future (in any major or meaningful way) was due not so much to a lack of effort or failure of methodology as to the inherent nature of the material we were handling. The future is, for the most part, not only unknown: It is unknowable.[2] The decision maker's dilemma, therefore, is how best to commit to a course of action in the absence of knowledge about the future.

Our author was surprised, therefore, by the volume and strength of the reaction—both pro and con—to this (he thought) simple statement. Beginning with the discussion period following his presentation, there was a barrage of comments either praising his honesty and powers of observation or berating his obtuseness and pessimism. Clearly he had hit a sensitive nerve.

Planning in an Uncertain World

We should realize that the fundamental issue here, and the main source of contention, was how senior managers involved with strategy should deal with uncertainty. In many organizations, strategic planning is organized on the premise that it is possible to plan for and forecast the future. And indeed

---

[1] The quotation is taken from a presentation by Ian Wilson on "Societal Change and the Planning Process," given at the annual meeting of the AAAS in New York City, January 31, 1975.

[2] This remains true even though there are certain elements of the future that are, in Pierre Wack's apt phrase, "predetermined" [see the identification of these elements in Chapter 15]—for example, the predictable movement of population age groups through successive age brackets. We know, for instance, that there will be a marked increase in the ranks of the U.S. retirement population, starting around 2010, as the "baby boom" population reaches age 65.

the pace and scope of change in much of the last century was such that this was a reasonable proposition. If this premise is no longer valid in most industries in an age of uncertainty, how does, or should, one plan?

Conceptually, there are at least three different answers to this question. The traditionalist response is, in effect, to throw more resources at the problem: Increase our data gathering and analysis, improve our forecasting capability, use better tools (and the computer) to expand our understanding of the working of complex systems—and (perhaps the favorite remedy) establish a new staff function to take care of the problem. The underlying assumption in this response is that the problem lies in the imperfection of our knowledge rather than in the unknowability of the future. The solution, it is argued, lies in increasing the reach and accuracy of our knowledge.

This reaction to uncertainty—"Let's use a bigger hammer"—is how most people respond to new problems: Use the old solutions, but in a better way. It can take a while before the recognition comes that something different is required.

Others concede that uncertainty is inevitable, but they go on to argue that any forecasting or speculation about the future is largely a waste of time and effort. They believe that the external environment is now so complex that the range of future patterns of change and possible outcomes cannot be identified or predicted. They consider themselves to be the "new realists," and their message can be summed up as follows: Given that uncertainty is both inevitable and unpredictable, our best way of dealing with it is to monitor for the early signs of change, then respond rapidly to stabilize or disrupt the new pattern, or even create the conditions for a favorable pattern. Now, while monitoring for early signs of change and being flexible to act quickly in response are admirable—indeed, essential—qualities to develop in an age of rapid change, they do not, by themselves, constitute a strategy. They say nothing about what we need to become as an organization; where we want to go; and how we want to get there. Even for complex environments, these are questions that we must strive to answer, if there is to be any degree of coherence in our strategy.

So we come to a third response that planning can make to uncertainty. We can speculate about not just "the future," but a *range of possible futures* that might arise from the uncertain course of the forces of change. And then, within the boundaries of these alternative possibilities, we can develop a strategy that is focused but resilient, specific but flexible. This approach has come to be known as "scenario-based strategy" and is the topic of this book.

What's in This Book

So while the book does deal with the basic theory, character, and uses of scenarios, it is principally a "how-to" book, a handbook for developing and using scenarios in a strategic decision-making context. With this in mind:

- *The book is organized mainly around clearly defined steps or stages in the development and use of scenarios, rather than around, say, differing theories and concepts or the historical development of the methodology.* These topics have already been well covered in the existing literature, as a review of the bibliography at the end of this volume will attest.
- *The book sets out the purpose of each step in the process*—Why do it?
- *It sets out the objectives of each step*—What is to be accomplished?
- *It specifies the tasks to be performed (and, if appropriate, who is responsible for them) and the resources (including time) required to attain these objectives*—How to do it?
- *It illustrates how these tasks can be performed, using examples drawn from past projects.*
- *It points out pitfalls—and how to avoid them.*
- *It describes the outputs and results of each step*—What are the deliverables?
- *It provides a lead-in to the next step.*

In short, the book provides the would-be practitioner with needed step-by-step guidance to complete a scenario-planning project successfully—*where success is measured not by a provocative report and "interesting" insights into the future but by changes in executive decision making and the creation of a more confident, flexible, and adaptive organization.*

It is true, for instance, that scenarios can be defined simply as "stories of alternative futures"; but we need to probe more deeply into their precise nature (what they are—and are not), how they differ from traditional forecasting, and how they fit into and change the strategic-planning system. Chapter 2 sets forth the context of why scenarios are needed and their organizational purpose. Chapter 3 then aims to pinpoint more precisely the nature of scenarios, their intellectual underpinnings, and methodology of development.

Make no mistake about it: Scenarios require (and, if they take root, they cause) a radical change in the planning and decision-making culture. That is why it is so essential to have a clear understanding of what scenarios are attempting to accomplish before embarking on a process which could change, to a potentially remarkable degree, the ways in which the organization thinks about, and plans for, the future. As Pierre Wack, the late guru of Royal Dutch Shell's scenario planning, so aptly put it, "if we want to make better strategic decisions, we need to change our 'mental maps' of the way the world works."

The introductory section of this book concludes in Chapter 4 with an overview of a scenario project we conducted with Nokia, the Finnish mobile communications company. This case study gives the reader a sense of the flow of the total scenario process, supplementing the detailed step-by-step approach described in the following sections.

Parts 2, 3, 4, and 5 then lead the reader and potential scenario planner through the step-by-step process of developing and using scenarios. In Part 2, "Getting Started," the emphasis is on forming the team that is going to drive the transformation (including the roles of outside facilitators and experts) and defining the focus and time horizon for the scenarios. On both points it is critical to get the input, if not the direct involvement, of top management, who, after all, will be the ones who actually use—or ignore—the contribution that the scenarios can make to their decision making. In some of the most successful projects in which we have been involved, the top management team actually was the scenario team. The resulting scenarios were, therefore, the product of their own critical thinking, and so were more easily assimilated into their decision making.

Part 3, "Laying the Environmental-Analysis Foundation," comes to grips with the initial steps in the scenario-development process. And the process begins not as one might think, by plunging into a discussion of uncertainty and forces for change and the differing futures they might create, but rather by getting clarification and agreement on how the scenarios are to be used. The key questions here are: What major strategic decisions do we have to make? And what do we need to know about the future in order to make them? The future is simply too complex, too multidimensional, for any one set of scenarios to encompass everything. To drive change—certainly, to be used—scenarios need to be "decision-focused," to use the term we stress at SRI and its associated subsidiaries and spin-offs.[3]

Having thus established the key strategic decision or decisions that we wish to support with the scenario-development process, we can better

---

[3] SRI refers to organizations related to SRI International, formerly known as Stanford Research Institute. The authors worked together at SRI International for a number of years; and Bill Ralston currently is a board member and officer of SRI Consulting Business Intelligence, the consulting and business research spin-off of SRI International.

determine what we need to know about the future in order to make this decision. If, for instance, the decision involves the strategy for introducing a new consumer product, then clearly our scenarios need to deal with, among other things, trends in consumer demographics and lifestyles, disposable income, and savings patterns. But these trends are of less importance if our sphere of interest and decision making lies in selecting the optimum portfolio of technologies that a company should develop. Our objective is to construct what one might call a "conceptual model," a decision maker's view of the dynamic forces shaping the future of whatever arena we are interested in. With such a model in mind, we can see more clearly the *total* pattern of events and trends, their interrelationships and cross-impacts, and their implications for our business.

There is another critically important reason for staying focused on a decision and what we need to know in order to make it. It dramatically increases the likelihood that the scenarios will actually be used (because they are linked to an important pending strategic decision) rather than set aside as an "interesting" but largely ineffective exercise. As we discuss later on, the inertia of most existing planning cultures will tend to resist the introduction of scenario-based thinking. Thus, success in introducing this new approach depends on initially linking it as tightly as possible to the needs of the current system.

Parts 4 and 5 then take the reader through a detailed methodology, first to construct the scenarios, and then to use them in the development of strategy. This is the core of the book and provides answers to the major questions raised by the scenario process, including:

- *How do we sort through the many forces and uncertainties to determine what's relevant or not?*
- *How should we develop a structure—an "organizing principle"—for the scenarios that satisfies the need for both clear focus and broad coverage?* There has to be some logical basis for the scenarios that we select and the way in which we develop them.
- *How many scenarios should we develop to cover the range of possible futures?*
- *How should we capture and use the organization's conventional wisdom about the future?*
- *How do we make the scenario descriptions interesting and compelling to experienced executives?*
- *What is the right balance between narrative plot and quantification?*
- *Should we assign probabilities to the scenarios?*

- *How much time and effort will be needed to construct these decision-focused scenarios?*
- *How do we use the scenarios to develop superior insights about strategic opportunities, strategic choices, and future decision making?*
- *How do we make sure the business uses the scenarios in the future to make decisions and acts in response to changing scenario forces?*

It is these last two questions that are the most perplexing and demanding, but also the ones to which the "decision-focused" approach to scenario development provides the clearest answers and the most useful guidance. While it is true that there is no single "best way" of using scenarios to make strategic decisions, there are some guiding principles, which we explore in later chapters.

Finally, in Part 6, the last major section of the book, we deal with the broader issues of the relationship between scenarios and the planning and decision-making culture of the organization. We have already noted that introducing scenarios into the planning system requires a change in the planning and decision-making culture—from forecasting to speculation, from force to resilience, from control to learning, from linear to circular patterns of thinking. Without this culture shift, our experience shows that scenario planning will soon succumb to the planning system's demands for "forecasts" rather than "alternative futures." This section deals, therefore, with the actions required for creating a "learning culture," one that tolerates ambiguity and uncertainty, that learns its way into the future, and that values consideration of a broad range of options before making a strategic commitment.

The SRI Model

Over the past 40 years since Herman Kahn first popularized the term "scenarios," a variety of approaches to scenario planning have been explored by companies, consultants, and academics. However, our objective in writing this book has not been to review the evolution of techniques in this arena, but rather to explore one specific approach in sufficient detail to provide a road map and detailed methodology that any organization could follow.

The approach we describe is the so-called "intuitive logics approach" that was developed in parallel by Royal Dutch Shell and SRI International during the 1970s and subsequently adopted by Global Business Network. This approach is "intuitive" in the sense that it builds on mental models, "soft" inputs, and the hunches and assessments of uncertainty by the scenario participants. But it is also logical, formal, and disciplined in its use of "hard data," analysis and a structured approach to the task.

Direct participation of the decision makers in the process puts the contribution of staff and outside experts in proper perspective; places responsibility where it should be; and ensures that the decision makers will truly understand, own, and so be more likely to act on the implications of the scenarios.

This approach encourages—indeed, depends upon—free and open discussion of differences of opinion about the dynamics of the business environment, uncertainties, and "wild cards." In this way, it encourages both individual and organizational learning.

Because it relies wholly on mental rather than computer "modeling," this approach has a good chance—perhaps the best chance of any approach—of describing alternative futures that will be both realistic and challenging to executives, thus influencing their mental maps of the future.

Because it is not tied to computer algorithms (which are, necessarily, reflections of the past), this approach is more likely to engender the sort of lateral thinking that is needed to anticipate future surprises and major "inflection points."

In our description of the process, and in the examples that we cite, it is perhaps inevitable that we may seem to suggest that scenario planning is only for corporations. Nothing could be farther from the truth. While the majority of our consulting assignments has been with corporations, we have also worked with hospitals, universities, not-for-profit organizations, and governmental agencies on alternative futures confronting these organizations. Indeed, the initial scenarios project that SRI undertook was for the U.S. Office of Education. And there can be little doubt that the power and uncertainty of the forces reshaping these organizations are every bit as great as those confronting corporations.

A Final Thought

As you launch into reading this book, be mindful of one thing. For all its usefulness in guiding you through the complexities of scenario planning, the most that this book can give you is a structured process, a framework for strategic thinking, the lessons to be derived from the experience of those who have pioneered this arena. It cannot, by itself, give you the new insight into the future, the inspiration that leads to an "Aha!" discovery, the vision that will reshape your strategy. Those qualities can come only from experience and from within.

CHAPTER 2

STRATEGIC DECISION MAKING AND THE PURPOSE OF SCENARIOS

Why Are They Needed?

At this point the question inevitably arises, "Why do we need scenarios? They sound very complicated and theoretical—and end up not telling us what the future is going to be. Isn't strategic decision making, based on a set of market assumptions and traditional forecasting—or something like it— still sufficient for our needs?" Given humanity's long history of searching, without much success, for certainty in seeking to know the future, we should not be surprised at this doubting and hesitant approach to scenarios. From the Delphic oracle through augury, tarot, and the crystal ball to the methodologies of the professional forecaster, we have developed a succession of tools in our efforts to know the future so we can make better decisions. All have failed to penetrate the veil between us and what is to come: None has given us the certainty we seek. As the old saying goes, "Those who live by the crystal ball are doomed to die of eating broken glass."

Another hard truth that we must face is that the problem of predicting the future has become more, not less, intractable despite the increased so-phistication of our forecasting tools. There has been a change in the charac-ter of change itself: With every passing year it becomes more rapid, more complex. Consider, for instance, the simple fact that more people around the world are working at the task of creating change, especially technological change. And with a large and growing population, even a small percentage can represent a substantial number and have a measurable impact on society. Then, too, we have witnessed in our lifetime a radical compression of the development time for new products and new systems, from their original invention to their diffusion through society.

We are, manifestly, dealing with more powerful technologies than ever before. Nuclear power, information technology, and the still-young biomed-ical revolution and nanotechnology have already had, and will continue to have, a more pervasive influence on human life than any previous technolo-gies in human history. The increasing scale of so many of our projects—not only in these technologies but also in engineering projects like China's Three Gorges Dam—also ensures that more people will be affected more deeply by changes that we set in motion. Above all, we should note that it is not just economic and technological change that affects, or afflicts, us, but social, political, and cultural change, too. There is, in short, virtually no aspect of our society that is unchanging.

And with every increase in the speed, complexity, and pervasiveness of change, there has been—and continues to be—a corresponding decrease in the accuracy and utility of traditional "single-point" forecasting (i.e., making a set of assumptions about external forces and projecting a specific outcome for a given factor at a specific point in the future). Even in such a sophisticated field as economic forecasting, we are constantly reminded of our inability to project, with any degree of accuracy, such "hard" factors as Gross National Product (GNP), productivity, or inflation.

But developing better forecasts is not the most important challenge to management: It's making the decisions about strategy in the context of all that uncertainty and change. In what direction should the organization move? What investments should be made now even though they probably won't bear fruit for many years? What is the strategy that enhances the organization's flexibility in the face of disruptions and changes in the external environment and that allows it to seize emerging opportunities and avoid the threats? How do you identify the many possible strategies that could succeed, and, after sorting through the different alternatives, select the one that leads to the most value? How do you come up with innovative ideas? How do you look broadly for the possibilities? How do you get the smartest thinkers of the organization involved? How do you develop strong passion and enthusiasm for the results?

For several reasons, many organizations stumble badly in how they deal with those issues:

- *They have poor means for linking strategic thinking to possible changes in the external environment.* Strategic decision making is a complex and amorphous process with innumerable information flows about internal and external issues, many participants with different incentives at several levels, and multiple subprocesses providing input and support. A critical problem in the process is that it's highly inefficient in aligning the organization's information, knowledge, and understanding about the external environment with the thinking about strategic alternatives and what the organization should do. There's typically no structured means for aligning the external with the decision.
- *They lack a common language about the marketplace and its future.* While it's possible that everyone in the organization could have the same understanding of the external environment, it's our experience that

they're usually different, and often very different. This is because of the complexity of the external environment, the different individuals' experiences and contacts with the environment, what issues everyone was last exposed to through their reading or entertainment, and so on. Without a common set of assumptions about the external environment and the possible futures, teams end up selecting strategies based more on the power and persuasiveness of the different team members than through agreement and consensus.

- *They lack innovative thinking.* Organizations often consider only one idea for their strategy of the future, which is usually an extension of the current strategy. This occurs because the decision makers either believe strongly in that strategy or don't want to change their thinking on the important causal dynamics of the marketplace. It's much safer and easier to justify what is already in place, even if the organization isn't performing well at the moment. Like incumbents in politics, much has already been invested in the current approach, and managers would be perceived as failures if the current strategy were abandoned or altered significantly. So the process adopted to develop the strategy often doesn't include exploration for new, value-creating ideas but simply begins with already defined alternatives.

- *They lack time or process.* Organizations often can't find the time to develop a long-term strategy because key decision makers are focused on meeting short-term goals and resolving current crises. The decision makers are unable or unwilling to divert their attention to long-term planning activities, particularly as a group. As a result, strategy-development processes are adapted to fit the limited time and resources available, resulting in short periodic discussions of the issues and alternatives ("Let's devote three hours at the end of October's monthly meeting to define our strategic direction for the next three years").

- *They have no leverage from the existing knowledge of the organization.* In many organizations, strategies seem simply to emerge from on high. The business unit leader or CEO announces the new direction of the organization without input or advice from lower-level managers and experts, and little explanation is given about how the strategy was chosen, what initiatives will be needed to execute it, what assumptions about market dynamics were behind the strategy's selection, and how things will be adjusted as the future unfolds.

To develop a new strategy for the future, organizations need to overcome these issues and apply a process that takes into account the possibilities of the future, that involves decision makers and critical thinkers of the organization, that seeks initially to explore the range of strategy possibilities before making a decision, that uses objective criteria and a transparent strategy selection process, and that communicates widely the results and how they were obtained widely.

Therefore, a process is needed—and we believe it should be scenario planning—to assist us in our longer-term strategy decision making. In place of single-point forecasting, we should focus our efforts on developing a deep understanding of the dynamics of change, and of the multiple possible futures to which they might lead. In place of making incremental improvements to our current strategy, we should take advantage of the changes that will come in the future and ensure our long-term prosperity. These are the tasks that scenarios are admirably equipped to perform.

Does this mean, then, that forecasting and short-term planning as we have known them are no longer useful—that indeed they may be counterproductive, misleading us into believing that there is greater certainty in our projections than is justified by the facts, and greater value in staying with the current strategy than is perceived by the marketplace? Almost certainly forecasts and short-term planning will continue to be much-used processes in our planning armory. For one thing, we need traditional single-point forecasting to describe the near-term future and provide a set of assumptions as the basis for our short-term planning. We are unlikely, for instance, to find it productive or feasible to develop scenarios covering just the next six months or year. The time and effort involved in developing those scenarios would be entirely disproportionate to the limited benefits they might convey. For another thing, we need short-term planning to set our operational priorities, define our tasks, and help us focus the organization's resources in the field.

There are always elements of strategic planning that need to be focused and decisive, but they should never constitute the entire process. Furthermore, as many point out, a strong strategic focus provides the means to specialize and develop advantages for competing in dynamic environments. And that is what makes them so dangerous. *Sooner or later the forecasts will fail when they are needed most:* in anticipating major shifts in the business environment that make focused strategies obsolete. Scenario planning, on the other hand, is most useful when such shifts are most threatening and uncertainty is at its peak.

The fact of the matter is that no single methodology will suffice to guide us through the confusing maze of change that confronts us. We need to examine strategy alternatives in the context of different possible outcomes. We need monitoring to keep track of the multifarious forces that shape our environment, and forecasting to project where these trends may lead us in the near term. We need a sensitive scanning system to alert us to the appearance of new and unforeseen forces that may channel the future in unexpected directions. And we need scenarios to give us a sense of the possibilities—the opportunities as well as the threats—that this uncertain future may present to us.

What Are "Scenarios"?

In recent years, the term "scenario" has become part of our everyday language. We encounter it virtually everywhere—in political campaigns and sports reporting, in international relations and technology forecasts, in societal analyses and environmental predictions. But its definition is vague, varied, and imprecise. In most cases, the term simply refers to a chain of events that unfolds to an imagined conclusion.

As we use the term in this book, however, we have in mind a more precise meaning which we need to define at the outset. To begin with, in the simplest and most straightforward terms, we could say that scenarios are simply "stories of possible futures." The term "scenario" is, after all, taken from the world of film and theater, so it is fitting that we should stress the narrative and dramatic qualities of the term even when it is translated to the world of business or other organizations. Scenario planning is or should be designed to help us see the present and the future as a continually evolving story.

As an aside but an important one, we should emphasize our use of the plural—"scenarios." Because the future is inherently uncertain, we need to consider a number of alternative futures (scenarios) if we are to cover the full range of possibilities that our planning must be prepared to confront.

Before moving on, it is worthwhile to pause to consider a number of implications of this definition. First, it underscores the *narrative* quality of scenarios. They should be designed to have a plot and a story line, tracing trends and developments, cause and effect, the interrelationships among events. Storytelling has been a powerful communications tool throughout history: Scenarios seek to use this tool in a new context—organizational planning, strategy development, and decision making.

Second, scenarios (like stories) seek to take a *holistic* point of view. Unlike trend analysis, which focuses on the progression of individual trends, or cross-impact analysis, which assesses the impact of one trend on another, scenarios focus on the total picture. Scenarios may, indeed, incorporate some form of trend analysis or cross-impact analysis in the process of developing their "stories"; but their aim is to depict the total gestalt of the future—which is, after all, the way in which we encounter the future with all its

---

BOX 2-1
Scenarios: What They Are and Are Not

Scenarios Are Not . . .	They Are . . .
Predictions	Descriptions of alternative plausible futures
Variations around a midpoint base case	Significantly, often structurally, different views of the future
"Snapshots" of endpoints (e.g., the market in 2010)	"Movies" of the evolving dynamics of the future
Generalized views of feared or desired futures	Specific "decision-focused" views of the future
Products of outside futurists	Results of management insight and perceptions

---

currents and crosscurrents. So scenarios should be encapsulations of the total picture that may confront the organization.

Scenarios, then, are stories in the sense that they describe the evolving dynamics of interacting forces rather than the static picture of a single end-point future (see Box 2-1). The futures they describe are possible and plausible: They are not posed as hypothetical extremes—utopia and dystopia. And, most significantly, they are not simply variations around a midpoint base case (high, medium, and low outcomes of essentially the same forces): They are rooted in views of the future that are based on the working out of structurally different forces.

But even this definition does not clearly or fully spell out the role that scenarios can, and should, play in our planning. We come closer to this goal when we say:

> "Scenarios are frameworks for structuring executives' perceptions about alternative future environments in which their decisions might be played out."

But then we need to parse this definition if we are to discern the full measure of scenarios' contribution to our efforts.

First of all, consider the phrase "scenarios are frameworks for structuring. . . ." In the planning context, scenarios have a specific, purposeful role to play. They are not loosely constructed stories, but carefully defined explorations of the future that planning must address and strategy will have to deal with. The structure needs to be tight enough to give discipline, coherence, and relevance to the final product, but loose enough to be able to embrace the creative, and sometimes unconventional, insights of the executives and planners who will develop and use the scenarios.

Next consider the phrase "... *executives' perceptions*...." Because scenarios (as we define them) are intended to be used as key frameworks for strategy development, it is vitally important that they reflect the thinking of the executives who will ultimately be responsible for developing and executing the strategy. This should not be taken to mean that the scenarios should simply reflect the current conventional thinking in the executive suite about the future. Far from it. As Pierre Wack insisted, scenarios should be designed to challenge, rather than reinforce, executives' "mental maps of the way the world works." But it does mean that the decision makers should understand and accept the reasoning that led to the development and selection of the scenarios if those decision makers are to have sufficient confidence in the final product to use it in their strategic decision making. Executive ownership of the scenarios is, thus, a sine qua non for their effective use.

Next consider the term "... *about alternative future environments*." The emphasis here is on the plural—"alternative futures." To cover what we might term "the envelope of acknowledged uncertainty," we need a set of scenarios, not just one. As a general rule, a set of two to four scenarios is usually sufficient to cover the envelope of uncertainty and act as test beds for strategy development. Any number above this range tends to become unwieldy and counterproductive.

Finally, scenarios should focus on the trends and issues in the environments "... *in which their decisions might be played out*." Although, it is, of course, possible to develop scenarios on a broad topic such as "The Future of the Globalized Economy," scenarios that are to be used in the strategy-development process should be more "decision focused"—that is, they need to concentrate their attention on the key trends and forces that we need to address in making and executing our decisions.

By and large, this approach to scenarios can be said to have all the strengths and all the limitations of a model that depends on the working of the human brain (or collection of brains). It may, for instance, need to be supplemented by computer modeling for the detailed quantification of trends. But it has the inestimable strength of capturing the power of both logic and imagination in creating stories of the future.

Using Uncertainty to Your Advantage

Scenarios make their main contribution to our future success by enabling us to turn uncertainty into a source of advantage. Taking advantage of uncertainty does not, of course, mean eliminating uncertainty; such an outcome is not feasible in our complex, interconnected world in which certainty remains forever a scarce commodity. But scenarios can help us deal with uncertainty (rather than be defeated by it) by teaching us to look at all the possibilities, "think the unthinkable," prepare for the unexpected and even the unlikely (or what we believe to be so), and develop the flexibility, resilience, and speed of response which are the essential winning qualities for any organization caught up in a confusing and rapidly changing environment.

The merits of scenario-based thinking and planning become clearer when we consider the innate qualities of this approach to dealing with uncertainty:

- *To start with, scenarios develop in us an* integrated approach to thinking *about our environment.* They are a practical way of integrating the voluminous, often incomplete, and sometimes contradictory information—both quantitative and qualitative—that bombards us from a variety of sources. They enable us to develop "pictures of the future" which we can carry in our minds and apply in a wide variety of situations.

- *Scenarios move us toward a* better understanding of the dynamics of change *that we must deal with.* Being forced to acknowledge the possibility of a variety of futures—rather than a single "most likely" future—we have to develop a rationale to explain why the future may follow differing courses. It is not merely a matter of describing different outcomes: Of greater importance is explaining why and how these differing outcomes come about.

- *By examining the trajectories of the various scenarios, we can get some clues as to the timing and nature of* key moments of change—*the points at which, say, one scenario becomes more likely, and another less likely, to become the emerging future.* And this, in turn, enables us to identify the *major leverage points* available to us—that is, the points at which we can take action to start, accelerate, or change strategic initiatives. Timing is so often of the essence in taking initiatives, and scenarios give us clues as to when our intervention is most likely to succeed.

- *The fact that we are examining the consequences of a number of scenarios, rather than those of a single-point forecast, means that we can give consideration to a* fuller range of opportunities and threats. This broadening of our horizon will often suggest new possibilities for our initiatives that we might otherwise have missed.

- *By evaluating the significance of a set of scenarios for an organization, and then engaging in "what if" thinking, we are, in effect, "*rehearsing the future." By anticipating different futures and the initiatives we might take in each case, we can move more rapidly in responding to changes in the environment if and when they occur. A classic case in this sort of anticipatory planning was Royal Dutch Shell's ability to outstrip its competitors in responding to the collapse of oil prices in the late 1980s because its scenarios had already envisaged this possibility and led the company to develop its response well ahead of the event. Most experienced users of scenarios can cite key periods in their organizations when they were ready to respond to disruptive events or discontinous changes and their competitors weren't.

- *A primary objective of scenario planning is to* reduce our vulnerability to surprises *by forcing us to envisage a variety of possible futures and to think through their implications for our organization.* It is unrealistic to believe that we can completely eliminate the element of surprise. But it is entirely possible to structure a set of scenarios that captures a much wider range of outcomes than conventional forecasting ever could. As a result, we are much better prepared to deal with the "slings and arrows of outrageous fortune."

- *As scenarios expand our understanding of the formative forces of the future, so do they increase our ability to perceive a* wider range of strategic options *that the future might present to us.* Each scenario presents us with a set of options, some of which may be opportune only for the conditions of one scenario. But, in total, this exercise will usually produce a larger and more diverse set of options for our evaluation than more traditional forecasting would. Particularly important, of course, are those options which appear in more than one scenario, indicating a greater degree of resilience in that course of action.

- *The strategy that emerges from scenario-based planning should exhibit a greater degree of resilience and flexibility because:*
  - It will have been tested against a set of scenarios, each presenting a different set of conditions that the strategy might encounter;
  - Contingency planning will have developed action plans needed to respond quickly to foreseen possible threats and/or opportunities;

- "Trigger points" will have been established to set contingency plans in motion as quick response to changes in conditions.
- *Scenario-based planning develops a better,* more thorough assessment of risks, *whether of missed opportunities or of developing threats.* Here again, contingency planning plays a critical role in preparing responses to risks foreseen by the scenarios.
- *Scenarios provide a* sound basis for continuous monitoring *of the environment and strategy adjustment.* Once they have been developed and interpreted for their implications for strategy, the scenarios must be tested for validity against the actual course of events as indicated by the output from a trend-monitoring system. Simultaneously, existing scenarios must be alert to the early warning signals of new trends detected by a scanning system that may indicate the need for new scenarios. In this tripartite system (scenarios–monitoring–scanning), scenarios have a critical role to play in providing a holistic frame of reference into which the output of monitoring and scanning can be fitted.
- *Finally, scenarios have the great merit of transparency; the reasoning underlying them, and the insights they provide, are readily available to managers seeking to use them.* (This is especially true, of course, in those cases in which the scenario team and decision makers are one and the same.) It is this quality which enhances both scenarios' communicability and utility in decision making.

A Final Thought

The benefits that virtually any organization can derive from scenario-based planning are, therefore, considerable. But one cautionary note needs to be sounded. For these benefits to be maximized, the decision-making culture as well as the strategic-management system need to be changed. Scenarios are more than a methodology: They represent a different way of looking at the external environment, a different approach to strategic planning and decision making. As we have already noted, and as we shall discuss in greater detail in Part 6, the introduction of scenarios requires that we change the emphasis in our thinking "from forecasting to speculation, from force to resilience, from control to learning, from linear to circular patterns of thinking" and develop the decision-making skills to examine multiple alternatives across scenarios, assess future risks and rewards, make choices under uncertainty, and adapt strategies and plans in response to future trends and events.

CHAPTER 3

THE SCENARIO-PLANNING METHODOLOGY

When we talk about scenarios in our everyday conversation, most of us do so loosely and casually. We put more emphasis on our own intuition and imagination than on discipline and formal structure in our descriptions of the future. Most often, therefore, the resulting scenarios reflect only our personal knowledge and prejudices rather than a more objective and comprehensive assessment of future trends and possibilities.

If, however, we aim to use scenarios more formally as a framework for decision making and strategy development in our organizations, we need to adopt a more disciplined approach. For one thing, if scenarios are to "push the envelope of uncertainty" and reflect the fullest range of possible futures, they need diverse inputs framed in a common structure. And, if they are to be communicated and used widely throughout an organization, they need a common language to ensure understanding and promote action.

As we note in Box 3-1, and further amplify in the bibliography, there is a considerable variety of approaches to the development and use of scenarios. Our experience has been focused predominantly on the SRI model, which is an "intuitive-logics" approach, and it is this experience and model which provide the substance of this book. As with any scenarios methodology, this intuitive-logics approach has its benefits and its limitations. Among its principal benefits is the fact that the methodology is completely "transparent." The step-by-step reasoning is laid out for critical examination, with no intervening "black box" or computer modeling. This makes for easier communication, understanding, and discussion of the scenarios and their strategic implications. Managers can pinpoint exactly where, and why, they agree or disagree with the reasoning.

The essence of this structured approach is captured in Figure 3-1 (Scenario Development: The SRI Model). Before proceeding to a step-by-step description of this model's implementation, we should emphasize three key elements that give this approach its character and strength:

1. The *starting point* for this process is agreement on the uses to which the scenarios will be put—the decision focus. We are not building a system

BOX 3-1

The Range of Scenario Methodologies

Without getting involved in a detailed survey of scenario methodologies, we can say that, in general, they exist along two dimensions: objective versus normative, and analytical versus intuitive.

Objective Versus Normative Approaches

The terms "objective" and "normative" are not perfectly descriptive, but they have traditional meanings in futures research. Objective scenarios evaluate the future external environment—trends, uncertainties, "break points," and so on—and then seek, through analyses of implications, to help an organization shift its strategy or improve its decisions to take the impacts of that environment into account.

Normative scenarios take the opposite point of view. They ask questions about alternative futures in light of company visions and points of leverage for the business in the external environment.

Characteristically, objective approaches treat the external environment as an uncontrollable factor, whereas normative approaches assume that a company can influence the external environment significantly through its actions. Both approaches have merit, and in practice, in comprehensive scenario planning, both kinds of thinking occur. But the starting point is quite different in the two approaches.

Analytical Versus Intuitive Approaches

Analytical scenario approaches use formal models or simulations to develop both broad alternative scenarios and their details. Intuitive scenario approaches focus more on qualitative visions of the future that reflect the "mental maps" of the people developing and using the scenarios. They, too, may have considerable analytical detail, but intuition plays a greater role in their initial development.

Again, in practice, most scenario work involves both approaches. However, their starting points are quite different.

A Balanced Approach

The trend in scenario methodology is toward more balanced approaches that incorporate both dimensions. Most futurists recognize the complementary values of intuition, vision, analysis, leverage, and truly uncontrollable externalities. And the field is likely, therefore, to continue to move toward richer methods that draw on the most useful set of tools for particular scenario issues and organizational cultures.

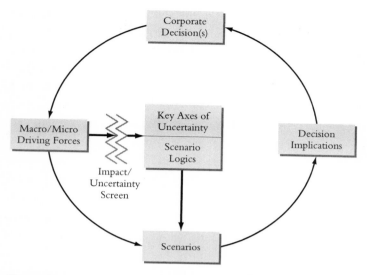

Figure 3-1   Scenario Development: The SRI Model

that needs to be continually fed with more and more input; rather, we are applying a process to help us make important decisions. It is not sufficient to say that we are interested in "the future." We need to be more specific as to *which aspects* of the future concern us, and what use we intend to make of this information. In effect, we should ask ourselves, "What is the key strategic decision confronting us? and what do we need to know about the future in order to make this decision?" By stressing this *"decision focus"* for the scenarios, we define the opportunities and circumstances in which scenarios should be developed.

2. The *heart* of the scenario process is in identifying the key axes of uncertainty confronting the organization and the alternative "logics" of how major driving forces could play out. For example, one obvious axis of uncertainty confronting most oil and gas companies today is the future cost and availability of crude. At one end of this axis, a heightened commitment to alternative energy sources tends, logically, to moderate increases in demand and so ease the upward pressures on price and supply. At the other end, a more global economic development policy tends to accelerate demand throughout the developing and developed countries, and so heighten price and supply problems. "Axis logics" are thus central, both literally and figuratively, to this approach to scenario development, so a thorough and complete

understanding of what this term means and entails is a prerequisite for success (see pp. 116 for a more detailed exposition of these terms).

3. The *conclusion* of the process comes not with the completion of the scenarios per se, but rather with the application of the implications to the decision making under way. Indeed, frequently one consequence of the scenario process is a complete rethinking of the decision itself—or of the strategic goals associated with it. The overall process has, therefore, elements that are in some sense circular and iterative rather than linear and singular. We find ourselves constantly reviewing our assumptions, re-evaluating our logics, replaying our decision alternatives against the possible futures.

At the outset we should stress two caveats that govern our approach to the scenario development process. First, we make a clear distinction between what we might call the "mechanisms" of the process and the knowledge, beliefs, and perspectives that are inspired by it. Indeed, using a structured approach to scenario planning has much in common with learning to speak a second language. In the early stages of learning, the would-be conversationalist practices speaking somewhat mechanically, uses grammar rules to create words and sentences, and uses carefully developed scripts to communicate descriptions, thoughts, and wants. It is only later, after gaining confidence and mastering the grammar and vocabulary, that a more fluent speaker moves beyond this mechanistic approach and communicates spontaneously with greater understanding and clarity.

So it is with scenario planning. Initially new practitioners rigorously, almost mechanistically, follow a step-by-step approach such as we describe here. In the process they tend to focus more on the structure of the process and the data inputs than on the meaning, insight, and spirit of the scenarios. With practice, experience, and good planning, however, structure becomes the means to an end, and the emphasis shifts—as it should do—toward generating the insight and heightened awareness of the strategic choices being made. The experienced management team can then "rehearse" its futures thoroughly and imaginatively and act decisively in response to changing events.

A second caveat attaches to the number of steps that we describe for the process. In the description that follows, we have identified 18 discrete steps that are involved (see Box 3-2), from laying the groundwork for the process through the actual development of the scenarios, to aligning the results to the rest of the strategy-development activities and setting up a continuous

BOX 3-2
A Step-by-Step Approach to Developing and Using Scenarios

Getting Started

Step 1:   Developing the case for scenarios

Step 2:   Gaining executive understanding, support, and participation

Step 3:   Defining the "decision focus"

Step 4:   Designing the process

Step 5   Selecting the facilitator

Step 6   Forming the scenario team

Laying the Environmental-Analysis Foundation

Step 7:   Gathering available data, views, and projections

Step 8:   Identifying and assessing the key decision factors

Step 9:   Identifying the critical forces and drivers (the dynamics of "the way the world might work")

Step 10:   Conducting focused research on key issues, forces, and drivers

Creating the Scenarios

Step 11   Assessing the importance and predictability or uncertainty of forces and drivers

Step 12:   Identifying key "axes of uncertainty" (forces and drivers with high importance and high uncertainty) to serve as logics and structure of the scenarios

Step 13:   Selecting scenario logics to cover the "envelope of uncertainty"

Step 14:   Writing the story lines for the scenarios

Moving from Scenarios to a Decision

Step 15:   Rehearsing the future with scenarios

Step 16:   Getting to the decision recommendations

Step 17:   Identifying the signposts to monitor

Step 18:   Communicating the results to the organization

monitoring process to ensure the necessary adjusting of the strategy. Such a detailed breakdown is needed to guide any new application of the approach and to better detail the critical requirements at each step if the overall effort is to succeed. There is, however, nothing sacrosanct about the precise number of steps in any given project because the process can and should be tailored to the needs of each situation.

Chapter 4

Nokia Case Study

A 32 percent market share of cell phones . . . that market dominant position of Nokia was worth U.S. $198 billion in shareholder value as of the end of 2000. How could Nokia grow that shareholder value with a product that was being increasingly commoditized; with aggressive global competitors constantly introducing cheaper, more innovative products; with large customers attempting to control all the product and service features, price, and even the brand names shown on the phones? How much would Nokia's mainstream businesses be able to contribute to future growth? Where were the innovations going to come from? Who would be responsible for developing the innovations that would be needed?

Even as Nokia recognized these issues, like most large organizations it was constrained by its need to exploit its current market position. How could it best explore for the new opportunities that would be needed to sustain the organization's growth and shareholder value?

Nokia recognized its predicament. A New Ventures Organization (NVO) was formed to identify possible new arenas and fund early seed investments, but like many corporate new venture efforts, it continually struggled to look broadly enough, beyond the current markets, and move promising investments to the next stage when they might compete for resources and market share with the existing business lines. In the late 1990s, Nokia management was aware of the challenges for NVO and that, as a corporation, it needed to look beyond the current business dominance into unknown market situations and circumstances that were more risky. So, realizing the need to develop new opportunities for the organization's long-term growth was not the issue. Rather, the issue was how to explore for those opportunities and provide shelter to early experiments—and not as a one-time initiative but continuously.

Nokia's efforts included a new business unit set up in the late 1990s close to Silicon Valley, California, to experiment with new innovation tools and create a flow of early stage opportunities for Nokia to invest in. The new unit was called Innovent, and it was established to operate with limited oversight by NVO. A key feature of the new unit was its executive sponsorship by the President of Nokia Corporation.

In the winter of 2001, Innovent had a staff of five, drawn from different parts of the Nokia organization and from the Silicon Valley community, all with strong backgrounds in technology commercialization. The group's early projects involved developing consumer frameworks to support the identification and evaluation of new ideas; creating an infrastructure of research capabilities, advisory councils, outside consultants, and internal specialists to apply to the ideas; executing several small development projects; and building awareness within Nokia of the charter, goals, and expected activities of Innovent.

Focused on developing the means to provide a clear vision to Nokia of how technology, the market, or consumer experiences could change the opportunity landscape, Innovent began a scenario-planning project focused on peer-to-peer (P2P) networks, with several elements in the project related to the broader change-management objectives of Nokia. These elements included:

• Extensive communication with corporate headquarters and leaders of the major functions. The support of the President for Innovent's mission and objectives was strong, but Innovent needed to develop other champions, supporters, and heroes at all different levels of the organization. Because many of those individuals were located in Finland and not likely to visit Silicon Valley very often, the Innovent staff planned frequent visits to Helsinki.

• Development of the skills and capabilities to manage innovation processes, particularly scenario planning, in creating commercialization opportunities. Special effort was reserved to evaluate the effectiveness of the scenario planning and to recast the approach to fit Innovent's needs.

• Creation of a flow of innovation opportunities that Nokia could invest in. Convincing Nokia management that structured innovation processes to create the next big area of opportunity could work posed a major challenge. Success in creating the seeds of new businesses was needed. Corporate functions like R&D and Strategic Planning naturally worried about the development focus of Innovent, about the involvement of unknown external partners, and about ensuring that intellectual property issues were managed properly.

• Implementation of an external issue intelligence process. A key factor in Nokia's future adoption of innovation would be the level of executive awareness and understanding of the disruptive changes and chaotic environments occurring throughout the world. Innovent needed to develop and maintain a discussion of new patterns of change that would help raise issues for Nokia management and would generate questions about how Nokia should respond.

Although Innovent had the critical support of the President for its efforts and the P2P initiative, the scenario-planning effort served as the springboard for accomplishing the change-management objectives.

Innovent had completed an earlier opportunity-development project, in cooperation with an operating group in one of the larger markets, that created surprisingly little appetite for pursuing new ideas. When combined with other tales of stifled innovation with the main operating units, this harsh experience jarred common assumptions about the corporation's willingness and ability to foster and develop innovations. Nokia senior management became convinced that Innovent needed to operate initially on the periphery of the traditional NVO organization and demonstrate independently whatever new innovation processes Innovent developed.

Getting the Initiative Started

On receiving the go-ahead from Helsinki, the director of Innovent reached out to the rich external network of entrepreneurs, market-research analysts, industry and technology thought leaders, and scenario-planning practitioners in Silicon Valley to begin preparing for the task of developing P2P scenarios. A team of 15, including the scenario-planning facilitators, was formed: seven from Innovent and Nokia, and eight from outside the Nokia organization.

Two 4-day workshops, approximately a month apart, were planned for May and June of 2001. In the first workshop, after an initial briefing on the scenario-planning process, the team would use the SRI scenario-planning methodology to complete basic outlines of the scenarios. The period between workshops was going to be used to draft scenario write-ups and conduct focused research on important issues. In the second workshop, the team would review the detailed scenario descriptions, make changes, and then use the scenarios to identify potential P2P opportunity areas for Innovent and Nokia. This workshop was to conclude with the selection of the best areas for Innovent and Nokia to pursue.

Eight days of workshop time were budgeted for the effort so that the workshops would conclude with the selection of a set of investment opportunity areas to pursue, having thoroughly reviewed a number of possibilities and having applied good decision criteria in selecting them. A key concern was that enough time be allocated to do a good job.

Secondary research on P2P networks was also developed, and briefing books were prepared and distributed to the entire team prior to the workshops.

Workshop 1: Creating the P2P Scenarios

The first workshop of the P2P scenario team set the tone for the initiative. When teams formed to address a difficult issue meet for the first time, they often struggle to have open, productive discussions. The reasons for this difficulty include the following: The focus is often still unclear, participants are preoccupied with making contributions in front of strangers, and participants are concerned about offending others early with critical comments. To minimize these issues, after some initial introductions and a scenario-planning briefing, Workshop 1 started with a discussion of a "straw man" decision focus that had been prepared in advance. This allowed everyone to make contributory comments without forcing anyone to defend the starting point. It also served to get all the participants on the same page as to the purpose of the initiative and how the assignment would require the entire team's skills and knowledge.

An important step was introducing a specialist for recording workshop discussions using text and graphics (also known as a graphic recorder) into the process to keep track of the results of the discussion in graphic, multi-color form in front of everyone. This helped to create an atmosphere in which participants couldn't wait to see how their input was going to influence the overall picture being developed. Using an assortment of figures and text, the graphic recorder covered large sheets of paper with the results.

Using the SRI methodology for scenario development, the team set the focus for the P2P scenarios by agreeing on the decision focus and the key decision factors. Team members then spent the better part of two days having an intensive discussion of all the forces and drivers that could affect how P2P networks evolved, of the markets that would develop, of the actions taken by local and national governments, of products and services that could result, and of the areas of the value chain that would generate the most revenue. Over 200 forces and drivers were identified and recorded by the graphic recorder. One thing that quickly became clear was that the uncertainty was very high about what markets would develop.

Applying the impact and uncertainty criteria, the team sorted out the high-impact, high-uncertainty forces and drivers from the over 200 forces and drivers and then identified three key clusters of uncertainty. These "axes" were:

• How would power and money be distributed in the marketplace over the next eight years? At one end of the axis, a guerrilla-like environment was thought possible; at the other end, an environment of large gorillas (major power-houses) was envisioned.

• How would the nature of the community evolve in that time frame? At one extreme, individuals could act very independently, not seeking support or being influenced by peers; at the other extreme, social groups become very important in everyone's behavior and activities.

• What was the scope of the P2P system? In this axis, at one end P2P networks could remain fragmented and difficult to establish while at the other end they become transparent, seamless, and easy to use.

After much discussion about the possible scenarios posed by these axes, four scenarios were selected.

	Power & Money	Nature of the Community	Scope of the System	
1	**Gorillas**	**Individual**	**Fragmented**	→ Battle of the Brands
2	Gorillas	Individual	Transparent	
3	Gorillas	Social	Fragmented	
4	**Gorillas**	**Social**	**Transparent**	→ Enlightenment
5	Guerrillas	Individual	Fragmented	
6	Guerrillas	Individual	Transparent	
7	**Guerrillas**	**Social**	**Fragmented**	→ Tale of Two Cities Revisited
8	**Guerrillas**	**Social**	**Transparent**	→ Community Coup

In the final half-day of the four-day workshop, the team developed the story lines for the scenarios, identified events and actors that might occur in each, and contemplated some of the P2P opportunities and threats that could emerge in each scenario. This raw material served as a valuable platform and set of ideas for writing the scenarios.

Writing the Stories

The intense discussions of Workshop One sparked the drafting of the scenario stories and the table comparing the outcomes of many forces and drivers across the scenarios. The stories provided a quick overview of each scenario's major dynamics and significant outcomes, while the comparison table high-lighted the differences, in detail, of scenarios and revealed their complexities. The initial drafts were written by a trio of authors and took three weeks to complete. They were then circulated to the entire team for review and comments.

The challenges in drafting the stories were to capture in a few paragraphs the key features of the alternate P2P environments and convince the Innovent and Nokia staff who would read them that the futures were real, plausible, and possible ways in which P2P networks could evolve, and that Innovent and Nokia needed to conduct in-depth discussions of their implications.

The stories were inserted in a PowerPoint file and required a total of 15 pages for all four scenarios. The comparison table required another 38 pages. This package of stories and comparison table was a relatively quick read; someone reading the package for the first time would need at least 30 minutes to go through the entire thing. The four scenarios are included in Appendix A as an example of four alternative scenarios defining the en-velope of uncertainty for an emerging opportunity arena.

Workshop 2: Moving from Scenarios to Opportunities

In Workshop 2, another four-day workshop, the team turned to identifying the specific opportunity areas that Innovent, on behalf of Nokia, should focus on. Instead of looking at all four scenarios and asking the team to iden-tify the implications for Innovent and Nokia across them, Innovent's direc-tor chose to look at the implications of each scenario on its own and then look across all four. The objective was to use the different dynamics of each scenario to stimulate the thinking about, "What areas of opportunity would have the most value for Innovent and Nokia if we absolutely knew that this scenario were going to occur?" To do so, the scenario team immersed itself in each scenario to the point where everyone forgot the other scenarios and began to identify the actions they would take in response to the conditions of that scenario. Two days were used to explore the implications in all four scenarios. Again, a graphic recorder captured the results in multicolor on large sheets in front of the team.

The specific questions raised for each scenario were:

- What would be important consumer and business needs in the scenario? It was important to start with the thinking about what consumers and customers would want and how they would behave.
- What would be the threats and the opportunities in this scenario, based on all those consumer and business needs?

- What would be good investment ideas for Innovent in the scenario? For each idea, the team identified:
  - A title
  - The markets served
  - The product or service provided
  - The technology needs
  - The success factors
  - The partners/needed acquisitions.

In all, the team identified 75 investment ideas.

In the last day and a half of the workshop, the team focused on sorting through the investment ideas for Innovent, evaluating them using criteria related to their attractiveness and risk, and selecting the ones that initially held the most promise. Through a voting process in which each workshop participant had five votes, the team selected 16 ideas for more in-depth evaluation. The team then considered each idea individually, assessing each according to four criteria:

- Robustness across the scenarios: Will the investment succeed in all the scenarios?

- Technology and other requirements: Do technology obstacles need to be addressed? Will there be other barriers?

- Market potential: What is the potential market size of the investment's product, service, or application? Can the investment help define an enduring market?

- Right for Innovent: Could the investment lead to a sustainable market position for Nokia? Would it be an important learning experience? How well does it complement Nokia's strategy?

All of this evaluation of ideas was completed in the workshop, where all the team members could listen, contribute, and debate the range of views on the different ideas. After reviewing the results of those evaluations, the team selected four ideas for further consideration by Innovent. Two opportunities were identified as having high potential for Innovent investments; two additional areas were identified for further research in the form of white papers.

The last step of the workshop was to leverage the expertise and knowledge of everyone in the room and identify key issues for each of the four opportunities; companies, organizations, and universities in the field, and a potential "elevator pitch" for each. This material would serve as valuable information in the coming months as the Innovent team further defined the ideas and began to communicate the scenario-planning results within Nokia.

Stimulating the Nokia Innovation Culture

The P2P scenario planning effort proved to be a gold mine of insight about future opportunities in the P2P space, highlighting "connection" market opportunities that few people in Helsinki could have anticipated. Over the next three years, the members of the Innovent team were on hand in Helsinki a number of times and communicated the insights and ideas about the P2P space that emerged from the scenario-planning effort in many parts of the organization. Through repeated effort and the support of key executives, the Innovent members were able to describe the range of opportunities that Nokia could face, and in doing so they gained a better understanding of Nokia's needs for innovation and capabilities for taking advantage of disruptive innovation.

A key lesson learned from all the effort was that even innovation-oriented organizations like Nokia need constantly to nurture exploration activities in the company while maintaining the focus on competing for growth in existing businesses. The balancing between existing business areas and possible new ones is a dynamic process, and extensive senior-management effort is required to manage the process and develop a change-oriented culture. Because of the exigencies of growing existing businesses in highly competitive markets, every high-tech corporation will orient most of its processes and systems to doing better in those businesses and will limit its investments, experiments, and thinking on other things. A key role of the senior executives in a change-oriented company is to sponsor and get involved in the exploration activities needed for innovation and carve out the necessary resources. Through Innovent's effort with P2P scenarios, the scenario-planning methodology was shown to be an excellent exploration-activity tool and a means for quickly— in a relative sense—communicating about future innovation opportunities throughout the organization.

One important discovery of this project was that executives, opinion leaders, and strategists continually talk to each other and to many others in the organization. Even though the Innovent team was not located in any of the main Nokia offices, the word about the P2P scenarios and ideas spread to many people—usually people in the mainstream businesses—some of whom were open to, and some were dismissive of, the P2P results. Since awareness of new patterns of change and potentially disruptive forces is a critical factor in developing a change-oriented culture, this word of mouth activity, albeit sometimes very slow, was an important part of the communication process.

Over the three to four years following the P2P scenario effort, Nokia began shifting the organization's orientation more from exploiting the full potential of its current businesses to developing business opportunities beyond its current ones, significantly altering the organization's openness toward innovation initiatives and marking the cultural shift to a change-oriented culture. At some point, the growth of every market begins to slow, and the cell phone manufacturing industry has been no exception. As market growth slows, it may be possible to continue growing by taking market share from competitors, but this will be very difficult in the high-tech cell phone industry, particularly given the power of the large telecommunications operators and the rapid change in technology. By 2005, Nokia had completely reorganized its senior management team and brought in new leadership to manage the next phase in Nokia's growth.

Five years later, the P2P scenarios are viewed widely in the organization as the type of activity needed to develop new business opportunities for Nokia, and they serve as an important example within Nokia on the value of scenario planning in long-term strategic thinking. Innovent continues to use the P2P scenarios in its innovation exploration activities because the stories and their representation of key issues affecting the emergence of P2P networks are still effective in stimulating new ideas and helping to evaluate investment opportunities.

In looking at Innovent and Nokia's experience with scenarios, we can conclude the following:

• Scenarios are an effective means for exploring the possibilities of new markets and the impact of fast-moving technology (seeing the future);

• Scenario planning provides a language and framework for an organization to learn about how markets could work in the future, to be challenged to think about how the organization could respond or take advantage of the uncertainties and disorder, and to prepare for the possibilities (preparing for the future);

• Scenarios provide the means to stimulate innovative thinking throughout an organization, serving as the means to develop awareness in the organization of key issues but also as the means to generate innovation ideas at all levels and functions, evaluate them, and select ones for future investment (exploiting the future).

This powerful set of capabilities—seeing the future, preparing for the future, and exploiting the future—empowers the organization when done well and defines the organization as one that is truly change oriented.

PART 2

STEPS IN GETTING STARTED

Part 2 of this book addresses the issues that have to be dealt with in initiating any scenario-planning project—issues of defining the scope and objectives of the scenarios, changes in staffing and culture, and revisions in planning procedures. Often these issues do not receive the attention they deserve, with the result that the scenarios have a short life span and little or no impact on the planning system they were designed to change. For scenarios to be successful, therefore, these issues must be central to our thinking and to the design of our system.

A compelling case for using scenario planning to improve strategic decision making in the organization lays the foundation for a successful scenario-planning project. Decision makers and staff need a clear sense of what can be accomplished by scenario planning and a change-oriented culture. Chapter 5 addresses the development of information that will be used again and again in planning and communicating what an organization's needs are for a new strategic approach, what benefits scenario planning will provide when creating a strategy in the face of uncertainty, how the approach compares to others, and what resources and change in culture the approach will generally require to be successful. In other words, Chapter 5 answers the "why" for conducting the project.

Executive understanding, support, and participation are fundamental to the success of any new decision-making process or change of culture. Chapter 6 describes how executive involvement is built into the process. It's simply a waste of time and resources to move forward without it.

Scenario planning is all about creating tailored scenarios to help make important decisions. These tailored scenarios are not generalized views about how the world could evolve, but specific descriptions of the possible marketplace dynamics, regulatory developments, and customer behavior that will influence the success or failure of those decisions. Chapter 7 describes how to create the focus that will deliver scenarios that will help in decision making.

Now that we know what we want to create, we need to plan the steps in the process to do so. Chapter 8 outlines the planning parameters for a project and provides some guidelines for organizing the project activities, methodology steps, outputs, and so on.

Chapters 9 and 10 finish laying the foundation for the project with the selection of the scenario-planning facilitator and the formation of the project team. As with any special project, the quality of the output and the willingness and ability of the organization to integrate the project's results are a function of the people chosen for the project team.

The sequencing of these chapters is not paramount. They can be read and executed in the order that makes most sense for the circumstances.

CHAPTER 5

DEVELOPING THE CASE FOR SCENARIOS (STEP 1)

The first step is developing the case for scenario-based decision making and beginning to introduce scenario thinking and the scenarios themselves into the strategic-management system.

Why Do We Need a Case?

Not every strategic-planning decision is suited to scenarios, and the case must be made that the circumstances are appropriate for scenario planning and the benefits clearly outweigh the costs. The case is particularly important for the initial selling of the methodology to key stakeholders and for ensuring that the initial application will be a success.

Whenever we introduce a new methodology into an organization, we should recognize the degree of inertia and resistance that individuals in the organization are likely to exert—consciously or unconsciously—and the extent of the changes in practice, structure, and, perhaps, culture that may be required. Very few changes are simple: Most are complex and demanding, if only because even the most limited change can have consequences and impacts throughout an organization because of complex lines of cause and effect.

Certainly the introduction of scenarios into a strategic decision-making or planning process is an example of such a complex change. Not only do we have to learn a new vocabulary and a new methodology, but in the most fundamental way, we also have to change the way we think about—prepare for—and make strategic decisions. Before embarking on such a venture, we must therefore be very clear as to what exactly scenarios are (and are not), why we need them for a particular decision-making situation, what we hope to gain from them, and how we plan to fit them into—or change—the way we develop strategies.

What Must We Accomplish?

Our first step, therefore, is to develop the information and arguments for conducting a scenario-planning assignment, perhaps for the first time. To do so, we will need to:

- *Lay out the needs for addressing the uncertainties in the external environment and identifying the potential strategic implications for the organization.*

What is the bet-the-business decision that the organization is facing and how could external issues such as new competitors, changes in market demand, regulatory change, and so on affect the success or failure of that decision?

- *Identify the costs of not developing a better understanding of macro and business forces and trends.* What would be the impact of missing the window of opportunity, choosing the wrong strategic course, being unprepared for new trends, not having options ready, or not acting quickly enough in response to events?
- *Identify the benefits of developing a structured means for integrating information about the external environment and aligning strategy development to that integration effort.*
- *Describe what resources, expertise, inputs, and so on it will take to develop and use scenarios to help make the bet-the-business decision.*
- *Develop references for using scenario planning.*
- *To help make the decision, provide an analysis of the planning techniques that are alternatives to using scenario planning.*

How to Do It

The keys to developing a good case for scenarios are to stick with a simple agenda, describe some of the major uncertainties in the external environment that are causing concern within the organization, and gather reference information on using scenarios for similar situations.

A tested agenda for the case includes the following:

1. Need. The need is the most important element of the case. It is the reason why a major initiative needs to be conducted at this time. It will include descriptions of:
    a) External Issues. What external issues are keeping people awake at nights? What's really uncertain? How much knowledge do we have about those issues?
    b) Potential Outcomes for Business (Good and Bad). What could happen to the business if certain developments occur? How ready is the organization for these developments?
    c) Decision Description. What strategic decision is the organization facing? What are some possible directions?
    d) Decision Process Problems. What cultural, resource, process, and organizational problems must we overcome to make a good decision?

2. Approach for Using Scenarios and Making the Decisions. What thinking and decision-making process should we use? What are the basic ingredients of that approach?

3. Benefits of Approach. What benefits will the organization receive by using the scenario-planning approach? How will the organization be better?

4. Competitive Approaches. What are the best alternative approaches to scenarios for meeting the needs? What are the strengths and weaknesses of the alternative approaches? How were decisions reached in the past?

5. Execution Requirements. What will the initiative cost? What will be the senior executive involvement? What resources need to be freed up? What doors need to be opened?

Typically, the case is assembled using presentation software slides, with 15 slides being the target number.

The compelling part of the case will be discussion of risks in making the decision without the benefit of scenarios. If the decision isn't significant to the business, then it will be hard to justify the use of scenarios. The case will identify important uncertainties for the future in the external environment that will determine the success or failure of the decision and highlight how inadequate existing management approaches are for understanding the future dynamics.

The development of supporting case and reference information for using scenarios is relatively straightforward, given the wide range of written material about scenarios available in books and articles and the number of experiences of corporations around the world in implementing scenarios. A quick online reference search will generate extensive sources of information. Please also note the bibliography of this book for some easily available reference material.

Who Needs to Lead?

Who is responsible for developing the case for scenarios? Who is in the best position to design and execute such a broad-based change in the planning system? Who needs to be the champion for using scenarios in the decision making?

The easy answer to all the questions, it is to be hoped, is the business–unit head or the chief executive officer, who is certainly the most responsible for developing an organization's strategy and ensuring its successful adaptation to change. As the chief strategists, therefore, such leaders should be the ones most concerned with assessing the likely dimensions and timing of change, and the extent of the uncertainties confronting the organization. However, while their support and involvement are critical to the success of the scenario process (see the next chapter for Step 2), in most cases they will assign responsibility for the detailed work in designing and executing this system to someone else, very likely the strategy or planning executive. Certainly the volume and caliber of the work involved justifies the appointment of a senior, experienced, and trusted executive to the effort.

In fact, in our experience, the introduction of scenarios into an organization is very often a bottom-up, rather than a top-down, process. Someone in the organization is motivated to focus on the evident limitations of traditional planning as the basis for making strategic decisions, searches for a "better way to do it," and eventually emerges as the initial champion for scenario planning.

Certainly that was the way in which the Royal Dutch Shell case—perhaps the best known and most respected example of the use of scenarios in the corporate world—evolved. It is true that the Committee of Managing Directors, the company's senior management group, deserves credit for recognizing, as early as 1972–73, that traditional forecasts were by then fast becoming a dangerous substitute for real thinking in times of uncertainty, and that scenarios provided a potentially better framework for thinking about the future. But it was the pioneering work of Pierre Wack, first at Shell France and then at Group Planning, that gave the then embryonic scenario-planning effort its focus, its structure, and its insight.

Indeed, Shell's experience underscores the critical importance of having a champion to build the case for scenario planning and lead the effort during the vulnerable early stages of introducing the new system. Such a leader, then, will have to address at least four critical and specific challenges:

1. *Articulating the case for scenario planning—in specific terms:* It is not sufficient to build a valid but generalized case for scenarios (such as we have summarized in Chapters 1, 2 and 3, and as is further articulated in the writings cited in the bibliography). What is required is a highly specific analysis of the critical uncertainties confronting the organization, the inadequacy of the current system to deal with them, and the potential role that scenario planning could play in developing a more effective strategy.

2. *Gaining top management support:* Because the primary customer for scenarios is the management team, the champion has to win their support for the new approach, and to help define the role they will play in first

developing the scenarios, using them to develop the decision implications, and then applying the results to the decision

3. *Designing and leading the initial effort:* In most cases, the champion is the one who is given, or assumes, responsibility for the initial investment in scenario planning. This requires that the champion think through how the current planning system will be used; how to work across organizational divisions; and how to maintain the respect of senior management.

4. *Changing the strategy-management culture:* As we frequently emphasize, scenario planning requires a planning and decision-making culture that differs from that in many organizations. Scenarios are, typically, most productive and useful in what we now term "learning organizations"—organizations that constantly challenge their assumptions about the marketplace, their beliefs about their strengths and weaknesses and future possibilities of their strategies; that recognize that change is inevitable and that they need to accommodate that change; that are open to new ideas and information and the sources of those ideas. Ultimately, therefore, the champion is a major catalyst for organizational growth and development.

What Are the Outputs of This Step?

The primary deliverable of this step is the written case for using scenario planning. Besides being used to gain initial senior management support for the effort, it can also be used as an internal communication tool about scenario planning for the various stakeholders during the project and as the plan for comparison purposes when reviewing the results of the project once it is over.

What's Next?

The next step is to gain the necessary senior management support and participation for making the scenario-planning assignment a success. Scenario planning involves significant decisions and issues for the company, and it's not possible to apply the methodology successfully without significant support and involvement by key decision makers. The case for scenarios plays an important role in the step.

CHAPTER 6

GAINING EXECUTIVE UNDERSTANDING, SUPPORT, AND PARTICIPATION (STEP 2)

Why Executives Need to Be Directly Involved

One of the first challenges confronting the person championing the use of scenarios is that of gaining the decision makers' understanding of, and commitment to, the scenario process. (By "decision makers," we mean the senior management team at either the corporate or business unit level, depending on the scope and positioning of the project.) After all, a key objective of scenario planning is to change, subtly but fundamentally, the way strategy is developed, and this can be accomplished only with a change in the mind-set of the management team.

The current mind-set usually revolves around "assumptions," "forecasts," and "most likely" assessments of the future. When confronted with scenarios, therefore, executives often have a strong innate tendency to identify, and focus on, what they judge to be the "most probable" scenario as the basis for their strategic thinking. To do this, however, would be to negate the true value of scenarios, and essentially revert to a forecasting mode of planning. If all we want is a range of high, medium, and low forecasts, there are quicker and less demanding ways of getting to them than through the scenario process.

The real value of scenarios, however, comes not from giving us more accurate forecasts but rather from improving our understanding of the dynamics of the world around us, seeing the range of possible ways in which the world could evolve, providing us the courage and confidence to make difficult decisions, and quickening our response time to events. A true commitment to scenario planning, then, requires more than simply parroting an openness about the future. It requires a deep understanding of the nature of uncertainty and a serious attempt to use that understanding in the decision-making process.

What Must We Accomplish in This Step?

Once the decision has been taken to proceed with the effort, the organization must decide on whether, how, and to what extent all the decisions makers or members of the senior management team should be involved in the process of developing the scenarios. Given that ultimately these executives will be called upon to use the scenarios in their strategic decision making, there should be no question about the need to involve them in the development process, at least to the extent that they have sufficient understanding of, and commitment to, the scenarios and are comfortable using them as the framework for their strategizing.

The general rule of thumb here is, therefore, "The more involvement, the better." Indeed, one of the most successful projects we ever witnessed—where success was measured in terms of the ease and effectiveness with which the scenarios were translated into strategy and with the subsequent use of the scenarios for a number of years—was with a European financial services company. In that effort, the entire management team (the CEO and his direct reports) was the scenario team and participated in key workshops to assess critical uncertainties, structure the scenarios, and interpret their strategic implications. (Only the detailed elaboration of the scenarios was assigned to staff work.) As a result, every step in the process clearly reflected the thinking of the management team; and the possibility of misinterpretation or disagreement in the hand-off from the scenario team to executives was eliminated. There can be little doubt that such an approach is highly effective, both in ensuring that the scenarios accurately reflect executives' perceptions of uncertainty, but also in ensuring that the scenarios are so internalized in executives' minds that their strategic thinking flows naturally from their interpretation of the scenarios.

Realistically, however, we should not expect that everyone on the management team will make such a large commitment of time to what is, for them, a nonoperational initiative, but will choose rather to assign subordinates to the effort. But even in these cases, some executives from the management team must play a critical role because, in the final analysis, the management team is the group that will have to use the scenarios and so must be comfortable and confident with the final product. To ensure this, some must be involved from the beginning and throughout the scenario-development process. Their participation is critical in:

- *Focusing the project*—As the ultimate decision makers, executives have the responsibility for understanding the decision(s) to be made, defining the scope of the scenarios, and so setting the agenda for the scenario-planning team.
- *Reviewing key trends and uncertainties analyses*—These analyses are a critical step leading to structuring the scenarios and evaluating

potential outcomes of strategic alternatives. It is essential, therefore, that the scenario team's insights be reviewed by the management team so any glaring differences in perceptions about key dynamics in the external environment can be identified and resolved before proceeding further with the process.

- *Reviewing the scenario structure*—The scenario team should review its proposed scenarios in outline form with executives to ensure that they can accept the proposed scenario logics and coverage of the "envelope of uncertainty."
- *Assessing the strategic implications of the scenarios*—Clearly this task is ultimately the responsibility of the management, not of the scenario team, although the team can and should provide executives with its preliminary assessment of these implications.
- *Communicating scenario-planning learning to the organization*—Support by executives in the communication of scenarios and their implications to the organization is essential, particularly in the initial efforts to use scenario planning in making decisions.

How Do We Get Their Involvement?

Soon after the project is initiated and the decision focus is clear, the person assigned to lead the effort should meet with the senior management group and/or the business unit head to develop initial commitments of executives to the project. At a minimum, one executive should be involved in all the steps. Those not involved in every step should be kept informed of the results and prepared with periodic briefings for using the results in the decision making.

Developing an understanding of the nature of uncertainty in decision makers and the confidence to apply it requires both time and effort. Reading materials on both the theory and practice of scenario planning can be a helpful introduction to the subject, so distributing appropriate articles (e.g., the Pierre Wack *Harvard Business Review* articles) or excerpts from books (see the bibliography for examples) can be a useful starting point. However, it is only a starting point. Simply reading will almost certainly raise questions—about the theory and practicality of scenarios, for example—and challenge deeply held personal convictions about how we should plan in uncertainty. Dealing with these questions and issues and building the case for scenario planning are best done in open discussion with those who will be most affected by the introduction of scenarios into the planning system. It is only through the give-and-take of open discussion that true learning and acceptance of the new system will take place. The case for using scenarios, developed in Step 1, is often the catalyst for this discussion.

Preparing the group for using scenarios presumes, of course, that there is, within the group, someone with experience in scenario planning, someone who can respond to questions, correct misconceptions, share experience, and help the group coalesce on a decision as to whether or not to apply the process. Sometimes that individual will exist within the organization, which is optimal because he or she will be likely to combine appreciation of the organization's needs and culture with an understanding of scenario planning. But often, it is necessary to work with outside specialists, who may not understand fully the group dynamics of the management team but who have broad experience with scenarios and the ability to respond persuasively to the team's doubts and questions.

An important tactic for conducting this step successfully is to organize the entire calendar of briefings, meetings, and workshops involving the senior executives at the beginning of the project. A typical schedule of executive time commitments is shown in Figure 6-1.

Figure 6-1   Schedule of Executive Time Commitments

When	Who	What
Month 1	Senior management team	2-hour presentation and discussion of scenario planning case; initial assignments of executive responsibility
Month 1	Executives involved in scenario-planning process	2- to 3-day workshop. Participate in detailed discussions of forces and drivers
Month 2	Senior management team	1-hour discussion of macro- and micro-environmental uncertainties
Month 2	Executives involved in scenario-planning process	2- to 3-day workshop. Participate in detailed discussion of alternative scenarios of the future
Month 3	Senior management team	1-hour briefing on future scenarios
Month 4	Executives involved in scenario-planning process	2- to 3-day workshop. Participate in assessment of decision implications of scenarios
Month 4	Senior management team	2-hour presentation and discussion of scenario planning results; alignment with decision-making process

What Are the Outputs of This Step?

The outputs include:

- *Awareness among the senior executives of the attributes of scenario planning, how it will be applied in the organization, the risks and benefits of the approach, and their roles*
- *Assignments of executives to the effort*
- *Calendar of meetings, briefings, and workshops to attend*
- *Briefing materials on the process, forces and drivers, scenarios, and decision implications.*

What's Next?

To create scenarios that help in making specific decisions, it's necessary to spend time early in the process clarifying the decision. This includes laying out the range of choices involved, the benefits the decision is expected to generate, the time period for realizing those benefits, and issues of scope.

Chapter 7

Defining the Decision Focus (Step 3)

What's the Purpose of the Decision Focus?

It would be difficult to overemphasize the importance of focusing the scenarios correctly. Too little focus tends to result in scenarios that take in too much of the environment and provide little guidance to decision makers. Too narrow a focus is apt to overlook factors that turn out to be critical in the future and see the future predominantly as a projection of the past. The best results, we have found, come from focusing the scenario effort based on the elements of the decisions to be made. The goal is to have the scenarios provide a clearer sense of future possibilities for the decision elements and the forces that influence them.

This decision focus essentially aims to do what forecasting has done in the past: Provide executives with insights into the future that will help them make the strategic decisions that confront them. Focusing the scenarios in this way has two immediate advantages:

- *It concentrates our thinking about the future on the trends and forces that most affect our organization and on the decisions we have to make.* Without such a focus, our thinking about the future is apt to drift into blue-sky speculation—interesting perhaps, but of dubious utility. With this focus, we can concentrate our imagination and our reasoning on the trends, issues, and possibilities that really matter.

- *It provides a link to action.* Without this focus, even the most imaginative scenario-building can lead us into a blind alley—"Now what?," we ask ourselves at the conclusion of the exercise. "What bearing does this have on our actions?" Having such a focus means that the link to action is built into the process from the word "go," and this linkage is particularly important in selling the benefits of scenarios.

This link to action relates to the strategic rather than the tactical decisions we have to make. This is so for two reasons. In the first place, scenarios deal more with major, radical shifts, rather than incremental changes, in the environment and so have greater significance for strategy. Second, the time frame for scenarios is usually 5–10 years, appropriate for strategy but not for tactical planning. Obviously, it would be unnecessary to develop scenarios with a horizon of only 1–2 years, which would be required for tactical planning, because the differences among the scenarios would be so small that it wouldn't be worth the effort to create more than one.

What Decisions Do Scenarios Support?

The range of strategic decisions to which scenarios can make a contribution is quite varied and extensive:

- *Large, capital-intensive projects with a long lifetime or payback, such as:*
  - Large manufacturing plants in basic industries
  - Exploration, exploitation, and reclamation of natural resources
  - Infrastructure projects
- *Business development decisions, including mergers and acquisitions*
- *Strategy for mature business lines facing decline or slowing growth*
- *Investments in emerging areas of business where little experience or knowledge exists.*
- *Investments in research and development or in unproven technology that will not move into the marketplace until some time in the future*
- *Political risk assessments in unstable countries or regions*

In fact, virtually any decision or area of strategic concern in which environmental factors are complex and changing may be appropriate for treatment by scenarios. When the stakes are high and when outcomes for the organization will be heavily affected by the external events and outcomes, then scenario planning is the appropriate tool.

The question sometimes arises as to whether scenarios developed for one purpose, say a corporate decision, can be used for other, related purposes, say a business unit decision. The answer depends mainly on the degree of diversification in the businesses or functions covered. For instance, in the case of Shell Canada (see Box 7-1), there was judged to be sufficient homogeneity in the key drivers of its various businesses that the corporate-level scenarios could be adapted relatively easily for use at the business unit level simply by adding environmental descriptors specific to each business. If, however, there are major differences in the drivers of the various businesses—if, for instance, one of the business units is a financial services business while others are predominantly manufacturing—then almost certainly there is a need to construct decision-specific scenarios.

What Must Be Included in the Decision Focus?

A decision focus is simple in its content. It includes:

- *An overall description of the decision to be made, usually a short paragraph in length.*

BOX 7-1
Shell Canada: A Case Study in Multitiered Scenarios

When Shell Canada decided, in the 1980s, to adopt the scenario-planning approach developed by its parent, Royal Dutch Shell, it used the group-level scenarios—at that time, "Fragile Compromise" and "Restructured Growth"—as a starting point and frame of reference for its work. These group-level scenarios provided the needed perspectives on global economic, political, and energy environments. Then, to "Canadianize" the scenarios, Shell Canada "cross-roughed" these scenarios with differing outcomes to the major political debate of those times—between centralization (or "country-building") and decentralization (or "province-building")—which had major implications for taxation, energy policy, resource development, and corporate regulations (see the following figure):

Shell Canada's Scenario Structure

Canadian Political Thrusts

	Centralization (Country Building)	Decentralization (Province Building)
Fragile Compromise	"Defensive Nationalism"	"Provincial Isolationism"
Restructured Growth	"Focused Growth"	"Confederated Provincialism"

Related International Economic Conditions

These four scenarios provided the environmental context for corporate-level strategy. They were then fine-tuned to demonstrate and assess their impacts on the supply and demand trajectories for each of Shell Canada's major business units (oil and gas, coal, chemicals, tar sands, etc.), in effect creating business unit–level scenarios.

The result, therefore, was a multitiered set of scenarios—group, corporate, and business unit—all closely interlinked, but each focused on the specific interests of its users.

- *Scoping statements of functions, geographies, and business units involved in or affected by the decision.* For example, does the overall decision affect marketing, product development, and research and development choices? Does the decision only relate to the one geographic area or is it global?
- *Scoping statements of what's not included.*
- *Time period in which the costs and benefits of the decision will be realized.*

Some examples of decision focuses are shown in Box 7-2. They are taken from actual projects, although some specifics have been altered to keep the identities of the companies and their specific products and market focuses confidential.

BOX 7-2
Decision-Focus Examples

For a car manufacturer's marketing group:

The decision is what should be the corporate marketing strategy to serve changing consumer needs in the major markets around the world over the next 10 years. The decision should consider how consumer needs could evolve in the 10 years and what will drive their choices of mobility so that the company can offer new concepts to consumers 10 to 15 years from now. Product development, production, marketing, and distribution and sales strategies are included.

For a U.S. financial-services company:

Consistent with the strategic focus of the company, what long-term opportunities should the company pursue that will provide the basis for growth over the next three to eight years? Key elements of the scope include:

- Focus on delivering financial solutions based on needs.
- Focus on opportunities for the company's current organization, skills, and capabilities.
- Focus on the voice of the end consumer (as opposed to the voice of the intermediary or the competition).

For a medical device company trying to launch a new product in the United States:

What actions should the business unit take in the next three to four years to ensure successful launch and implementation of New Product X for medical procedures Y in the outpatient procedure room environment? The time frame is three years for the decisions that will play out over eight years. The U.S. marketplace is the focus. Major decisions for the product will occur in public relations strategy, market segments, product features and design, marketing activities, communications messages, regulatory affairs, clinical trial design, supply chain, resource allocation, intellectual property management, timing, training, services, sales, and pricing.

For an international petrochemical company:

What technology strategies and goals, aligned with the company's business interests, will create major earnings growth?

- Geographic scope: global
- Time horizon for business options over next 10 years, for businesses over next 10 to 20 years
- Full range of technologies and businesses affecting the company's business areas and interfaces (external and internal)
- Hydrocarbons and related products focus
- Exclude the following potential business areas:
  - Providing products and services to Industry X
  - Producing Product Category Y

How to Develop a Good Decision Focus

While the focus description is simple in its content, its creation often involves extensive consultation and deliberation. The first task is to conduct interviews with the executives who will make the decision in order to identify the underlying needs for the decision, the goals to be achieved with the decision, some of the alternatives to be considered, and so on.

Following those discussions, the project leader should create a draft for the decision focus, following the outline. He or she should then review it with the executives in a group session, make necessary changes, and obtain everyone's agreement with the result.

After this step is completed, the decision description can still change, but generally it doesn't. Instead it serves as a beacon for why the work is being done and what needs to be considered.

What Are the Outputs of This Step?

- *A written description of the decision focus, often on one page*
- *Agreement on the focus among the key executives*

What's Next?

The last steps in getting started are to design the process in detail, select a facilitator, and form the team that will carry out the scenario-development steps. This can be done now that the overall case has been made for the scenarios, the executives have been assigned to the process, and the decision focus has been agreed upon.

CHAPTER 8

DESIGNING THE PROCESS (STEP 4)

Overview of the Process Design Issues

With the purpose and focus of the project clarified, we can turn our attention to organizing the scenario-development effort. Designing the process, setting the schedule, selecting the facilitator, and forming the scenario team typically are the next tasks.

The focus of the scenario process is to create scenarios specific to the decision, so that the decision makers, who must consider the different alternatives and their risks and rewards far out into the future, have an effective tool for examining decision implications and evaluating risks and rewards. Given the scope and complexity of the task of developing sophisticated descriptions of the future, it may well be asked how an amateur team with diverse interests and perspectives can address such a task. Our experience shows categorically that the most effective approach to this task is through a set of carefully structured and executed steps conducted in a series of workshops. The specific sequence of steps eliminates the uncertainty about creating useful scenarios for the decision makers. The steps ensure that the scenario team is stretched to think broadly about the forces and drivers that could influence the decision; this also reduces the possibilities of being surprised. But the steps also force the team to sort through the various issues to identify those that could have the biggest impact and those that are the most uncertain for the decision. Finally, the steps generate compelling stories that allow decision makers to quickly grasp the major issues and provide a common framework or language for discussing the external environment.

How much work, over how long a period, does the scenario-planning process require? In our experience, the answers to these questions vary from one week to six months, depending, for instance, on the scope of the decision focus, the experience of the scenario team, the supporting research involved, and the importance of the project. (For instance, is it just a "learning experience," or is it a part of a corporate strategy-development effort?). Nevertheless, it is possible to make some generalized observations about a "typical" scenario project (see Box 8-1).

BOX 8-1
Calendar/Time Line of a "Typical" Project

- *Initial meeting(s): Discuss decision focus, conduct scenario briefing, arrange teams, set schedule, collect data, interview key thought leaders.*
- *Workshop 1: Agree on decision focus and key decision factors; identify environment forces/drivers; set topics for "focus papers."*
- *Edit workshop results; prepare focus papers.*
- *Workshop 2: Discuss focus papers; conduct impact/uncertainty assessment of environmental forces; agree on scenarios logics/structure; select scenarios for elaboration.*
- *Write scenario drafts (qualitative and quantitative descriptions).*
- *Workshop 3: Review scenario drafts; assess implications— opportunities/threats, issues, strategy options.*
- *Prepare project report.*

Overall duration of project: 3–4 months

- *A structured process with a number of sequential steps is required.*
- *Workshops are needed to help process the voluminous information and proceed through the sequential steps.* A team of experienced persons in a workshop environment can be highly productive in processing and making sense of a lot of information.
- *A series of workshops is required, each lasting two to three days, spread out over a three- to four-month period.* This time commitment allows team members to maintain other responsibilities yet make significant contributions in the scenario effort.
- *Staff work is required between workshops to assemble background material, plan the workshop activities, conduct special tasks in the methodology, and document the results of the workshops.*
- *First drafts of the scenarios are not written by the scenario team in the workshops, but by individuals outside of the workshops.*
- *Focused research is conducted on important issues, but always summarized before being presented to the team.*

Figure 8-1   Characteristics of Different-Size Scenario-Planning Projects

	Small Size	Typical Size	Large Size
Type of Decision	Routine Functional or Business-Unit Decision	Large Strategic Decision	Bet-the-Company Decision
People on Scenario Team	4–6 each	8–12 each	8–20 each
Workshops	2 workshops, ½ day each	3 workshops, 2–3 days each	4–6 workshops 2–3 days each
Number of Workshop Days for Scenario Team Participants	1–2 days/ participant	4–6 days/ participant	8–12 days/ participant
Number of Days for Team Leader, Facilitator, Core-Team Members	4–6 days	25–40 days	30–70 days
Total Pages of Scenario Text	5–10 each	10–30 each	15–40 each
Days to Write Scenario Drafts	1–2 days	5–10 days	8–15 days
Days to Research Key Topics	1–2 days	5–15 days	10–40 days
Project Duration	2 weeks–1 month	2–4 months	3–6 months

While many first-time efforts follow the "typical" formula, the scope and scale of scenario-planning efforts do vary depending on the decision-making circumstances. Figure 8-1 provides some benchmarks on how projects can differ.

The use of workshops leverages the capabilities of the human mind to process varied inputs rapidly, to detect patterns amid volumes of information, and to reflect on stored knowledge and experiences, providing a powerful and effective means of integrating the diverse viewpoints needed for successful scenario building. It is in workshops that the interplay of ideas, opinions, and facts can lead most effectively to an understanding of the diverse, interacting forces that constitute the fabric of scenarios. At the same time, the workshop approach to the task is economic in its demands on participants' time: By encouraging discipline and structure in the process, while permitting—indeed encouraging—freedom and innovation in thinking, this approach is both efficient and productive.

As with any management process, a number of tradeoff issues need to be addressed in planning the effort. Not obtaining the right knowledge or information for the project, not allocating sufficient resources and time, moving too quickly through the process, or not properly organizing the workshop details can all jeopardize the project. Consequently, the scenario-planning project leader and senior executive sponsor must allow planning time to think through the organizational issues and give the project the best chances for success.

How Do We Design the Process?

In the design process, three types of issues need to be addressed: 1) management requirements, 2) process steps, and 3) workshop management details. The approach is to start with the typical project template (see Box 8-1) and then adjust that scheme depending on the needs of the situation and the resources available. Basic management issues that need to be decided include:

- *When do the results of the project need to be done?*
- *How much background research needs to be conducted?*
- *What expertise is required to develop the needed scenarios?*
- *How much time can the scenario team members afford to devote to the effort?*
- *What budget will be needed for off-site facilities, consultants, travel, and so on?*

Process step issues are those related to the steps carried out by the team to create and use decision-focused scenarios. See Figure 8-2. These issues are the primary focus of this handbook and are described in detail in the chapters. In this process design step, it is recommended that the scenario-planning champion use Chapters 9 through 22 as the agenda for developing the design.

Once the process design is set, then workshop management details can be addressed. Scenario-development projects should follow standard workshop-management practices. The workshop issues that need to be addressed include:

- *Defining the objectives of the workshop.* What are we trying to accomplish in the workshop(s), and for whom?
- *Identifying the desired outcomes.* If all the workshop steps are effectively conducted, what specific results would be achieved?
- *Planning the workshop format.* What type of workshop activities will best achieve the objectives? Short presentations followed by discussion? Physical movements around the room by participants? Breakout groups for focused analysis?

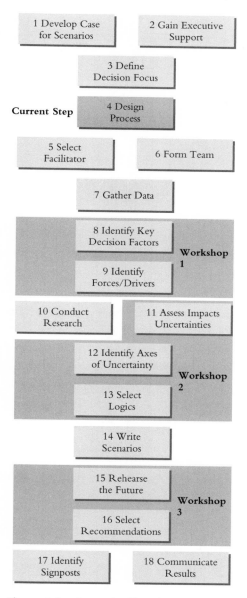

Figure 8-2 Scenario-Planning Process Steps

- *Holding everyone responsible for carrying out their assigned role.* What roles are needed for successful workshop management, and what are their responsibilities?
- *Involving the proper participants.* Decision makers? Guests? Observers?

- *Maintaining a creative atmosphere.* How to get everyone involved, avoid "idea killers," and establish the appropriate psychological climate?
- *Encouraging open minds.* What needs to be done to achieve the right balance between openness and imagination in stretching the boundaries of the team's thinking and maintaining discipline and logic in structuring the scenarios of possible futures?
- *Following an agenda.* What does it take to keep the group moving toward a goal and not floating aimlessly?
- *Leveraging the interaction.* How to get the best ideas by contributions of many participants?
- *Preparing the participants beforehand.* How to focus the time of the workshop and avoid walking into a workshop discussion "cold"?
- *Leveraging the power of visual aids.* What are the best techniques for supporting scenario development discussions?
- *Creating the appropriate physical setting.*

One important recommendation should be noted here: The workshops—however many, and of whatever duration—should be held off-site, away from the disruptive demands of an active office. With modern telecommunications being what they are, the team leader will, in any event, be severely tested to keep the team focused on its task and not be distracted by calls to or from team members' offices.

A more thorough discussion of how scenario-development workshops should be organized and managed is found in Appendix B: Workshop-Management Practices for Scenario Development. Issues related to application of new information-technology tools in scenario planning are discussed in Appendix C: Future Impacts of Information Technology on the Scenario Planning Methodology.

For first-time efforts, the involvement of a scenario-planning specialist is recommended. That person will have a good sense of the tradeoffs and alternatives in accomplishing each step, time requirements of activities, and needed resources and expertise. This person is also often skilled in acting as the facilitator for the scenario-planning workshops.

At the end of this step, a project plan should be prepared that includes a time line for all the activities, a description of what will occur in each workshop, some methodology templates, and a list of the resource and expertise requirements.

What Are the Outputs of the Step?

- *The plan for the scenario-development activities*
- *Example templates to be used in the process*
- *Decisions about the requirements for a facilitator and expected time commitments for the scenario team*
- *A schedule*
- *A budget*
- *List of background research and expertise requirements to be filled*
- *List of logistics and administrative requirements.*

What's Next?

The next steps are to arrange for a workshop facilitator and assemble the scenario team that will be responsible for conducting the rest of the process activities.

CHAPTER 9

SELECTING THE FACILITATOR (STEP 5)

Early in the process, before work on developing the scenarios actually begins, a decision must be made about how the workshops and process activities will be facilitated. For first-time developers of scenarios, that usually means bringing in a facilitator with experience in scenario planning. Senior management of the organization most affected by this change in planning procedure must have input to the decision because they must have confidence from the beginning that the facilitator will be able to guide the scenario team through the many steps in meeting the project's objectives.

Why Do We Need a Facilitator?

The question immediately arises as to why a facilitator is needed in the first place. After all, it may be argued, the organization doesn't always use facilitators in other strategic-planning processes, so why here? Regardless of how other processes have been managed, the need remains for a facilitator to ensure the smooth and effective introduction of scenario planning, for the following reasons:

- Scenario-based planning involves a new approach to thinking about the future—a change from single-point forecasting to speculation about alternative possible futures—that will take some time to get used to. It takes a while to appreciate what alternative scenarios really are, and it takes even longer to understand why each step in the methodology does what it does. Throughout the process, first-time (and often second-time and third-time) participants require constant guidance and frequent reminders about what is going on and why.
- Scenario-based planning involves a new approach to making choices about strategy—change from a fixed commitment to a single course of action to a more flexible strategy in the face of uncertainty. This new approach requires a new set of beliefs about what an effective strategy is and how should it be developed and executed. Scenario team participants need a strong image of what the final output will look like, and for first-time efforts, that needs to come from a scenario-planning specialist.

- Scenario-based planning requires an open exchange of ideas about external forces and drivers and how well the organization's possible strategies will fare in the face of those forces and drivers. This includes both structured brainstorming, in which many ideas are desired, and analytical thinking, where it's often necessary to struggle to integrate everyone's perspectives. The process is well designed to elicit inputs from many sources on both the future and strategy, but it will fail if a small set of the participants, or even one, dominates the discussions and doesn't brook other ideas, disagreement, or alternate views.

The appointment of a facilitator is, therefore, both a way of signaling a commitment to this new approach to planning and an effort to deal with the problems inherent in managing a group of smart, strong-willed people who have been charged with reaching an agreement on an important issue.

What Is the Facilitator's Role?

Essentially, the facilitator's role is (as the name would suggest) to maximize the benefits of scenario-based planning, to ease the problems inherent in the change from one system of planning to another, and to guide group discussions. The responsibilities of such a role include:

- Keeping the process moving and on track
- Suggesting new approaches when the process appears to be bogging down
- Ensuring that the scenario team understands, and plays by, the rules
- Cheering the scenario team on when the process is progressing smoothly
- Constantly challenging the reasoning behind the team's conclusions— not to suggest that the reasoning is necessarily wrong, but to ensure that it is debated and made explicit
- Highlighting—and encouraging debate about—seeming contradictions in the team's conclusions, for these may be the basis for alternative futures
- Ensuring that a record is made (in front of the workshop and in a computer) of the major conclusions reached by the team

Who Should Be the Facilitator?

This role can be played by either an "insider" (a member of the scenario planning team—see Step 6) or an "outsider" (e.g., a consultant). In either case, the individual must have a deep understanding of the nature and role of scenarios and some "hands-on" experience with scenario-planning projects.

And in either case—but particularly if an outsider plays this role—the facilitator must adhere strictly to the rules governing the facilitator's role and, at all costs, resist the temptation to lead by imposing his or her own views and conclusions on the group.

What Qualities/Strengths Should the Facilitator Possess?

The most important strength that we should look for in the facilitator is an ability to stimulate open-mindedness and a reach beyond conventional thinking on the part of the scenario team. He or she must exemplify these characteristics in leading the workshops and in encouraging the scenario team members to "think the previously unthinkable," provided there is a sound rationale for it.

The facilitator must have the confidence of decision makers, because they are the ones who will, in the final analysis, actually use the scenarios. They must, therefore, be convinced that the facilitator has guided the team to a set of scenarios that will challenge the decision makers' thinking rather than lead the team astray into the "land of improbable futures."

The question then arises as to whether or not the facilitator should be considered an expert authority in the arena and issues covered by the scenarios. The answer is "Not necessarily." Indeed, the argument can be made that too much expertise can get in the way of the facilitator raising the right questions (because an expert may consider the answers are "obvious"). Other members of the team will bring expertise in various areas to the team's deliberations: The facilitator should bring other talents to the exercise—while knowing enough about the arena in question in question to raise the right questions and evaluate the answers that are offered.

Who Appoints the Facilitator?

The answer to this question depends mainly on the management culture ("the way things are done around here") of the organization—that is, how hierarchical the structure is, and how receptive the organization is to new ways of doing things. However, it is probably safe to say that this appointment, if not made by, has at least to be approved by the senior executive of the organizational unit most affected by the scenarios project—that is, either the general manager of a business unit or the CEO of the company. This makes sense, because they will be the ones most immediately and powerfully affected by this change in the organization's approach to planning, and so need to feel comfortable with the individual selected for this position.

What Are the Outputs of This Step?

A key position in the structure of the scenario team will have been filled and, in the process, the "comfort level" of executives who will eventually be called upon to use the scenarios in their planning will have been raised.

What's Next?

The next step in the process builds on the selection of the facilitator by moving on to the formation of the scenario team—a step in which the facilitator can provide some guidance in suggesting the areas to be covered and the characteristics of individual team members who should be sought out.

CHAPTER 10

FORMING THE SCENARIO TEAM (STEP 6)

What Are the Responsibilities of the Scenario Team?

Basically, the team has three primary responsibilities:

- Defining the critical uncertainties in the business environment that the company must address.
- Developing a set of future scenarios that effectively cover the key alternative outcomes to these uncertainties ("the envelope of uncertainty").
- Initiating the process of thinking through the strategy implications of these scenarios. (It is important to note that the scenario team only *initiates* this process: The aim is to ensure that this consideration of the scenarios' implications permeates strategic planning wherever it occurs in the organization.)

To satisfy these responsibilities, the team will need expertise in a variety of external issues, time to examine the issues and develop scenarios, communication channels to senior executives and key functions of the organization, a team-management process, access to resources, and accountability for generating results.

How Should the Team Be Composed?

Scenario development is, first and foremost, a team effort, typically requiring diverse viewpoints, various kinds of expertise, personal and communication skills and good links to information sources throughout the business—and beyond. Most effective is a group of eight to twelve people who meet these requirements and form the core team, doing most of the work and coordinating the work of others. Their areas of expertise should include the strategies and decisions under consideration and knowledge of the external forces that influence them. As a group, they should be able to represent, at least by proxy, differing points of view held by key executives (assuming, that is, that the top management team is not also the scenario team).

The team should represent a good mix of educational and professional backgrounds as well as differing analytical capabilities. Developing and fleshing out scenarios requires both quantitative and qualitative skills, specialists and generalists, and "hard" analysis balanced with good intuition. The team must be willing to consider new, unconventional, and sometimes controversial ideas about the future: Few situations are deadlier for scenario development than gathering together a group that is unable or unwilling to go much beyond a "business as usual" scenario. And they should be able to work as a team, with no one individual dominating the group's thinking. The importance of this last point was underscored in one project in which the advantage of having the senior executives act as the scenario team was completely nullified by the overriding views of a dominating CEO who brooked no view of the future except his own. But generally this doesn't happen because the methodology is designed to avoid political or biased thinking from dominating the discussion and analysis of the future. The group's task is to develop the best *set* of scenarios to cover the possible futures. None of the scenarios in the set is actually expected to occur; each simply represents one of the plausible directions for the future.

It is advisable not to include too many "numbers" people in the team, to avoid bogging down the project in excessive or premature quantification. There is nothing wrong with elaborating scenarios quantitatively—indeed, doing so is often important, if not essential—but scenario design is initially qualitative.

Two further caveats are worth noting. First, participants should stick with the scenario process from beginning to end. A continually changing membership is highly disruptive and costly. And second, excessive bureaucratization of the process is nullifying: The broader the ownership of the scenarios among relevant decision-making groups, the better. Nonetheless, too many cooks and too much feedback will slow down the process and make it boring—which scenario-development work should never be.

The leader of the scenario team should be a committed generalist who is knowledgeable about the decision areas, familiar with the company's business and culture, and credible to both senior management and staff. It is especially important that the project leader should be able to motivate reluctant participants, mediate among differing views, and translate and communicate the scenarios and their implications to different users.

One critical question arises about the composition of the scenario team: What role, if any, should consultants or other outsiders play? The answer is that they can be stimulating and supportive, but must never, in any way, diminish the essential quality of ownership that executives must have if they are to act on the scenarios. Initiating a scenarios project for the first time means working with an unfamiliar, new approach to planning and dealing with the future business environment holistically and comprehensively. Outside expertise is, therefore, often desirable, particularly in companies that embark on scenario planning to challenge traditional ways of thinking about their business. Ideally, consultants bring the following qualities to a project:

- Methodology and process expertise.
- Knowledge of the company's business. (Strictly speaking, this knowledge is not essential if client and consultant establish a close working relationship beforehand, and the client can bring this knowledge to the table.)
- Specialized expertise about topics and issues outside the client company's range of knowledge.
- Capabilities (in individuals or processes) for pushing participants beyond conventional frames of reference in looking at the company's future business environment.
- Usual consulting-project management skills and the ability to work smoothly with both planners and senior executives.
- Willingness to involve clients in the scenario development process and ensure the needed transfer of know-how in the course of the project.

Corporate culture and available resources are, of course, significant determinants of how firms use consultants over time. Typically, firms that implement scenario planning as a key management process continue to use consultants in the following roles:

- Process experts, who return to lead or assist with scenario development, help refine methodology, and introduce new techniques
- Substantive experts, who provide independent information and insight on key issues
- Providers of information services for environmental monitoring and scanning

How to Form the Team

Because many of the best people of the organization will be wanted for the scenario team (who typically are the most busy), it will be necessary for the executives who are involved to make the resources available or negotiate their release.

The scenario-planning champion should develop a list of the desired scenario team members and then meet with the senior executive responsible for the effort to agree on the team members and how to obtain their participation on the project.

Once the team members are set, it helps considerably if, before the first workshop, the team meets to review the total project, the team's role in it, and the amount of time (and ideas and information) that team members will be expected to contribute. We have found that such a meeting often has the additional advantage of giving team members an opportunity to start getting to know one another. All too frequently, in today's functionally segmented corporate organizations, this is the first opportunity many of them have to work together.

The greatest need at this stage for the team is to develop an understanding of exactly what scenarios are (and are not), how they should be used, and what changes they require in the organization's approach to strategy and its execution. A distribution of selective background materials on scenario planning, including excerpts of this volume, can serve to promote this understanding. However, this learning process can be heightened and accelerated by bringing the scenario team together before the start of the scenario development process.

What Are the Outputs of This Step?

- A scenario team of eight to twelve members committed to the objectives of the project

What's Next?

With the team formed and the planning complete, the next step is to start the process of developing the scenarios. In the next few chapters, the steps for gathering the necessary background information, identifying the key external issues, and exploring potential external-environment dynamics will be described.

PART 3

STEPS IN LAYING THE ENVIRONMENTAL ANALYSIS FOUNDATION

Part 3 of this book deals with the steps of the scenario-planning methodology that are focused on gathering all the necessary information about the external environment to address the particular decision or strategy issue.

As the quote by Ian Wilson at the beginning of the book suggests, all our knowledge is about the past, but what we need is insight about the future. This dilemma is heightened by our experience that the future rarely plays out as we expect and that this always seems to be maddeningly true when the stakes are the highest for us. Adding to our frustration is the realization that when we go back and review what happened, the evidence for how the future was going to play out, for the discontinuity that occurred, for the new markets that emerged was there in front of us. We simply didn't have the means, or never took the time, to look for the evidence and seek to understand what it could mean.

At this stage in the methodology, the team members' responsibilities are to identify the key strategic levers in the external environment, bring forward all the best insights and knowledge on the topics that exist within the organization, and fill gaps in the knowledge and understanding of key issues.

Chapter 11 covers the gathering of information and views about the external environment, the new signals of change, and new models for how the environment could work in the future. It addresses what information to gather and where to go do it.

Chapters 12 and 13 describe the initial workshop activities in the scenario development methodology. Chapter 12 grounds the scenario team in the purpose of the scenario planning effort by focusing on the overall decision and key external uncertainties that could affect that decision. This focus ensures that the scenario-planning outputs will support the strategic needs of the organization.

Chapter 13 addresses the identification of the forces and drivers that could be important in the future and that determine how the specific world in which the decision will play out will work. It describes how to identify the relevant social, political, economic, market, competition, customer, and technological forces and drivers, and what information is needed about each to develop alternative models of how the future will work.

Finally, Chapter 14 describes filling in of gaps in the scenario team's knowledge and understanding of the external environment. Even an ideal team won't have individuals knowledgeable on every conceivable topic of importance. Gaps in the team's knowledge become apparent through the in-depth workshop discussions about the external environmental forces and drivers. Priorities for filling those gaps are identified, and then appropriate team members are assigned the responsibility of conducting focused investigatory activities before the next assembly of the team.

While the sequencing of the chapters in Part 2 is not important, the sequence of steps described in Part 3 must be followed. The chapters are meant to read in order, although each stands alone as a specific step in the scenario-planning methodology.

CHAPTER 11

GATHERING AVAILABLE DATA, VIEWS, AND PROJECTIONS (STEP 7)

Why Do We Need to Gather Information?

Scenarios depend equally, for their success and utility, on ideas and information. That is to say, they require both data on what *has* happened and insight into what *may* happen—and why—in the future. For most decision-making situations, much of the data and insight needed already reside within the organization; it's a matter of finding and unveiling them.

Many organizations find that the process of internal discovery generates two important benefits: (1) integration of the various, voluminous, and often disparate information about the business environment that is spread throughout the organization, and (2) reconciliation of the differing views and projections of key managers and executives about the future. An important early step, then, in the overall scenario-planning effort is to gather the available materials, studies, and knowledge bits that exist, and ensure that the important views of the organization are being represented. These data will then be shared with the scenario team as part of the process of creating the scenarios.

What Must We Accomplish?

The overall objective of this step is to prepare for the start of the scenario-planning effort by bringing forward the information, knowledge, and views about key trends in the business environment that relate to the decision and by gathering expert insights about how the business environment could play out in the future. Much of the information about the past will be obtained from internal files and databases or from sources published electronically and will include market and business studies, speeches by industry and company leaders, business media reports, government studies, sales force reports, and so on. Information about future trends and uncertainties will be found in many sources, but particularly in the minds of senior managers and executives.

It is important to be selective in the amount of data and viewpoints that the team members are asked to absorb. Passing on too much information is open to two conflicting problems. On the one hand, information overload can set in and militate against effective usage of what data are available. On the other hand, too much reliance can be placed on existing materials to the detriment of engaging in new insights.

From one week to four weeks are required to gather the information that is available and needed for the project. This abbreviated search for information forces the project team to be focused in what it collects from sources, and doesn't allow new extensive analyses. In general, there already is too much information available about the issues, and we don't need to be creating more. What we want to accomplish is pull together information to:

- Remind the scenario team members of the range of issues involved.
- Stimulate their thinking about what's possible and the potential implications.
- Fill in gaps of knowledge within the team.

How to Conduct This Work

Three avenues are followed to obtain the desired information: (1) Gather available studies and data from inside the organization; (2) conduct secondary research of external sources; and (3) interview key internal experts, managers, and executives for their knowledge and views. The members of the scenario team are charged with doing this work.

Pulling Together What's Available Internally

For the first avenue, the scenario team quickly scours the organization for whatever studies, assessments, and information exist on the main focus. Very often the organization has purchased or gathered reports on many relevant subjects, and the scenario team usually has to make a specific request to gain access to the reports. Some organizations have well-developed intelligence or knowledge-management functions that can be leveraged for this task.

As a general rule of thumb, the search for internally available materials that might be of assistance to the scenario team should focus more on materials that try to explain the changing dynamics of the present and the way they might play out in the future rather than on materials that purport to predict exactly what the future will be. After all, one major reason for making the move to scenario planning is presumably dissatisfaction with the product of the current forecasting system—its obvious *in*ability to forecast the future with any degree of accuracy. The search should, therefore, be focused on studies that will stimulate the team's thinking about the present and the future, rather than on single-point projections of the future.

Once these studies and reports have been gathered, it's usually evident that additional information is needed. Often a major reason for this is that the information available internally is old and dated. Another reason is that the decision focus is not within the current scope of the organization's activities, and little information has been developed.

Conducting Secondary Research

In the second avenue followed, the team conducts secondary research of external sources. The activities include identifying the potential topics for which information should be gathered, selecting the best set of topics, collecting what is readily available, reviewing the gathered information, and compiling a summary of the information, to be presented to the rest of the scenario team.

As a guide to how much information to compile by this means, we recommend developing 10 to 20 "chunks" of information to achieve the purposes of providing understanding of the range of issues, stimulating thinking, and filling knowledge gaps. Each "chunk" will include some background information and facts about a topic, identification of major uncertainties, and a discussion of the topic's implications for the organization; each "chunk" is assembled by scenario team members. Often an article from a magazine or journal or a chapter from a book will have all the information that's needed.

The 10 to 20 topics are selected from many possibilities. The team prompts itself on the possibilities by using some management frameworks for analyzing the external environment. In projects we've managed, we've found the following frameworks to be helpful:

- S-E-P-T. What Social, Economic, Political, and Technology issues could be important to how the future plays out?
- Porter's forces driving industry competition. What are the threat of new entrants, the bargaining power of buyers, the threat of substitute products or services, and the bargaining power of suppliers?
- SRIC-BI's trilogy. What customer-demand issues will shape the future? What technology and product/service innovations will influence the future? What competition issues will be important?
- Determinants of corporate success. What elements of company strategy will determine future success in the business arena? These could include product mix, innovation, marketing, sales and distribution, operations, research and development, cost structure, finance, organization, human resources, and management and leadership.
- Geographic coverage: What are the geographic issues? Developing versus developed countries? Western Europe, North America, Asia?

Once a group of possible topics is identified, the scenario team members select 10 to 20 topics from the possibilities by applying three criteria:

1. Does the topic help represent the range of issues involved?
2. Will it stimulate the thinking of the scenario team?
3. Does it fill a gap in the team's knowledge of the external environment?

Individuals are then assigned to develop the information for each topic, based on their backgrounds and expertise. It's not necessary to be an expert on a specific topic to develop the needed information for the scenario process; one must simply be capable of reading inputs on the topic from different sources and summarizing the key issues for the group.

The desired deliverable on each topic is a short written summary. If a magazine or journal article isn't succinct enough, or if several sources need to be integrated, then a summary will need to be prepared. Typical instructions to the members responsible for producing these summaries are:

- Spend no more than a day on a topic.
- Use readily available information that can be gathered quickly from internal or external sources.
- Prepare a Word document that is no more than two pages long (or a PowerPoint document of 10 pages).
- Answer no more than three to four basic questions in the document:
  - What is important about this topic?
  - What are the key trends and uncertainties?
  - What are potential developments and outcomes in the future?
  - What are potential implications for the decision focus?

Interviewing Key Thought Leaders

The third avenue for gathering information is interviews with key thought leaders on the future. Since only a limited number of people can be directly involved in the process of developing the scenarios, it's important to identify the differing views in the organization on the important forces that will shape the business environment, understand what issues keep people awake at night, and survey beliefs on what the future dynamics will be. An effective technique for developing that information is to conduct 30-minute to 2-hour structured interviews with key individuals who have something to contribute. If the interviews are with internal personnel, then in-person interviews are preferred, although telephone interviews are appropriate when talking to individuals in remote offices. When interviewing external personnel, it's often too expensive to schedule and conduct the interviews in person, so telephone interviews are used.

Standard interview protocols should be observed to ensure that the interviews are productive and that they generate the desired information for the process. It's good practice to send a topic outline and selected questions to interviewees ahead of time. Issues of answer confidentiality, attribution, and so on should be addressed before the interview starts so that interviewees understand how their input or views in the interview might be used or communicated.

Although a list of questions for each interviewee should be developed in advance, each interview is usually conducted in an open-ended fashion. This will encourage interviewees to make unforeseen connections with the various forces, drivers, and the decision focus, so as to develop alternative views of the future. Ideally, two interviewers are used in each interview so that a question is always ready for the interviewee and complete notes are taken.

Interview notes should be prepared immediately after an interview is completed. When we conduct the interviews as consultants, our practice is to finish the notes before the day is over (or when traveling, before allowing ourselves any food in the evening). Depending on the confidentiality commitment made, the results can then be quickly shared.

What Are the Outputs?

The outputs of this step are selected articles, summary presentations on key forces and drivers, and notes on the views of key thought leaders. These often are packaged together in a binder or folder for the scenario team to review. They can then be referred to in the subsequent steps.

How Do We Make This Information Gathering a Success?

The key to this step is to stay focused and not let the time or costs expand beyond the plan. Strong project management is needed to make choices on what information is needed, to assign someone to get the information, and to produce quick summaries of results. Given the emphasis on keeping to a schedule and the need to interview people who have busy schedules, it's helpful for the senior executive or sponsor of the project to make the requests for information interviews.

This step generates very valuable information for the scenario team and it's important to schedule presentations of this step's results into the agendas of the scenario-planning workshops. Every person on the scenario team should learn the results of this step to help build the common base of understanding about the external environment that is needed to develop good scenarios.

Later, when the results of the scenario planning are being communicated to the organization, the interviewees can help sell the results by vouching for the fact that their inputs were used and are represented in the specific scenarios.

CHAPTER 12

IDENTIFYING AND ASSESSING KEY DECISION FACTORS (STEP 8)

Typically this is the stage at which the first scenario workshop is held, with an agenda covering three major topics:

1. Clarification and elaboration of the decision focus for the project
2. Identification and assessment of the key decision factors
3. Identification of the critical forces and drivers in the macro- and micro-environments

In this step, the scenario team clarifies the decision focus and then identifies and assesses the key decision factors.

Why Do We Need to Focus on the Decision Again?

By now, the decision focus for the scenario planning will have been developed by senior executives (see Step 3) who then delegated responsibility for the development of the scenarios to the scenario team. This is not to say, however, that the focus is well defined or that the key issues are very well understood. Consequently, as the team begins building the foundation for the scenarios, a great deal of insight and clarification can be gained by discussing such questions as:

- What is the reasoning behind the selection of this particular decision focus? Are there underlying assumptions of imminent major changes in this area? If so, what are these assumptions?
- Would the decision in question represent a major departure from the organization's current trajectory? Or would it represent just a modification of existing strategy?
- How does the decision relate to other goals, objectives, and values of the organization?

Through the give-and-take of open discussion of such questions, the scenario team can "internalize" the reasoning behind the selection of this decision focus and so make it the basis for their own reasoning and for the next steps in the process. The importance of this elaboration and clarification of the decision focus becomes even more apparent later in the methodology when emphasis is on the strategic implications of the scenarios.

In addition, though, the team typically needs to develop a more complete description of the decision focus. Early descriptions often don't adequately address all the scope issues, including:

- The time frame for when the decisions will be made
- The time period for the scenarios of the future (they can range from less than five years for some high-tech industries to more than 20 years for some energy industries)
- Geographic coverage
- Business areas, functions, technologies, markets, and so on included and excluded

The discussion of the decision focus typically requires one to two hours. To guide the discussion, the facilitator often will prepare a "straw-man" description of the decision focus for everyone to read. This helps define the scope and nature of the discussion to be conducted.

Introducing Key Decision Factors

Having established the central focus and purpose of the project, the scenario team can then identify and analyze the key decision factors (KDFs) of the decision. What are KDFs? In simple terms, they are the key externalities affecting the decision; or—put another way—they are the events or outcomes about the future that we would like to know more about to improve the quality and relevance of our decision. KDFs thus become critical elements in grounding the scenarios in operational utility.

Obviously, these factors will vary from one decision or organization to another. For example, for a decision about an anticipated major expansion of manufacturing facilities, decision factors might include market size, growth, and volatility; competing products or substitutes resulting from new technology; long-range economic conditions and price trends; government regulation; and competition. Other typical decision factors include capital availability and costs, human resources, material and energy resources, technological availability and capacity, economic performance of particular businesses, profit margins, and so on. Information about the future "value" (or range of values) of these factors will come from the scenarios.

The important thing to note about these decision factors is that they all relate to *external, largely uncontrollable* conditions. This is not, of course, to suggest that the more controllable internal factors—such as a company's strengths and weaknesses, culture and organization—are unimportant and irrelevant to the decision, Of course, they are, but because they are controllable, decisions about them belong more appropriately in the strategizing phase rather than in the scenario-development phase of the decision-making cycle. Scenarios, we should remember, are designed to give us insights into the sort of market and competitive environment, the social and political climate, that we may encounter. Then, and only then, should we make our decisions about what we should do.

How to Develop the KDFs for a Decision

The steps in the workshop are to brainstorm potential KDFs, conduct some clustering to combine similar issues and eliminate duplicates, and then select the most important ones to be addressed by the scenarios. The specific steps are to:

1. Identify as many decision factors as seem relevant. The typical means for drawing out the KDFs is to pose questions to decision makers and thought leaders about what external issues they're most concerned with. In the workshop an effective technique is to pose the "Oracle" question: If there were a business oracle that you could go to and ask one question about the future, what would you ask? (To help stimulate the workshop participants, we tell them to assume that their entire career depends on what they recommend for the decision. Given this, what one question would they ask the oracle?) In surveying the scenario team members in the workshop, there typically is very little agreement on what the questions should be and the step generates a raft of interesting requests. It's common for 20 to 35 requests to emerge from the discussion. One technique for recording the questions is to have each participant write their requests on 8" × 5" cards (one per card), using the back of the card to record details. Then the cards are posted on the wall in front of the entire workshop group.

2. Examine the requests and cluster them by focus or topic. The facilitator will often ask the workshop members to develop five to eight clusters from the submitted requests. Through discussion, the workshop members identify possible clusters, experiment with different arrangements of the requests, and finally agree on a set of clusters to be addressed in the scenarios. Some individual requests end up as single-item clusters, but typically there are two to five requests in a cluster.

3. Apply a label or title to the cluster.

In a workshop setting, the development of the key decision factors will typically require from two hours to four hours to complete.

In 2003-2005, SRIC-BI conducted several scenario projects for financial services companies focused on developing new opportunities to serve the aging baby boomers in the United States. KDFs in those projects included the consumer behavior of the boomers, U.S. and state regulations and tax policies, the economic prosperity in the United States, innovations in products and services serving the aging population, and healthcare practices. An example of the individual oracle questions from workshop participants, clustered into five KDFs, is shown in Box 12-1.

BOX 12-1
Example: Key Decision Factors for Serving the Financial Needs of U.S. Boomers

If I could ask the oracle one question about the future as I get ready to make new investments in innovative products and services for serving the financial needs over the next 15 years of retiring boomers, what would it be?

Key Decision Factor Cluster: Consumer/Retiree Behavior

- What will the different segments of boomers do?
- What will the pre-boomers do?
- What will high-end, early-adopter boomers do?
- How will boomers and pre-boomers make retirement-related decisions? What will they value in the process? How will they get information? What will they believe/understand?
- How will consumers interact and use the media?
- What technology will consumers use?

Key Decision Factor Cluster: Financial System and Economy

- How will the U.S. economy perform?
- What will the financial system look like?
- Will there be significant scandals and fall out?

Key Decision Factor Cluster: Government Policies

- What will federal, state, and local tax policies be?
- What will social security look like?

- How much will government intervene or be part of the services provided?

Key Decision Factor Cluster: Social and Health Issues

- What will the "border" situation look like?
- What healthcare solutions will emerge and be used in the future? How will consumers receive healthcare?
- What will healthcare cost?
- What will work look like, particularly for employees over 60?

Key Decision Factor Cluster: New Services and Solutions Provided

- What new services or solutions will emerge?
- How will services be developed, "manufactured," and delivered to consumers?
- What will be new industries/markets?
- What will things cost?

To some, this detailed analysis of the decision focus might seem to be overly laborious, but we have found the step essential to constructing effective scenarios for decision making. The oracle question highlights those external issues that scenario team members (and decision makers) believe will have the biggest impact on the success or failure of the decision. And it never fails to stimulate a robust set of interesting and challenging questions from the participants. When viewing the diversity of important questions presented, participants often become energized by the range of issues they see and the challenge to make sense of all of them on behalf of the organization. Important team building occurs at this point as members realize it will take their collective insights and effort to succeed.

Output of This Step

The output of this step includes a clear statement of the focus of the scenarios and identification of important areas of uncertainty that the scenarios need to help address. The rest of the scenario-development activities then are oriented to developing the potential outcomes for the KDFs. One way to think about it is that the KDFs will become the chapter headings for each scenario. Not only do the KDFs serve to focus attention on what is truly important about the future for the decision in question: They also, importantly, sharpen the strategic thinking of the scenario team.

CHAPTER 13

IDENTIFYING THE CRITICAL FORCES AND DRIVERS (STEP 9)

The Importance of Developing a Model of the External Environment

Having thus defined the external arenas that the scenarios should cover, the team can now turn its attention to identifying the key trends and uncertainties that will form the warp and woof of the scenarios. In simple terms, there is no oracle to respond with answers to the key decision factors (KDFs) questions, and so the team must analyze the forces and drivers that will determine the outcomes for the KDFs.

The goal of the step is to construct what we can think of as a conceptual model of the dynamics of the business environment. To do this, we need to develop as inclusive a list as possible of forces and drivers—a complete set rather than an elegant one—and then build a simple model of the environment from that list.

There is no particular framework for ensuring that all the relevant forces and drivers have been identified, but Box 13-1 provides a checklist to help in identifying the key forces that the scenarios should cover. Such words as "trends," "conditions," "forces," "factors," "events," "areas of uncertainty," and the like are all examples of what deserves attention.

The diversity of backgrounds, interests, and professional competencies among members of the scenario team should be an asset in ensuring a comprehensive listing of key forces—provided that we have some way of capturing (and organizing) the diversity of the team's input. A relatively comprehensive, yet simple, way of doing this is to construct a schematic of the dynamics of the business environment. Figure 13-1 shows a three-tier structure that we've found very useful for showing the interaction of forces that will shape the future environment for which we have to plan. While not possessing the mathematical precision of a computer model (though this can be created at a later stage), this approach has the twin merits of structure and comprehensiveness.

To reiterate, we must make every effort at this stage to ensure that our mapping of external forces is as complete as possible. We should not be deterred by the seeming impracticality of manipulating as many as 100–200 forces,

BOX 13-1
Frameworks for Characterizing External
Environmental Forces

Many different frameworks are useful for identifying relevant forces. A common one is the S-E-P-T scheme in which environmental conditions are organized in terms of Social, Economic, Political, and Technological forces. This S-E-P-T scheme can be elaborated by considering forces in terms of local, national, and global consequence, for example. A more elaborate scheme is listed below.

Category	Examples
Demographic patterns	Age, family, household and ethnic structures and trends
	Regional and national migration
	Labor force structure and trends
Social and lifestyle factors	Consumer values, needs, and wants
	Psychographic profiles
	Education levels
	Employee concerns and issues
	Special interest groups
Economic conditions	Macroeconomic trends (gross national product, trade, inflation, and the like)
	Microeconomic trends (markets, competition, unionization, consumer spending)
	Regional and national variations
	Economic structure
Natural resources	Energy prices and availability
	Raw materials prices and availability
	Land resources
Physical environment (ecosystems)	Effluents and toxic wastes
	Environmental quality
	Land use policies

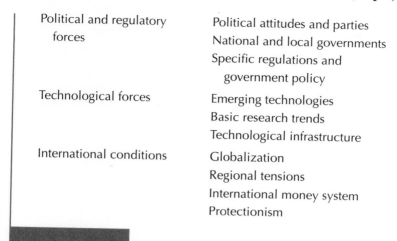

Political and regulatory forces	Political attitudes and parties
	National and local governments
	Specific regulations and government policy
Technological forces	Emerging technologies
	Basic research trends
	Technological infrastructure
International conditions	Globalization
	Regional tensions
	International money system
	Protectionism

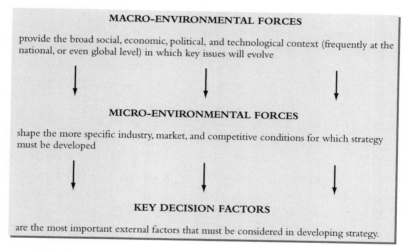

MACRO-ENVIRONMENTAL FORCES

provide the broad social, economic, political, and technological context (frequently at the national, or even global level) in which key issues will evolve

MICRO-ENVIRONMENTAL FORCES

shape the more specific industry, market, and competitive conditions for which strategy must be developed

KEY DECISION FACTORS

are the most important external factors that must be considered in developing strategy.

Figure 13-1

which is frequently the case at this stage. This multiplicity of forces in our model is an accurate reflection of the complexity of the real world. And it is easier (and more systematic) to take the time to build up a complete inventory of these forces at the start, and then to prioritize them down to what we term the "key axes of uncertainty," than it is to make additional inputs later in the process.

How Does the Team Conduct This Step?

The workshop is an ideal stage for building the conceptual model of how the future environment could operate. In a very short period of time, which will vary from four hours to two days depending on the assignment, the scenario team will map out the major external dynamics and issues that will ultimately determine the success or failure of the decision. At first glance, this seems an almost impossible task to accomplish in such a short period of time. But the workshop activities take advantage of the human brain's ability to synthesize inputs, creatively and rapidly, on a myriad of forces. Structured workshop activities provide the means for scenario team members to learn about inter-actions among the many forces, to absorb new details, and to make connec-tions across a variety of functions, disciplines, markets, technologies, and so on. Each scenario team member is called upon to provide input about the im-portant trends, uncertainties, and issues that he or she is familiar with, but is also expected to listen carefully when the others are speaking, so as to learn about the many issues and possibilities.

The facilitator of the workshop manages the discussion by asking the scenario team members to describe the major forces and drivers that will determine how the KDFs play out. Over the four-hour to two-day period, the facilitator expects to draw out 100 to 200 forces and drivers from the team members.

To assist in capturing the force and driver descriptions by the team mem-bers, notes are taken on white boards or large easels placed in front of the group. To ensure accuracy and completeness of the notes, the person describ-ing the force or driver is often asked to fill in a form with pertinent details about the force or driver before discussing it with the team. The specific top-ics to be filled in on the form include (see Figure 13-2 for an example):

- Name of force or driver
- A sentence describing the force or driver
- Possible outcomes in the future for the force or driver
- What the force or driver will influence
- What the force or driver is influenced by

A simple way to organize this discussion is by KDF. The facilitator poses the question, "What forces and drivers will determine the outcomes for KDF number one (e.g., the nature of healthcare services delivered to individuals over 50 years old in the United States from 2010-2015)?" The facilitator then gives the group approximately 10 minutes to begin filling in description forms. The discussion begins when the facilitator asks someone to briefly

Figure 13-2   Sample Force/Driver Description

Force/Driver Name: INTELLECTUAL PROPERTY LAWS AND RULINGS

Describe What It Is:

Patent offices around the world are under siege by new applications. Practices vary from one country and region to another. The scope and benefits of patent rights are being challenged in legal and legislative forums.

What Are Possible Outcomes over the Next Five Years?

- WTO countries agree on a worldwide patent rights system; alternatively, the situation stays largely the same.
- Technology changes could expedite the processing of patent applications to reduce waits in the United States to one year on average; alternatively, the increase in applications may continue and the wait time could increase on average to five years.
- The criteria or standard for awarding a patent could tighten significantly to reduce the number of patents awarded by 50% from today's levels and severely limit the coverage of the patent.
- Costs per patent application and maintenance could be restructured such that fees on average rise by 100%; alternatively, they could remain unchanged.

What Other Forces Influence It?

- Court rulings on patent rights
- Number of patent applications received around the world
- WTO influence

What Other Forces Are Influenced by It?

- Number of patent applications received around the world
- Technology development activities of companies interested in drug delivery and patient monitoring
- Lawsuits on patent-right infringement in drug delivery systems

---

describe one of his or her forces or drivers. This approach generally results in approximately one hour of discussion per KDF.

This step is an open brainstorming activity, and all inputs by group participants are accepted. It's important for the facilitator to emphasize that the objective of the step is to identify as complete a set of forces and drivers as possible, and to remind participants not to worry about which ones are more important than others or whether they deserve to be mentioned at all. Later in the process, critical thinking activities will be used to sort out the most important forces and drivers and how uncertain their future dynamics and outcomes appear to be compared to others.

Once the group has finished attempting to identify the forces and drivers that will be relevant to projecting the outcomes for the different KDFs, group members typically have exhausted the forces and drivers that might be relevant to their decision. The facilitator or group then begins the process of organizing the forces and drivers that were identified. A simple structure to follow is to organize them by macro-environmental and micro-environmental and then by subgroupings within each. An example of a conceptual model for a forest products company wishing to make environmental management decisions is shown in Figure 13-3.

We can, however, get a better sense of the dynamics of this environment by tracing the varying impacts of macro- and micro-forces on the key decision factors—for instance, in this example, on the regulatory (Figure 13-4) and competitive (Figure 13-5) setting.

What Are the Outputs of This Step?

The outputs of this step include individual force and driver descriptions prepared by scenario team members and the schematic of the external environment. With these outputs the group has, in effect, created a clear map of the forces and drivers that will define the group's future, and the group has accomplished this in a relatively short period of time. In addition, by concentrating on how one force or driver influences another and by listening carefully to what everyone else is describing, the group has begun the process of creating alternative mental models for how the world could operate. Much work is still needed, and the outputs are not yet useful to decision makers, but the scenario foundation has been set.

Global and U.S. Economy
- Overall performance
- Industrial production
- U.S. housing starts
- Advertising
- Retailing
- Packaging trends
- Business communications
- Global paper/paperboard consumption
- Energy prices
- Exchange rates

Regional Business Environment
- Economy and structure
- Business climate
- Costs of doing business
- Demographics
- Quality of life
  - Urbanization
  - Migration
  - Income

Regulatory and Legal Setting
- Focus and style of regulation
- Dispute resolution systems
- National versus local preemption
- CO emissions
- Federal Laws
- National energy policy
- Trade (taxes, tariffs, environmental regulations)
- Liability
- Pollution prevention

State of the Environment
- Old growth timber/tree farms
- Water quality
- Landfill capacity and economics
- Global issues
- Global warming
- State of the ecological science

Environmentalism
- Attitudes about
  - Reuse/recycling
  - Sustainability
  - Nature and species
- Knowledge about the environment
- Nature of environmentalism
- Nature of activism
- Aesthetics
- Business Positions and practices

Socioeconomic Trends and Values
- Demographics
- Work force sophistication
- Two-tiered society
- Political priorities
- Education priorities
- Economy/environment trade-offs

Stakeholder Positions
- Electorate and politicians
- Environmental groups
- Neighbor communities
- Regulators/governments
- Customers
- Employees
- Investors
- Media
- Unions
- Others

Market Demands
- Solidwood products
- Paper
- Paperboard
- Pulp
- Chips/fuels
- Log exports/imports
- Homes
- Customer needs
  - Quality
  - Life-cycle costs

Forest Products Inputs
- Timber/asset base changes
- Regional variations in costs
  - Pulp
  - Recycled fibers
- Regional production
- Raw material imports/new supplies and exports

Residuals and Recycled Materials
- Market demand
- Markets/uses
- Prices
- Supplies
- Costs
- Waste composition

Regional Energy Issues
- Demand
- Natural gas (Canada, Texas , LNG imports)
- Costs
- Electricity supply
- Cogeneration

Industry Regulations
- Mandated technologies
- Environmental
  - Endangered species
  - Forestry practices
  - Chlorine use
  - Recycled content
  - Water quality
  - Solid wastes
  - Landfills
  - Slash burning
  - Quarantines
  - Air quality
- Energy production
- Timber import/export policy
- Enforcement

Industry Technologies
- Closed-cycle manufacturing
- Waste management and handling
- Efficiencies and process yields
- Monitoring technologies
- Customer technologies (e.g., new inks)
- Recycling
  - Sorting and separation
  - Mill residuals
- Forest designs
- Thinning

Industry Structure
- Capital availability
- Regional manufacturing capacity/investment
- Regional industry structure
- Relative regional competitiveness
- Direct foreign investment
- Environmental posture and practices
- Alliances

Key Decision Factors → Environmental Management Alternatives → Environmental Regulatory Setting → Residuals → Competitive Setting → Stakeholder Views

Figure 13-3 Mapping the Forces for Environmental Management Scenarios

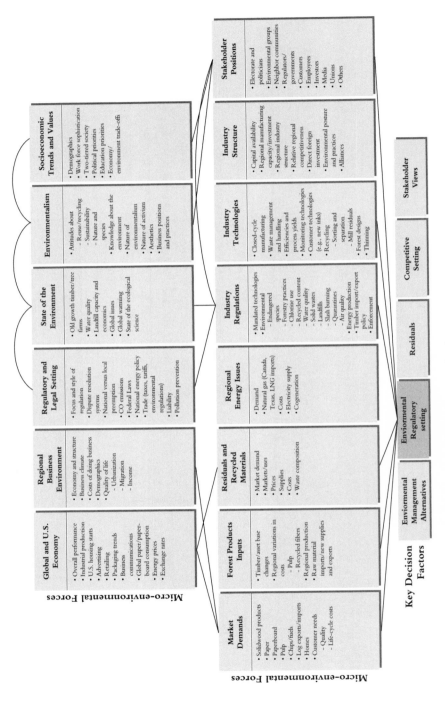

Figure 13-4 Dynamics of the Environmental Management Setting

94

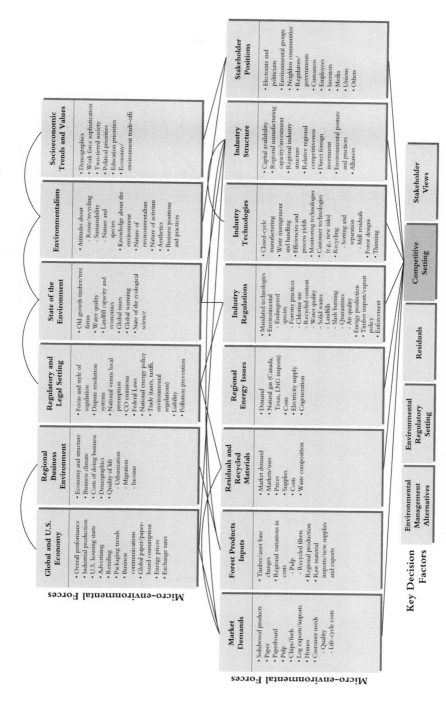

Figure 13-5 Dynamics of the Environmental Management Setting

95

CHAPTER 14

CONDUCTING FOCUSED RESEARCH (STEP 10)

Why Do We Need Research Now?

In a scenario project, the period between the first and second workshops is devoted to editing and distributing the results of the first workshop to team members and to preparing focus papers on key forces and issues (see Box 8-1, "Calendar/Time Line of a Typical Project").

Up to this point, the research to support the scenario effort has consisted of gathering readily available articles, reports, and analyses within the company and surveying the managers and decision makers on what they think the key issues are. Now that a wide-ranging discussion of the external environment has been completed, the team probably sees an immediate need for sharing currently available information among members of the team and for filling important gaps in the team's knowledge and understanding of the external environment. The team has a clearer sense of what information (about key trends, issues, branching points, forecasts, etc.) is needed to proceed to the next stage of scenario development and who or what is the best source of current information on these subjects. In this step, therefore, we ask these sources to do a "dump" of their *currently available* ideas and information for the scenario team.

However, we should distinguish between this need for a dump of information and the need for basic in-depth research on new forces and trends that have come to light through the scenario process. At least these forces and trends are "new" in the sense that they are not factors in current management thinking and planning. In these cases we need to assign long-term responsibility for conducting the required research and reporting back on the results to ensure that future rounds of scenarios take these new perspectives into account. Clearly this type and level of research is time-consuming and stretches beyond the limits of a single round of scenario development.

Because the team doesn't want to be sidetracked at this stage by a series of large research tasks, it needs to stay focused on producing the best set of scenarios describing the future, largely using the (probably) abundant resources already at hand, in a reasonable period of time. The team needs a quick sharing of information on key issues, delivered in easy-to-understand ways. Large research assignments should be defined and scheduled for future scenario efforts. At this stage, the objective is simply to bring the other team members up to speed and to fill gaps.

What Must We Accomplish?

The basic purpose of these focus papers is to develop a shared understanding among team members of the future prospects for key formative forces that the scenarios must deal with—what the major trends and uncertainties are; how the forces are interrelated; which are most important in influencing the course of the key decision factors; and which best represent underlying or driving forces for significant change in the future.

Given the normal time schedule for a scenario-planning project, it is standard practice to limit the focus papers both in number and length—perhaps half a dozen or so key topics, each of, say, three to six pages of text (or 10–15 slides).

The step should not be allowed to affect the overall schedule and should be completed in a two-week to one-month period. This will also allow the team to remain generally familiar with the issues and maintain enthusiasm for learning about the external environment.

How Do We Do It?

At the end of the discussion of the external forces and drivers (Step 8), the facilitator should ask the group to identify the biggest gaps in its knowledge or expertise and which issues should be understood in more detail for the purposes of creating decision-support scenarios. The scenario team does a quick brainstorming and selection process and then assigns responsibility for conducting the studies and presenting the results back to the team.

In the environmental management decision case (see Figures 13-3, 13-4, and 13-5) for example, the team elected to have focus papers prepared on:

- Public views and attitudes toward the industry, timber, and manufacturing wastes
- Conflict resolution structures and practices
- Recycling markets and economics
- Timber supply restrictions
- Market dynamics of forest products residuals
- Characterization of manufacturing wastes
- The structure of the forest products industry
- The energy issues by region

The question arises here as to whom the team should turn for this work. There is much to be said for using team members as authors of these focus papers. They, after all, are the ones who will interpret and use this information in their subsequent work on the scenarios, and so have the greatest stake in the quality and relevance of the information contained in the papers. This doesn't mean the authors must do all the work, but they must be sufficiently involved to explain the paper's key findings and to deal with questions of interpretation or the need for supplemental information in later stages of the project. Other things being equal—it is also preferable to use inside rather than outside sources as authors of these papers. But in the final analysis, the key question to be asked in this assignment process is: "Who can best, and most quickly, prepare these focus papers with an in-depth understanding of the scenario process and the team's needs?"

The key to success in this step is not to plan extensive research but to organize quick dives for information. The information that the team needs will be readily available through secondary research or a few interviews with outside experts. If it isn't, then the issue probably isn't one that deserves additional attention at this stage in the project. One significant benefit of going through the scenario-planning process is the sorting and organizing that occurs of the many external issues that relate to a decision and the overwhelming amount of information that is available on those issues. The process is not about uncovering bits of information that no one else has found, but about making sense of the complexity of information that is already there.

Effective instructions that we've given to scenario team members charged with preparing a focus paper include: "Spend no more than three days of working time to create a written report of no more than three pages (or a slide presentation of no more than ten pages)."

To harmonize the work of the various authors, it is helpful, if not essential, to develop guidelines for the preparation of the focus papers. For example, authors should be encouraged to:

- Cluster forces together, where possible, in ways that make sense
- Analyze major clusters of forces in terms of:
  - Their apparent direction today; that is, current trends
  - Major uncertainties; that is, how much, in what ways, and how fast might current trends change in the future?
  - Their impact on the key decision factors; that is, which forces are of most, moderate, or least importance
- Identify the most important underlying forces that can best serve to explain how other forces will change. For example, birth and death

rates are key elements of changing demographic patterns. But economic conditions and changing consumer values come closer to being more significant underlying forces of change.

- Discuss potential implications for the decision. What opportunities might be created for organizations in the future, or how might current competitors be threatened by potential developments?

How Are the Results Delivered?

The most effective means for delivering the results of each study is a crisp presentation by the responsible scenario team member of the critical points. These presentations should be included in a workshop agenda because the discussions will stimulate much learning in the scenario team about specific challenges the organization will face in the future, how the world could operate, and what will be important issues to monitor, going forward. We often suggest scheduling 30 minutes for each topic, 15 minutes to show slides and 15 minutes for discussion.

These discussions—requiring perhaps some two to four hours of the opening day of the second workshop—serve to stimulate the group's thinking, highlighting significant agreements and differences of opinion (which may turn out to be the bases for differing scenarios), and set the stage for a systematic ranking of the macro- and micro-forces.

Copies of the presentations should be distributed to all the team members. It's usually sufficient to do this during the workshop, and not before, since the key points are being made in the workshop.

In the Future

The search for insight and background materials, it is important to say, should be a continuing effort, not restricted to the period of the team's preparation for this step. Frequently we have found that it is only in the course of (or even after) the first workshop that the full extent of the need for new data or new insights becomes clear.

At the conclusion of this step, many organizations realize the potential importance of systematically gathering and sharing key external information across the organization and begin thinking about how this could be accomplished in the future. Further discussion of this important issue and how it can be done is presented in Chapter 23.

PART 4

STEPS IN CREATING THE SCENARIOS

Part 4 is focused on the steps to construct alternate scenarios of the future from the analyses already completed of the forces and drivers. A strict sequence of activities is needed to ensure that the stories created add significant value to the strategic decision-making process. The sequence results in carefully constructed descriptions of the future that reflect the organization's most recent information and perspectives about the key challenges it faces in the external environment. But the sequence is also designed to create stories that will be persuasive. Decision makers or users must be convinced that the scenarios of the future are possible and that the consequences need to be analyzed. The scenarios that emerge from these activities will be far more instructive than traditional single-point forecasts of one or two variables in the future; they will be more comprehensive and useful than scenarios created around the latest crisis or hot issue in the media; and they will be much more inspirational than a deck of PowerPoint slides.

As in Part 3, the sequence of steps described in Part 4 must be followed. The output of one chapter becomes the input to the next.

Chapter 15 sorts the forces and drivers in the conceptual model on the basis of their relative impact and uncertainty. Up to this point in the process, the workshop and research activities have been focused on expanding the team's thinking about potential dynamics in the external environment. Now, the team performs some critical analysis steps to identify the most important forces and drivers.

Chapter 16 develops the axes of uncertainty around which the scenario story lines will be built. An axis of uncertainty is a grouping of forces and drivers that influence each other. Given the uncertainties of the forces and drivers in the axis, the number of ways in which the forces and drivers could interact and the possible outcomes is infinite. In this chapter, we identify the major axes and then describe the range of possible outcomes for each axis by defining two extremes. For example, two alternate outcomes for the dynamic between buyers and sellers could be called a buyers' market and a sellers' market. We call those alternate outcomes *logics*. A logic includes both the dynamic of how the forces and drivers interrelate as well as the outcomes that they produce.

Chapter 17 selects the scenarios or stories of the future to be written from the axes of uncertainty and the logics. A scenario is an integrated view of the external environment. Outlines of possible scenarios are suggested by mixing together the alternate logics from the axes. From the possible combinations, the team selects two to four scenarios that best cover the envelope of uncertainty and will be challenging to the decision makers.

Chapter 18 describes the writing of the scenarios. Scenarios are stories about how the future unfolds and the events and outcomes that are witnessed. In this chapter, we lay out a structured means of creating compelling, realistic stories for management.

CHAPTER 15

ASSESSING THE IMPORTANCE AND PREDICTABILITY/UNCERTAINTY OF FORCES AND DRIVERS (STEP 11)

We Need to Focus on the Key Issues

Up to this point, the primary objective of the process has been to identify the environmental forces that our planning—and scenarios—must consider. These are the threads that, when woven together, will form the pattern of the future and so determine the range of differences among our scenarios. The result of this effort, as we have seen (Step 9), is likely to be an array of 100 or more forces identified through the brainstorming of the scenario team. Clearly, it would be impractical to develop and interpret the almost infinite permutations and combinations of those 100 or so forces. In addition, they will vary greatly in their impact on the arena that concerns us, and so in their importance to our scenario building. They will vary, too, in the degree of certainty or uncertainty that we feel in predicting the trajectory of their future course. On both scores—impact and (un)certainty—we have suspended judgment up to this point, in the interest of building as complete an inventory of trends and forces as possible. "Better to err on the side of redundancy rather than of omission" might be said to have been the guiding principle.

What Must We Accomplish?

The assessment of uncertainty lies at the heart of developing scenarios and of all that is gathered under the umbrella of strategy learning. Uncertainty is more than incomplete and ambiguous information about individual forces and how they could play out in the future; it is the inspiration for the strategic thinking that occurs throughout the scenario-planning process. In this step of the process, therefore, our objectives are to make the uncertainties about the future explicit and to zero in on those uncertainties that will form the backbones of our scenarios.

The simple, but highly effective, innovation for accomplishing the prioritizing and sorting of the forces we've identified is the application of a two-step analytical framework, called the impact and uncertainty matrix, to the forces and drivers. (See Figure 15-1.) Using this matrix, the team analyzes

Degree of Uncertainty

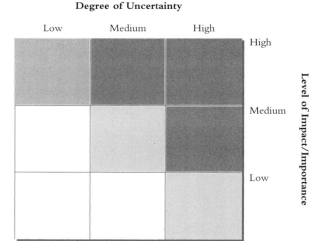

- Impact/importance: How great an impact will each force have in shaping the future of the key decision factors? And so how important will it be in determining the differences among the scenarios that we develop?
- Uncertainty: What level of uncertainty—high, medium, low—do we feel in projecting the future course of each force?

Figure 15-1   Impact/Uncertainty Matrix

each force or driver as to its future importance to the decision arena and the degree of uncertainty that exists about future outcomes.

How to Do It

After completing Step 9: Identifying Critical Forces and Drivers, and Step 10: Conducting Focused Research, the order of business for the scenario team is to rank and sort all the forces that have been identified. To ensure that all members of the scenario team share common perceptions (not necessarily agreement) regarding the key forces and issues, we should conduct this ranking and sorting step in an open workshop session. Again, the purpose of these sessions is not to give exhaustive treatment to individual topics but, rather, to stimulate thinking about the overall forces shaping the future of the key decision factors.

This ranking will be based on two key factors—level of impact/importance, and degree of uncertainty—and recorded on the impact and uncertainty matrix. Figure 15-2 highlights ranking results for an oil company in Europe developing an R&D strategy, and Figure 15-3 shows the summarized reasoning behind this ranking in tabular form.

At the start of this ranking and sorting, the workshop facilitator should communicate to the group the goal of identifying no more than 25 percent

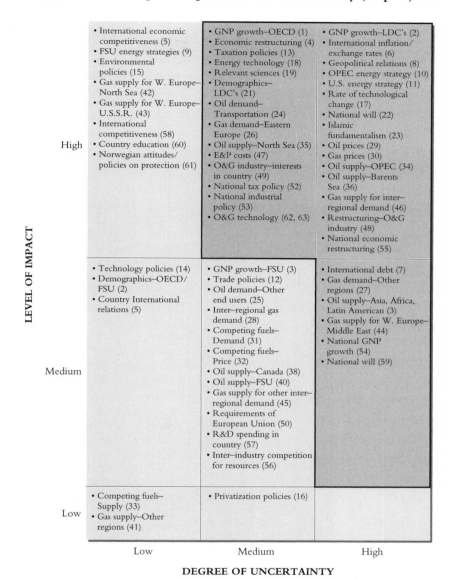

Figure 15-2 Tabular Summary of Ranking of Macro- and Micro-Forces

of the forces as high impact/high uncertainty forces, and that it's the group's responsibility to achieve that goal using the matrix. The high impact/high uncertainty forces will be used in subsequent steps to design the basic story lines and structures of the scenarios; the matrix provides the means to focus on those essential forces. Assigning 15 to 30 forces to the high impact/high

Figure 15-3 Assessment Rationales

| Macro Driver/ Micro Force | Assessment | | Notes on Assessment |
	Impact	Uncertainty	
55. National Economy Restructuring	High	High	High impact rating stems for the perception that this issue is central to Norway's (and possibly Statoil's) economic future. The future in this regard is clouded with many political and economic uncertainties.
56. Inter-Industry Competition for Resources (in Norway)	Medium	Medium	Impacts will be felt in R&D funding and availability of needed professional skills. And the extent of this competition will depend, in large part, on the extent of economic restructuring.
57. Norwegian R&D spending • Government spending • Private sector spending	Medium	Medium	The level of R&D spending determines the general "climate" of Statoil's technology environment, including the availability of Norwegian technology and R&D funding.
58. Need for Norwegian International Competitiveness	High	Low	Given the general increase in international competitiveness, Norway's ability to compete in the economy is clearly crucial. The low uncertainty rating stems from the belief that Norway faces a continuing struggle over the next 20 years—regardless of whether or not economic restructuring is successful.

uncertainty cell out of the 100 or so total forces will give the scenario team the necessary information and cornerstones to design good scenarios. Using more than 30 forces to create the scenarios would be hard to accomplish in a workshop setting with a scenario team of 10 to 15 persons, and the result would likely be less useful. Stating the goal at the beginning of the evaluation process also provides the team with a target and metric to help with the choices between high and medium, and medium and low, for both the impact and uncertainty factors.

It's important that the impact/importance of any force be assessed first. That avoids the problem of trying to assess the impact of a force when one outcome is "no effect." For example, if a packaging-company scenario team first evaluates the uncertainty of the force, Future RFID (radio frequency identification) Applications in the Packaging Industry, as "high" and sees potential outcomes in five years ranging from "Embedded in every package used to transport goods in the supply chain" to "No implementation yet in the supply chain due to costs," then if some on the scenario team believe the "No Implementation" outcome is much more likely, they may argue that the impact/importance of the force is "low." However, if that same team analyzed the impact/importance first, most everyone would probably view the impact/importance of the force as "high." It would then assess the "uncertainty" as high and identify the range of possible outcomes as part of that rationale. Needless arguments among team members can be avoided by assessing impact/importance first.

There are a couple of techniques for analyzing all 100 or so forces. The first technique is the more rigorous one: In the workshop, the team considers together each force in turn and agrees on its level of importance and uncertainty. In the event of a disagreement about the level of importance, the team discusses the different viewpoints until some agreement can be reached. Often the definition of the force needs to be modified so that everyone understands the force in the same way. In the event of disagreement about the level of uncertainty, the process is different for resolving the differences. If there is disagreement about whether the outcome can be predicted (does everyone agree on what the outcome will be?), then by virtue of the disagreement, the force is deemed either medium or high uncertainty. For all low uncertainty forces (i.e., where the outcome is predictable over the time period), the team should record what it agrees that outcome will be. Demographic factors, like the number of persons in the United States approaching the retirement age of 65, are often low uncertainty forces, whereas forces like the acquisition strategies of major competitors in the scenario period are usually high uncertainty forces.

The second technique for sorting through the 100 or so forces is to ask each team member to select no more than five high impact/high uncertainty forces and five high impact/low uncertainty forces from the total. Then the facilitator goes around the room and asks each individual to nominate the forces he or she has selected. Once all the nominated forces have been stated, the facilitator opens the discussion about whether anyone disagrees with any of the nominations. The facilitator then facilitates resolution of the differences. If more than 30 forces have been identified as high

impact/high uncertainty forces, the facilitator challenges the group to eliminate some items.

[As a precautionary measure, it is sometimes advisable to widen the
focus to include forces in the two adjacent cells—medium impact/high
uncertainty and high impact/medium uncertainty to allow for the fact that
this ranking process is not a precision tool.]

Even though the upcoming scenario-design steps will focus on the high
impact forces for developing the basic story lines and logics for how the
future environment could work, the low and medium impact forces are not
discarded or forgotten and will be used when filling in the details of the
scenarios later on.

It should be noted that execution problems can occur in this step when
workshop participants don't develop a common understanding of the factor of
uncertainty. Participants also sometimes resist using the ungainly expressions of
"high uncertainty" and "low uncertainty" and prefer "low certainty" and
"high certainty" instead. Before starting the individual assessments, it's important for the team to agree on the definitions for impact/importance and uncertainty. We've found the following definitions and examples work well:

- *Definition of impact/importance.* Strength of the force's influence on future
outcomes of the key decision factors and consequently on the entire business
environment the decision makers will face. Example: As shown by the lines in
Figure 13-4, forces related to the state of the environment will have high impact and be of high importance to the future environmental regulatory setting;
whereas forces related to the socioeconomic trends and values will not.

- *Definition of uncertainty.* The degree to which future developments and
outcomes are not predictable. If the team can agree on what the outcome of
a force is likely to be in the future (in the time frame of the scenarios), then
the force has low uncertainty. If there is disagreement among the team
members on what this outcome will be, then the degree of uncertainty is
medium or high. That is, when experts can't agree, then there is some level
of uncertainty. Future behavior of competitors is usually given a high uncertainty rating, whereas future demographic trends or Moore's Law are usually
given low uncertainty assessments. Another trick for generating consensus
on an uncertainty rating is to ask, "Would you bet your paycheck on one
outcome?" If there isn't enough information or it's too ambiguous to bet on
a single outcome, then there's medium or high uncertainty.

Often in the process of assessing the importance/impact and uncertainty
of a force, the team discovers that the description of the force is too general,

vague, or misleading and needs to be changed. For example, an issue such as "Need for Better Material X" is not a good title or description of a force. A force, for the purposes of this process, must be described in a way that it has different possible outcomes in the future. "Material X's Characteristics in Three Years Time" or "Market Size of Material X in Ten Years Time" would be appropriate descriptions.

What Are the Outputs of This Step?

Once this analysis is complete, we focus the scenario-development effort on the forces in the high impact/high uncertainty cell (and maybe on those in the medium impact/high uncertainty and high impact/medium uncertainty cells) because these will most likely lead to significantly different futures depending on how these uncertainties play out. We should search among these forces, in Step 12, for the key "axes of uncertainty" that will provide the structure for the scenarios.

We also take note of forces that we have placed in the high impact/low uncertainty cell, for they come closest to being predictable or, in Pierre Wack's term, "predetermined." Their importance stems from the fact that these are the forces most likely to be common elements in all our scenarios and therefore should be factored into all our planning.

Clearly, these rankings are highly judgmental and seemingly imprecise (what, exactly, is "high" uncertainty?): There is no "right" or "wrong" answer in each case, and different teams might well come up with differing rankings. But despite these limitations, we have found that this approach not only provides an important stepping stone toward structuring the scenarios, but also stimulates the shared learning that is an invaluable benefit of the scenario process.

What's Next?

While we have congregated the high impact forces into the two cells of interest (high impact/high uncertainty and high impact/low uncertainty), we still have too many individual elements to juggle to identify the basic outlines of the scenarios. In the next step, we will look to make sense of the interrelationships and dynamics of the forces in the two cells and to develop new, compelling logics for how the external environment could work. In doing so, we will also create the means for identifying and selecting the decision-focused scenarios that we need.

CHAPTER 16

IDENTIFYING KEY AXES OF UNCERTAINTY (STEP 12)

Defining the Great Tensions of the Future

This step—identifying the key axes of uncertainty confronting the organization and the alternative "logics" of how the major driving forces could play out—is both literally and figuratively the heart of the scenario process. It builds upon the preceding analyses but depends mainly on the insights and judgments of the scenario team. It may take the least time, but it is the most difficult step.

We can begin to get a better understanding of what "logics" mean by looking at its historical origins. In the early 1970s, Pierre Wack, while still at Shell France, started to detect the early warning signs of what he felt might be a radical shift in the dynamics of the global oil market. Up to that time, the working of this market had been determined by the power of the major energy-consuming nations—the United States, Europe, and Japan—and their need for stable and expanding supplies of oil at the lowest possible price. Wack summed up the impact of these forces in the term "consumer logic": that is, the market was, and might continue to be, determined by the logic and power of the consuming economies. However, his studies led him to believe that there were already signs of the growing power of the major producing nations, with their main interests in balancing the expansion of production against the need to conserve a nonrenewable resource and in obtaining the highest possible price for oil to finance their economic development plans. There was, therefore, he felt, the possibility that the future market might be determined principally by "producer logic," that is, the needs and growing market power of OPEC. The tension between these two forces—consumer logic and producer logic—effectively defined the major uncertainty then confronting the global oil industry and became the focus and driving force for the initial scenarios that Wack developed.

This concept of alternative logics has proved to be a robust and resilient approach to developing scenarios. However, reliance on a single axis of uncertainty, while having the merit of elegant simplicity, is the exception rather than the rule. In most cases, we have found that there is a wider and more complex range of uncertainty, and the best scenarios spring from the interaction of two (or more) critical axes of uncertainty, as shown in Figure 16-1.

Economic Restructuring \ Power Shift	Accomplished	Failed
Success	Transformation (Corporation as agent of social change)	Reregulation (Corporation as regulated utility)
Volatility	Neomercantilism (Corporation as national competitive weapon)	Turbulence (Corporation as populist target)

Figure 16-1 Alternative Futures of the Corporation

Take, for example, the uncertainties surrounding the future social, political, and economic environment for the private corporation. They can be summarized in two dimensions, each with a pair of alternate logics (phrased here as questions rather than statements):

- Will the "power shift" (to more democratic and market-oriented systems, privatization, and deregulation) continue and take root? Or will it succumb to countervailing forces, fail, and even be reversed?
- Will the multiple-level economic restructuring (global, national, industry) proceed successfully and relatively smoothly? Or will it result in considerable volatility and only partial (at best) success?

Playing the logics of these two axes against each other provides a convenient and useful matrix of four alternative scenarios.

What Must We Accomplish?

The basic objective here, then, is to identify, and describe two, three, or four key axes of uncertainty that:

- Encompass all—or at least the majority—of the high impact/high uncertainty forces.
- Push the envelope of uncertainty—so that the resulting scenarios will be distinctly different from one another, not merely modest variations of a central theme. (However, the scenarios that we select will exclude "wild cards" i.e., very unlikely, but very high impact, events or trends: These will be dealt with separately.)
- Are logical—the alternative outcomes of the axes are logical consequences of the driving forces (see Box 16-1 for an illustration of this point).

BOX 16-1
Axis Logics

Axis logics provide the beginning outlines of story lines of the future. As such, they are the product of imagination and creativity as much as of logic, as the following examples (taken from an environmental management strategy project for a pulp and paper company) will show.

Outcome	Logic
Market-driven recycling business dynamics	Customer and consumer acceptance of recycled products increases steadily because of environmental attitudes and improving product quality. Mandated recycling, the early stimulus for recycling, declines in relative importance as market demand for recycled fiber, wood, and other products increases to catch up with supplies. The forest products industry takes advantage of this opportunity and of steadily improving recycling process and conversion technologies to exploit new resources as feedstocks and produce new recycled products economically. Vigorous, increasingly sophisticated recycling industries and segments emerge.

Or

Regulation-driven recycling business dynamics	Social good, rather than economic realities, continues to drive much of the supply and demand for recycling. Customers and, increasingly, consumers are required to return paper and package wastes, and industries such as newspapers and packaging firms are required to use more recycled products. Supplies of recycled materials exceed market demand, as demand for nonvirgin products is limited by high costs (less economical recycling technologies and relative quality). Recycling remains a chaotic and immature business area.

- Are plausible—they may surprise, but do not strain credibility with decision makers who focus on them.

How to Develop the Axes

The first task in this step, then, is to organize the forces in the high impact/high uncertainty cell(s) into tightly linked clusters of related forces that become the key axes of uncertainty, with each axis later defined by a pair of alternate logics. In a workshop process, this is accomplished by conducting activities that leverage the collected knowledge and pattern recognition capabilities of the participants. One approach is to display the array of high impact/high uncertainty forces in front of the team, using 5" × 8" cards or 3M Post-it™ note paper, and then ask the participants to nominate the possible axes and determine what forces they would include in each by looking at the unstructured arrangement, mentally developing possible clusters or groupings, and then volunteering possible combinations.

We often use the Affinity process[4] to sort the cards/Post-its into groups. In this process, the team members assemble in front of the randomly displayed cards or Post-its, and then begin moving the cards or Post-its around so that forces related to each other are located together. Each team member is empowered to move any cards/Post-its when he or she sees a relationship(s) or disagrees with one. The process works particularly well when the team members initially move the cards without talking and simply react to what they see. This seems to stimulate innovative thinking and encourage the different perspectives of the participants to find their way into the process. Also, starting with an unstructured array of forces—in effect, with no preconceived models for how the forces relate to each other—also encourages participants to think creatively about potential cause-and-effect groupings.

At the beginning of the activity, the facilitator makes it the team's responsibility to work toward grouping all the forces into no more than four axes and encourages the team to try for three or two. But the facilitator also asks the team not to force-fit single cards/Post-its into clusters to which they don't belong. It's okay for single cards/Post-its to stand alone as an axis or never be part of any grouping.

The facilitator also should state that if someone disagrees over the location of cards, then that person should simply move them. Through action

---

[4] A detailed description of the Affinity process in included in the book, *The Memory Jogger Plus+* by Michael Brassard. The book was published by GOAL/QPC in 1996.

and then reflection, a consensus eventually emerges. Near the end of the activity, team members generally resolve their differences via discussion.

Frequently, before the scenario-planning process begins, concerns are expressed about the senior decision maker(s) in the group dominating the discussion or insisting on getting their way. The rules of the Affinity process help greatly to prevent those circumstances.

In our experience, this activity goes very fast, often being completed in 30 minutes or less, largely because the Affinity process works so well. It also is our experience that the initial groupings, developed by working silently, often are changed several times as the group works to limit the number of groupings to less than four and tries to incorporate outliers or single cards, and as various individuals try to impose their perspectives about possible groupings on the team.

The final task, after a consensus on the axes is reached, is to name the axes. The purpose of naming is to capture the idea that links all the cards together. The facilitator should challenge the group to create names that are compelling and communicate clearly the idea. Typically, several suggestions are made for each axis before the team can settle on one.

Sometimes naming of the axes occurs after logics for the endpoints of the axes are developed. This is because the thinking to identify the logics serves as an excellent catalyst for developing possible names to convey the idea and scope of the axis.

How to Develop the Alternate Logics for Each Axis

A logic is a hypothesis about the dynamics of the external environment in the future, about how the world will work. For each axis of uncertainty, the group will develop two alternate logics for how the clusters of forces will play out in the time frame of the scenarios. Each logic will have a central theme or dynamic that describes how the forces in the group will interrelate, and some specific outcomes. The goal of the step is to identify two logics for each axis that are plausible, yet at the extreme. The facilitator should remind the team of the goal to develop scenarios that cover the "envelope of uncertainty" for the decision focus, and that it's critical for the axis logics to be at the limits of what the team thinks is plausible.

This step usually involves a great deal of trial and error, making explicit (but not necessarily resolving) significant differences of opinion and perception about how major uncertainties could evolve. The ideas for the logics come from the "mental models" of change that are based upon the perceptions of the scenario team, those of key decision makers (who may not be present in the actual workshops), those of other experts, and established theories of social, political, economic, and technological change. The scenario team brings all these elements together to identify plausible and useful logics. The facts and uncertainties from previous steps shape, constrain, and make realistic the logics; models of change point to what kind of change—and how much—can occur and what basic dynamics are possible in the time period of the scenarios.

It is often necessary for the facilitator to challenge the team to stretch itself in defining what is plausible for the endpoints of an axis in the time frame. Typically, teams are too conservative in what they would define as the extremes.

It is also sometimes difficult for the team to move away from purely economic logics, especially the "high, medium, low growth" sort of logic. While it is true that economic forces are often among the key drivers of change, and differing assumptions about future economic growth may provide part of the scenario logics, other forces—notably technology innovation, new business models, social change, political factors, and international developments—are often at least as important. The facilitator should challenge the group to develop interesting and challenging logics. The logics must ultimately communicate well, get people's attention, and stimulate the strategic thinking of the organization.

We've found that a couple of techniques work well in developing the logics. In the first technique, using an easel with flip charts or cards/Post-its on an open wall, the team systematically develops two extreme outcomes for each force in the axis cluster, combines extreme outcomes together that are consistent with each other, and then develops a description for the central cause-and-effect dynamic that results in those outcomes.

In the second technique, which is more of an open-ended, brainstorming approach, the participants look at the forces of one axis as a group and then brainstorm two alternate logics for that axis. The facilitator guides the discussion by asking for clarification of the logics when suggested, by asking for alternative logic ideas, and by asking how the suggested logics capture the forces in the cluster. This technique usually works well as long as the participants are given five to ten minutes to reflect silently on possible logics before the discussion begins.

Invariably, it's a mix of the two methods that finally generates the two challenging, plausible, extreme logics for each axis.

The group needs to continue working until it's happy with the results. Often a break is needed in the middle when the team isn't making progress so that everyone can step back and rethink the possibilities. A break also allows the facilitator and a small set of the team to identify some process changes to break the logjam, once the discussion begins again.

What Are the Outputs of This Step?

The final activity, which occurs outside of the workshop, is to prepare paragraph descriptions of all the logics. These paragraphs are important not only for documenting the workshop discussion results but also for communicating the key strategic issues facing the organization.

What's Next?

With completion of Step 12, Identifying the Axes of Uncertainty, the team has made significant progress in getting its arms around the pressing issues of the external environment. Through the activities completed so far, it has integrated a voluminous amount of disparate, often contradictory, information about the forces and drivers of the external environment; it has sorted that information to identify the most important forces and drivers for the decision focus at hand, and, within those most important forces and drivers, the ones, that because of their uncertainty, will define the different futures the organization could see; and it has identified the primary dynamics or logics that will be relevant for how the world could operate in the future. It's now time to select the alternative scenarios that will effectively incorporate the results of this work.

CHAPTER 17

SELECTING SCENARIO LOGICS TO COVER THE ENVELOPE OF UNCERTAINTY (STEP 13)

What Must We Accomplish with This Step?

The overall goal of the project is to develop a set of alternative scenarios that describes the detailed possible futures for the organization in a language and form that decision makers can use. The scenarios must describe the important trends and driving forces as well as the major uncertainties and their possible outcomes, and do so in such a way that decision makers can understand them, learn from them, and apply them in decision-making circumstances. A key issue, then, is the number of scenarios that should be developed.

At this point in the methodology, the team could conceivably create tens to hundreds of scenarios, using the possible combinations of outcomes of all the forces and drivers that have been identified. But this result would be unusable by the decision makers, and the benefits of having so many individual scenarios would never be greater than the costs of creating them. Decision makers would be overwhelmed by all the scenario descriptions produced, and never find time to learn from them. To be useful, then, we need to restrict the scenarios to a small enough number that decision makers will be able to remember them, understand their differences, and communicate about them with others. At the same time, the set of scenarios needs to cover the range of possible futures the organization could face.

Based on our experience from many assignments, we've found we can accomplish the overall goal by developing no more than four scenarios using the axes of uncertainty. Very rarely, we have developed five scenarios, and almost always felt afterward that we would have benefited by only having four. Often, we've only created three or two, and felt we effectively described the important uncertainties facing the organizations and covered their envelopes of uncertainty.

The axes of uncertainty derive their importance from the fact that they provide the basic structure for our scenarios. We have already noted, in Step 12, cases in which either one or two axes have constituted a stable and sufficient structure. For instance, Pierre Wack's early efforts relied, in effect, on a single critical axis—"Who will wield dominant power in future oil and gas markets? The major energy-consuming nations, or the major producing nations?"—and he was able to use this simple but powerful structure to develop two critically important scenarios that raised some important questions that Shell's strategy of those times needed to address.

In our experience, however, this single-axis structure usually does not cover the full range of the uncertainty confronting a company, and a two-, three-, and sometimes four-axes structure is required. Indeed, a structure made up of two axes of uncertainty, each with its own bipolar logics, does a much better job of covering the envelope of critical uncertainty (see, for instance, Figure 16-1). And the resulting four-cell matrix provides an easily assimilated set of scenarios which provide good coverage of the envelope of uncertainty.

There are occasions when the scenario team's analysis of the critical future uncertainties results in identification of three axes of uncertainty, each related to, but in some measure independent of, the other two. For instance, in the environmental management study for a forest products company already mentioned (see Chapter 13), the team identified three critical uncertainties in the future: the nature of environmental attitudes and regulations, the structure of the forest products industry, and the dynamics of the recycling market. Certainly there is no merit in carrying on the debate within the team merely for the sake of reducing the structure from three to two axes. If all three axes are judged to be critical, and independent of (though related to) each other, then a three-axes structure can be managed—with one proviso. Some way must be found to deal with the fact that three axes, each with bipolar logics, results in eight potential scenarios (2 × 2 × 2), which is clearly an unmanageable number of scenarios to deal with. However, it is usually possible to reduce the number of potential scenarios by identifying and then eliminating those combinations that are logically inconsistent. For instance, the team argued that it would be logically inconsistent, and so highly unlikely, that environmental concerns would be "confrontational" at the same time that the recycling market was driven by market driven rather than by regulatory driven. By this sort of reasoning, it was possible to reduce the number of scenarios to a more manageable set of four.

In most cases, two scenarios will not adequately cover the full range of future possibilities and will also suffer from the tendency of most people to interpret one scenario as "good" (for the organization), the other as "bad." Similarly, selecting three scenarios suffers from our all-too-common tendency to interpret such a set as a "most probable" future (in the middle) with a "high" and "low" alternative. There is, therefore, a good case to be made for developing a set of four scenarios (more is too many).

Regardless of the number of scenarios that the team selects to develop, the scenarios must meet the following criteria:

- They must be plausible—that is, they must fall within the limits of what might reasonably be expected to happen. This is, admittedly, a highly subjective criterion, and the limits of plausibility will change, and probably expand, as the team gains experience with scenarios.
- They must be structurally different—that is, they are not simply variations of a base case. The futures they describe take radically different courses in some important respects.
- They must be internally consistent—that is, no scenario has any built-in inconsistencies that undermine its credibility.
- They must have utility—that is, each scenario (and all the scenarios together) must adhere to the decision focus of the project and be useful for identifying strategic options for the organization.
- The scenarios should challenge conventional wisdom about the future—that is, they should encourage us to expand our horizons and broaden our definition of "probability."

It is important to note that we do not select scenarios on the basis of our judgment as to their probability of occurrence. Probability has more to do with forecasts than with scenarios; and scenarios are not forecasts, for one cannot reasonably "forecast" three or four quite different futures. Scenarios, as a collection of possible futures, are intended to establish the boundaries of our uncertainty and the limits of plausible futures.

However, we should recognize that there is a very powerful human tendency, born of past experience and culture, to assign probabilities at the end of the scenario process. Every individual on the team ends up with his or her own private assessment of probability, and it is almost certainly better to bring these assessments into the open for group discussion than to leave them suppressed in individual minds. Indeed, doing this usually serves to underscore the wide diversity of opinion—and the consequent foolishness of trying to reach some sort of consensus on this matter. However, whichever course of action one elects—to engage in this group discussion or not—the critical point is to avoid focusing on one "most probable" scenario to the exclusion of the others. To do so would negate the whole value of the scenario-planning exercise.

How to Do It

The process of selecting the scenarios starts with displaying the possible combinations of the axes' extreme outcomes, from Step 12, in a table

Figure 17-1 Scenario Selection Table

Scenario	Environmental Attitudes Axis of Uncertainty	Industry Structure Axis of Uncertainty	Recycling Market Axis of Uncertainty
1	Cooperative	Manufacturing Focused	Market Driven
2	Cooperative	Manufacturing Focused	Regulatory Driven
3	Cooperative	Wood Products Focused	Market Driven
4	Cooperative	Wood Products Focused	Regulatory Driven
5	Confrontational	Manufacturing Focused	Market Driven
6	Confrontational	Manufacturing Focused	Regulatory Driven
7	Confrontational	Wood Products Focused	Market Driven
8	Confrontational	Wood Products Focused	Regulatory Driven

(see Figure 17-1 for the scenario-selection table for the forest products company). In the columns, the two extreme outcomes for each axis are entered so that the rows show the different possible combinations of the extremes. Each row represents one possible scenario. With two axes, we have four possible combinations; with three axes, we have eight possible combinations; and with four axes we have sixteen combinations. In the workshop process, the team members discuss the different combinations and then select the best set of two, three, or four scenarios for further elaboration.

The table serves as a guide both to developing the central dynamics for the scenarios and to making the selection. The central dynamics emerge as team members envision the possibilities for how the extreme outcomes in a row could occur together in the future, with one idea leading creatively to another. Typically, one or two ideas can be developed for the plausible dynamics that will result in the extreme outcomes of each row.

Once the team has considered the possible dynamics, then using the selection criteria listed on the previous page, it selects the best set of scenarios to be described in detail. In helping teams to develop the best set of scenarios, we often use a figure that is shaped like an amoeba to represent the envelope of uncertainty (see Figure 17-2). We ask the team to imagine that all the possible ways in which the world could play out in the future are represented as points inside the amoeba-like shape. Because of the uncertainties involved, just like with scenarios, there are infinite possibilities. Points near the edge of the shape are considered extreme, near the edge of plausibility.

Using that figure as a guide, the task for the team is to identify the two, three, or four points at the edge of the shape that, when connected by lines to make a line, triangle, or square, will effectively cover the entire shape. With

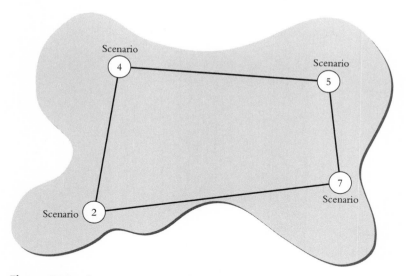

Figure 17-2   Scenario Coverage of the Envelope of Uncertainty

this visualization, team members quickly understand several key points:

   • The goal is to identify points, or scenarios, that are extreme. Otherwise, it won't be possible to cover the entire envelope

   • None of the points being selected is likely to occur. They are being selected because they're plausible and in a particular region of the figure. Therefore, it doesn't make sense to assign a probability to a point. None of the points selected would have a high probability of occurring.

   • If two points are near each other, either one could be selected. This means that the details of a scenario can be adjusted to improve the scenario's utility (in effect moving the point to a new position) as long as those adjustments don't alter the overall scenario logic significantly (i.e., move the point out of the area).

   In workshops, we select the best set of scenarios out of the various combinations by asking the team members to vote on what they think are the three best scenarios. We give them 15 to 30 minutes to reflect on the possible dynamics that could explain each row, pick their three rows, and develop a rationale for their selection. The facilitator then asks for all the votes.

   Typically when voting is used, one or two scenarios will initially emerge as consensus winners. A discussion then ensues about why members voted for particular scenarios and what dynamics they were considering. A good technique for exploring the different possibilities and not settling too

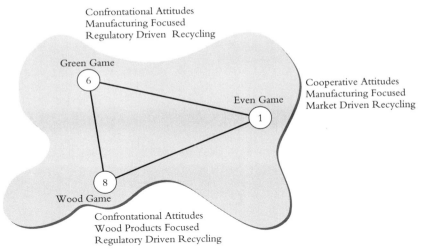

Figure 17-3   Three Scenarios Covering the Envelope of Uncertainty

quickly on the majority vote getters is to start the discussion by asking for explanations of some of the minority vote getters. Often a team member will make a very compelling argument for a particular row and will persuade the rest of the team members to switch their votes. The discussion continues until the team reaches agreement on the best set of scenarios for capturing the envelope of uncertainty. Figure 17-3 highlights the three scenarios selected by the forest products company from the eight possible choices shown in Figure 17-1.

What's Next?

With the basic outlines of the scenarios selected, the next step is to turn those outlines into persuasive descriptions of alternative futures. The challenge is to write stories that will stimulate strategic thinking in the decision makers and communicate to anyone that reads them the critical strategic issues facing the organization. In Step 14, a small group or an individual from the scenario team will be responsible for authoring the scenarios, using a template that ensures key information is included in the stories.

CHAPTER 18

WRITING THE STORY LINES FOR THE ALTERNATIVE SCENARIOS (STEP 14)

What Must We Accomplish?

This is the critical integrative step in the scenario process—weaving together the threads of the alternative logics into coherent, distinctive patterns; spelling out the cause-and-effect relationships among a multitude of macro and micro forces; seeing the future whole rather than as a collection of discrete trends. The purpose is to provide the organization with a coherent and comprehensive view of alternative possible futures for developing and testing strategies resilient enough to deal with the inevitable uncertainties that we shall encounter.

The main activity of this step is essentially one of storytelling, describing how the differing scenario logics might play out to create different futures. As we have already noted, scenarios should be designed to have a plot and a story line, tracing trends and developments, cause and effect, and the interrelationships among events. It is this trait that makes scenarios so very different from forecasts. The role of a forecast is to predict the future, and its value is determined largely by the accuracy (or otherwise) of its prediction. The role of scenarios is to describe the differing ways in which the future might evolve, and their value is determined largely by the understanding, flexibility, and speed of response that they promote.

Storytelling is an art, not one that is normally practiced in most organizations. But it is a capability that can be adapted to the needs of strategic planning and developed with learning and experience. We have found, for instance, that it is possible to focus and hasten this learning process by:

• Spelling out the implications of the scenario logics. As we noted in the previous chapter, each scenario is defined by the logic of its position on the two (or three or four) axes of uncertainty that denote the range of possible futures. So these logics provide us with the outline of a story. To take the example of alternative futures of the corporation (Figure 16-1), if we postulate a future defined by a failed "power shift" and volatile economic restructuring, we can start to "tell the story" of a turbulent economic environment in which the corporation becomes the target of populist legislation.

• Tracing cause-and-effect chains. We can expand the scope and detail of our "stories" by extrapolating the consequences of a relatively small number of events. For example, we might postulate a chain of events triggered by new evidence of the seriousness and imminence of global warming . . . leading to accelerated initiatives by the private sector to deal with the problem . . . which, however, continues to escalate . . . and forces a dramatic increase in governmental regulations and research on a global scale. Given three or four such chains, we will have the making of quite an intricate story.

• Highlighting critical events. Scenarios take on clearer focus and greater meaning when we define them with specific events or developments: the outcome of trade negotiations, the result of an election, a technological breakthrough, a major corporate merger. The precise event that we describe in the scenario may not, in fact, occur—and its nonoccurrence might not affect the overall validity of the scenario—but the level of detail it provides gives added meaning and clarity of the overall thrust of the scenario. It is important to recognize that, by this action, we are not making a forecast, only a statement: "Given this sort of future, these are the sort of events that might occur."

• Incorporating conflict. Scenarios become interesting and challenging when conflicts among industry participants' goals, assumptions, and expectations about the future and a new reality are included. A story that is simply a series of events from beginning to end describing how future outcomes meet expectations of industry participants is boring. Instead, we need to describe how, from today's world, something happens that causes participants' expectations to crash into an uncompromising reality. Totally positive or totally negative pictures of the future don't ring true. We need to develop stories that contain conflict, that force the readers to struggle with the consequences. In our experience, the scenarios that typically generate the most interesting discussions and innovative strategic ideas are the dark ones, the ones decision makers most dread. Even rosy scenarios need to have conflicts built in to them.

At the conclusion of this step, each scenario description would include the following:

SCENARIO TITLE

As a practical matter, it is essential to give each scenario a brief, descriptive title that facilitates understanding, comparison, and discussion. We should avoid simplistic and misleading titles such as "High/medium/low growth" or "Best case/worst case," because such titles give very little clue as to the driving forces at work in each case and may be misleading. Rather, we should try to distill the essence of each scenario, using its logic and position on the axes of uncertainty as clues. Turning to the recently published Royal

Dutch Shell global scenarios to 2025, for instance, we can see that titles such as "Low Trust Globalisation, A Legalistic 'Prove It to Me' World," "Open Doors, A Pragmatic 'Know Me' World," and "Flags, A Dogmatic 'Follow Me' World" would capture the principal dynamic of each scenario and serve as a convenient—and memorable—shorthand in planning and discussion.

Brief Description

Expanding and elaborating on these titles, one paragraph descriptions serve to convey the essence of each scenario in a one paragraph story line. The aim here is to capture the essential dynamics of each scenario, highlighting the major forces at work and the differing outcomes that they produce. For example, one scenario in the environmental management project referred to in Chapters 13 and 17 was titled simply "Green Game" and was described as follows:

> *A strong coalition of environmental groups and urban publics, strong growth in other regional industries, and the declining competitiveness of the U.S. forest products industry set a context in which the conventional wisdom becomes: "Forest products are 'dying' anyway, so let's save the forests." Environmental regulations impacting the industry are strict and severe, and conflicts remain high. Virgin pulp and paper activities are targeted as major polluters and the industry is forced to move aggressively into recycled fibers, despite the problematic economics of that business. The industry is severely restricted in the range of options it can use to handle pulp and paper wastes.*

Narrative

This is the detailed account of how each scenario might evolve, describing a fairly detailed "history" of the future. It is here that storytelling capability is most needed, pulling together the main threads of the developing trends into coherent patterns and "seeding" the story with specific events that may not be inevitable parts of the scenario but that give substance and detail to the plot. This level of detail is needed to make the scenarios useful as test beds for developing strategy rather than merely "interesting" stories: They are, after all, supposed to be planning documents.

Comparison Table

Finally, it is helpful to develop a table comparing how the key elements of the future "play out" in each scenario. See Figure 18-1 for an excerpt of such a

Figure 18-1 Example of Comparison Table

Scenario Title	Brave New World	The Shakeout	Mad Max
Catastrophes	• The scenario decade is characterized by the lack of devastating physical catastrophes. • Technology improves seismographic instruments and earthquake prediction models. In 2010 USGS successfully predicts a 5.7 magnitude earthquake on new fault line in Marin County.	• No unusually large catastrophes, except for one category 4 hurricane in Florida in 2005 causing $1 billion in damage to homes and businesses. • California experiences no major earthquakes. • Global warming causes unusual weather patterns, increasing the number of tornadoes, hurricanes and flooding; damage is minor.	• Severe catastrophes throughout the scenario period. • Category 5 hurricane hits Long Island in September 2002 causing $20 billion in damage. • In 2005 solar flares interrupt satellite communication for 2 weeks and result in $5 billion in business interruption and property damage. • Los Angeles experiences its worst brush fire in 2007.
Terrorism	• International terrorism against U.S. citizens and property is modest because of international cooperation against terrorist groups throughout the world. No attacks on U.S. soil occur. • Cyber attacks in U.S. and across the globe continue but are largely contained because of computer-security technology advances and increased FBI sophistication. • Chemical weapons are introduced with lethal effects in the Congo and Northern Iraq in 2004 and 2006 respectively. International boycotts are imposed.	• Cyber attacks in U.S. and across the globe continue against businesses and government agencies. • Chemical weapons used in parts of Eastern Europe and Asia. Some major injuries but no deaths occur.	• Widespread terrorism throughout the world. • Cyber-terrorism became part of the new economy, stimulated by several foreign governments. Blue chip companies, in particular bear the brunt of the attacks. • Iraq's leadership position in the Arab world leads to rampant terrorism against Western nations. • In 2006 Russian terrorists release a chemical weapon in downtown Philadelphia causing panic, but no injuries.
Politics	• Bush wins re-election in 2004 after a relatively easy campaign against Gephardt and H. Clinton. In 2008, a centrist democratic President is elected. A republican majority in House and Senate remains throughout the scenario	• Open trade and international competition are high priorities for the Bush administration and Congress. Bush is surprised in 2004 and loses the presidency to a moderate Democrat. Democrats also regain control of the Senate, but Republicans continue to hold the House.	• A democratic President is elected in 2004 and the democrats win Congress as a result of the economic chaos and social problems. • Strong federal regulations influence the economy.

Economics	• A minor recession occurs from 2000 to 2002. • The U.S. experiences a very prosperous economy (4% GDP growth from 2003 to 2010), driven by technology advancements and a hands-off fiscal policy by the federal government. • Economics dominate politics worldwide as seen in a gradual opening of Chinese markets. The European Union continues to improve its ability to be a strong competitor to the U.S. Japan initially experiences economic woes, but by the end of the decade is growing the fastest amongst the large economies.	• The U.S. is experiencing a moderate-growth economy with a 3.0% GDP growth rate. • From 2001 to 2008 the world experiences a roller coaster of economic highs and lows. • Due to the unstable global economic environment China is hesitant to open its market; South Korea thrives.	• Economic downturn results in U.S. recession from 2001 to 2005 with double-digit inflation most years. • The GDP growth rate is 1% from 2001 to 2005, and 2.5% from 2006 to 2010. • The U.S. recession spreads internationally and Russia faces an economic nightmare.
Laws and Regulations – Financial Industries Related	• States continue to regulate the insurance industry. Individual state requirements remain largely unchanged. • At the federal level, efforts to eliminate separation of banking and insurance fail. • Capital regulations remain the same. • Tort liability laws remain unchanged.	• Single-market experiences in the European Union are highly positive. • The Oxley-Gramm Act of 2003 ends the separation of banking and insurance, ending the last vestiges of Federal legislation passed during the Great Depression. • U.S. Congress passes controversial Federal Insurance Act of 2005 (and repeals the McCarran-Ferguson Act) to establish an open competition system for rates at the national level. • States continue to operate their own commissions and oversee insurance practices and agent licensing. • Tort liability increases for insurance and financial firms.	• U.S. Congress passes the Insurance Reform Act of 2005 that creates a federal insurance system. • The federal government limits Insurance rate increases to 5% p.a. • States continue to create their own requirements, creating regulations that do not always coincide with the federal ones. • The federal government requires insurance firms to cover uninsured patients and underprivileged children.

table from a project conducted for a property and casualty insurance company at the end of 2000. In principle, this table could cover all the macro and micro forces identified earlier in the project as drivers of the future; but, as a practical matter, such a table is usually limited to the more important forces in our story line. The value of such a summary table lies in providing us with a line-item approach to examining the differences in the ways in which each macro and micro force plays out in each scenario, to reassure ourselves, first, that the differences we have imputed to the scenarios are reasonable and plausible; and, second, that they cover the full range of possibilities.

In summary, the objective of the scenario writer is to create alternative stories of the future that capture all the discussions of forces, trends, and uncertainties that have occurred and that will challenge how decisions makers think about future threats and opportunities. Each detail, character, or event used in the story is part of that effort. The paragraphs of the story must allow experienced, knowledgeable readers to understand complex environments quickly and readily and be stimulated by them. The scenario drafts will fail if they are long, boring, and tedious, even though they may be very accurate and complete.

How to Do It

We have found that, in most projects, the development of scenario story lines is best accomplished by a combination of group and individual work, with the general scoping out of the stories being done by groups and with the detailed writing left to individual effort. For instance, if we were following the calendar of a "typical" project (see Box 8-1), we would conclude the second workshop by starting the process of "putting flesh on the bones" of each scenario structure. This can be done by the entire team, working on one scenario after another or by breaking the team into three or four work groups, each taking one of the proposed scenarios.

What we want to do prior to the start of the writing is brainstorm the possible ideas, events, time line, characters, mini-dramas, outcomes, and surprises of each scenario. In this way we provide the scenario writer with key input and insights for each story, leverage the detailed perspectives and expertise of the participants, and further test the scenario structure that we plan to use.

The detailed drafting of the scenarios is, however, best left to one individual who is both familiar with the subject matter and an accomplished and imaginative writer, on the principle that anything "written by committee" generally lacks integrity and coherence. The drafts are circulated for review and comment by the scenario team and then become the first agenda item in the next workshop for discussion, amendment (if necessary), and approval.

In developing these "stories," there are a few guidelines to follow:

• Give each story a beginning, a middle, and an end. Every good story has these elements. And every scenario should give the reader a detailed understanding of the forces at work at the start of the story; describe how they evolve and interact, and what new forces develop, in the period covered by the scenario; and highlight the changes in the strategic picture that have developed by the end of the period covered by the scenarios (not the end of the story, but the limit of the horizon for our scenarios).

• Remember that not everything changes. Some key elements remain reasonably constant across the scenarios (or change in relatively minor and [predictable] ways) and it is important for our planning to know this.

• Populate the scenarios with characters. Every period of history, every arena of human activity, has its change agents—individuals who sense the need for a change of emphasis or direction and who act as catalysts for new values, new programs, new products, and new directions. Although this has to be done carefully, introducing such critical actors into our scenarios (even if just for purposes of illustration) can serve to bring our "stories" to life and give them focus and added meaning.

• Include dramas or conflicts to help convey how the world is changing. To make the scenarios realistic to the users and decision makers, within each scenario we need to describe situations that start in balance but then get thrown out of balance by key incidents or events of the scenario. The scenario should describe how the characters try to restore their balance and where their optimistic programs for the future meet a new, uncompromising reality.

• Use present tense verbs so that the story is written as if we were omniscient: We know what happened in the past (there are no *might haves* or *could-haves*); we can see exactly what is happening now; and we know what will happen in the future (there can't be a *might be, would be,* or *could be*). For example, "In 2010, a new product weighing 50% less is introduced by the largest Chinese competitor. By the end of the scenario, overall demand for the product is exploding, increasing at a rate of 25% per year." The voice that is created by this technique helps readers to quickly get involved in the stories and accept the possibilities being described.

• Make each story unique. Given that the scenarios have been selected to represent very different futures, the story line, characters, and events of each need to convey an alternate perspective. Often the story line and sequence of events are described in a different order to help convey the dynamics of a different world. One scenario story might start from the vantage of looking back on events from end of the scenario. "In retrospect, the entire period from 2006 to 2015 for the telecommunications industry was a time of boom, bust, and consolidation of global giants." Another might begin at the start of the scenario period. "In 2006, AT&T surprised the entire telecommunications industry, particularly big media competitors, by slashing all consumer rates for phone, wireless, and broadband services by 50%." While there could be symmetry in describing the same events differing only in outcomes, it's not a good technique for describing very different future dynamics. The descriptions of the scenarios will feel forced and not very plausible.

The length of the scenarios will vary based on their purpose, on the topic, on the resources and time available to do the writing, and on the needs and culture of the organization. Typically, for strategic-planning purposes, we write scenario narratives that are two to three pages in length each and comparison tables that are ten to twenty pages in length.

The typical time required to draft the scenarios is two to three weeks, although we have completed one-paragraph summaries in an hour, one-page narratives overnight, and full descriptions in a week.

A good plan for conducting the writing is to write drafts for all the one-paragraph scenario descriptions first. Then a two- to three-page narrative description for one scenario is written, followed by details of the different forces and drivers for the first scenario in the comparison table. After that, the second scenario narrative can be written, followed by the details in the comparison table for the second scenario, and so on until all the scenarios are completed. Once the details of the comparison table have been filled in for one scenario, many writers find it easier to complete the details of the other scenarios in the table first before moving on to the narratives for the rest of the scenarios. In practice, most writers go back and forth between the narratives and the comparison table as they strive to create logical, extreme, yet plausible descriptions of the future.

After the initial drafts are completed, they are circulated and read by the rest of the team. The team members are asked to suggest changes to make the stories more complete, correct errors in logic, and suggest a more plausible and challenging dynamic. In the end, all the team members need to agree on the scenario descriptions. Do the descriptions accurately reflect the inputs by the team on what will be important in the future and the possible dynamics?

Since a scenario is not a forecast, scenario descriptions and details frequently get changed during the reviews of the drafts by the scenario team and after they are initially used. Often as the scenarios get used, better ideas emerge for how to describe the dynamics in the scenarios and make them more challenging for the decision makers. When those ideas emerge, the team should simply makes the changes if everyone agrees.

A frequent technique for conveying the atmosphere and dynamics of future scenarios is to write each scenario as if it were a news report on radio, television, or in a newspaper about what has happened, with analytical commentary included.

In several projects we've facilitated, clients made videos of some of the scenarios using Hollywood-like scripts, sets, and actors. This type of investment in the scenario descriptions can be very worthwhile if the scenarios are to be used by many people in many different locations and when the scenarios and their differences need to be communicated quickly. Movies and videos can communicate a lot of information quickly and spark valuable discussions by many people.

The Insurance Company Example

The guidelines we have presented for developing scenario story lines should prove helpful but may still leave the reader uncertain as to what the final product may look like. To give an example of a finished product, therefore, we present the detailed story line of one of the scenarios developed in the course of a project for a property and casualty insurance company at the end of 2000. The scenario in question, "Mad Max," was based on three key scenario logics: a society of turmoil and disruption; federal regulatory leadership and states resistance; and evolutionary change in industry competitive dynamics (see Appendix A for the complete set of written scenarios for the Nokia case study).

MAD MAX

In Mad Max, the world feels like it is going backward—physically, socially, and economically. Natural disasters are frequent and severe, the social order is severely stressed by terrorism and health scares, and an economic recession prevails. To fix and ameliorate the situation, the U.S. federal government promulgates a wide range of new measures. But many—including state governments—feel the new federal laws hurt more than help. The property and casualty insurance (P&C) industry slowly grows worldwide because of the demand for protection in an increasingly risky business and social environment. But this growth is severely tempered by the lack of supply created by a federally imposed 5 percent per year rate increase ceiling.

The scenario begins with a major economic recession from 2001 to 2005 in the United States, accompanied by double-digit inflation, which quickly spreads to much of the rest of the world. In retrospect, the California energy crisis of 2000–2001 was the stimulus, not only in the United States, but also in Europe and Asia. Corporations find it difficult to raise money, few new businesses start, and existing corporations struggle to maintain their valuation in a difficult financial environment. Capital availability is extremely low because of the economic recession and skepticism toward new opportunities. With strained resources and poor prospects for growth, firms struggle to comply with the new regulatory landscape, to meet loss requirements, and to meet new customer needs.

Beginning in 2002, Congress passes President Bush's plan for social security reform, allowing individuals to place portions of their social security contributions in fixed-income securities. But other social issues quickly arise with the deteriorating economy, widespread cyber terrorism, and hacker attacks. The digital divide and economic gaps between the haves and the have-nots widen dramatically, and privacy infractions are abundant as firms struggle to survive in the harsh economic environment. U.S. citizens blame the Bush administration for the economic recession and lack of controls on dangerous technology and elect a liberal, Democratic president in 2004, along with a democratic majority to Congress. The new Democratic administration, responding to rising skepticism about technology's benefits, spearheads new federal laws to protect consumers and clean up broken regulatory systems.

One target for reform is the insurance industry, which is besieged by massive claims from the Long Island hurricane in 2002 and the Berkeley-Emeryville earthquake of 2003. As a result, the federal government passes the Insurance Reform Act of 2005 to impose a federal insurance system and prevent insurance companies from taking advantage of state differences. A key feature of the new federal system is that it effectively prevents insurance providers from increasing their rates above 5 percent per year. The new rules also encourage more bundling of P&C services. Unfortunately, the new federal regulations fail to establish order, and states continue to impose their own new requirements, with little consideration for how all the laws interact. Insurance companies have to invest heavily to reorganize their back-office infrastructure in response.

An important driver of Mad Max is the public's (and politicians') perspective that many technological advances need stricter control. New cloning of human tissue in 2002 and disease detection through DNA analysis make many people question the controls behind advanced technology development, the ethics of many commercial organizations, and the risks to individual sovereignty. In 2008, researchers announce substantive evidence that human brain chemistry can be affected by electromagnetic pulses from a variety of common electrical appliances. Special-interest groups quickly blame the electromagnetic pulses for dramatic increases in cancer and mental illnesses in various geographic locations. Major individual and homeowner lawsuits are filed against most major manufacturers and distributors of electronic products, as well as the many corporations that supply products to their employees. Homeowners in California who have installed wireless networks in their homes and subsequently sell those homes are required to dismantle the networks or have them certified as safe.

As the public forcefully voices its fears, the U.S. and European Union (EU) governments take action to redress the damages and harms to their societies. Because of the alarming spread of the HIV virus and AIDS, insurance firms in the United States must provide coverage for patients and underprivileged children without healthcare coverage. Restitution cases for tobacco and holocaust victims continue with broad public and court support. New cases for American slaves, female World War II Japanese slaves, and child workers enter the court systems around the world. Protests on restitution cases for families of black slaves result in street riots in Los Angeles, Chicago, and Miami, with 30 deaths and $2 billion in property damage to small businesses.

Although the United States and the European Union attempt to respond to their citizens' problems, they snub developing countries on the same issues, leaving them to find their own solutions. Russia's economy fails to get on its feet and the state of anarchy continues throughout the scenario. Iraq's rise to being the leader of the Arab nations leads to emboldened terrorist attacks against the United States and other Western countries. Cyber attacks from the developing world become constant, particularly against blue-chip companies and symbols of U.S. capitalism, like Microsoft and Oracle. In 2006, a terrorist group from Russia successfully detonates a chemical weapon in downtown Philadelphia, causing widespread panic for three days but few injuries.

As P&C companies are threatened by the global mayhem, they are at the same time challenged by the unusual weather events across the globe. A Category 5 hurricane hits Long Island in September 2002, causing damage totaling $20 billion. California experiences a magnitude 7.6 earthquake (the Berkeley-Emeryville Quake) on the Hayward fault in January 2003. The earthquake causes more than $20 billion worth of damage to homes, businesses, and city infrastructure in the East Bay and leaves the East Bay without power in many areas for three weeks. Solar flares in the summer of 2005 interrupt satellite communications for two weeks in Seattle, Portland, and Cleveland and cause $5 billion in business interruption and property damages. Los Angeles County suffers its worst brush fire ever in 2007.

The P&C insurance industry is in a position to benefit from all the up-heaval and catastrophes because consumers and businesses are highly alarmed by the unfolding events and want new coverage. In addition, using the latest technologies to gather information and determine appropriate events, companies can better assess risks and determine appropriate rates. And on the supply side, the outgrowths of the social and environmental difficulties are such that financial-services companies experience minimal competition from new entrants, and the industry structure remains largely unchanged. However, the combination of rate increase caps and difficulties in settling claims from all the disasters results in an extremely tight supply structure.

Traditional firms still sell traditional sets of products through the same basic distribution channels. But the firms find themselves chasing after new, often conflicting requirements rather than developing new products and services. Legacy systems are extremely expensive to reprogram for all the new requirements, and the new systems are all still highly susceptible to cyber attacks. Widespread adoption of XML provides some help, but implementation is slow.

Consumers and small businesses are desperate for solutions and companies they can trust, and this desperation often translates into competitive advantages for firms with established brands. Small companies attempt to overcome the brand advantage by offering innovative new products and services. In the insurance industry, small companies attempt to fend off larger brands by developing such new products as geriatric healthcare insurance and "first-car" insurance for graduating college students. These products can also be fully priced for two years before the rate hike controls come into effect.

In such a different environment, many small businesses struggle to avoid going out of business. Demand for the expensive, albeit high-quality, products and services they sell is down, and small organizations cannot apply their scarce capital to developing more competitive products and services but must support business infrastructure needs. A large number of bankruptcies occur throughout the scenario period, contributing to a significant decline in the number of new businesses. Outsourcing of professional services continues, but overall demand is down.

In the end, Mad Max could have been an attractive environment for P&C insurance companies, but the combination of disastrous regulatory controls and a difficult economic environment results in an industry under constant attack for not providing services or coverage when needed. By the end of the scenario, both the European Union and United States governments realize that their controls have made the situation worse, and while still blaming the insurance industry for many consumer and small business woes, they begin to reassess what they should do.

It may be tempting to evaluate this scenario in terms of its "accuracy" (or otherwise), asking "How well did this scenario predict the future?" and therefore "How useful was it in the insurance company's planning?" It is, however, a temptation that should be resisted. For one thing—as we have constantly reiterated—scenarios are not forecasts; they are descriptions of possible futures. For another, the reason the company developed this particular scenario was not because the company thought it was the "most likely" future, but because if the future did evolve along these lines, the scenario would be the most challenging for the company and its long-term planning. It was critically important, therefore, that the company commence contingency thinking and planning on how to respond to such a future.

What's Next?

Once the scenarios are written, the process moves to the true purpose of the effort: deciding what to do after developing and evaluating options for the organization under each scenario. The preparation is complete, and now it's time to do strategic thinking. Activities will include leveraging the realistic stories about the future to identify threats and opportunities for the organization; thinking through the risks and rewards of the alternative courses of action in the different environments that might be encountered; focusing on the courses of action that provide the flexibility to succeed under different scenarios and take advantage of the strategic insights gained by the scenario planning; and developing scanning, monitoring, and contingency plans for the future.

PART 5

STEPS IN MOVING FROM SCENARIOS TO A DECISION

What strategy will generate the most value for us in the future? What decisions will the organization need so as to make developments of the future play out? How will our competitors act as information about the marketplace emerges and events occur? What investments by us will carry the most risk? What could be the unintended consequences of our actions? What signals should we watch to forewarn us of new market developments?

Although imaginative and thought-provoking scenarios can be generally useful in preparing our minds for dealing with what would otherwise be the unexpected, their main value lies in the contribution they make to strategic decision making. It is appropriate, therefore, that the climax of our process should lie in bringing the implications of our scenarios for the specific decision(s) before us, and for our strategy in general, into the sharpest possible focus.

Our aim at this stage of the process is threefold:

- Expand and consolidate our language about the future, using the scenarios,
- Identify and assess the strategic implications of the scenarios for our organization as a whole, and
- Specifically, develop conclusions for the decision that has been the focus of the whole exercise.

As we noted in the preceding chapter, the detailed drafting of the scenarios is best left to one individual to ensure harmony of style. In the current phase, therefore, the scenario team as a whole should immerse itself in the detailed "stories" presented by the scenarios, both to take ownership of the scenarios and to commence the process of interpreting their significance for the overall strategy of the business and, more specifically, their implications for the "decision focus" of the project.

What, then, are the implications of the scenarios? From the point of view of strategy development, we can say that the scenarios make the following contributions:

- Opportunities—scenarios highlight the potential for expansion into new products/services/markets and for new sources of competitive advantage.

- Threats—scenarios can alert us to the possibilities of new sources of competition, changes in market structure and customer needs, technological change, and shifts in regulatory policy.
- Options—scenarios suggest the need and possibilities for changes in strategy to adapt to these and other new conditions.
- Resilience—scenarios provide us with test beds for assessing the resilience and potential payoff of both old and new strategic thrusts that we might deploy.

Part 5 is divided into four chapters, following a logical sequence from looking broadly at the strategic implications of the scenarios to developing strategic recommendations and, finally, to preparing to transfer the results of the scenario-planning project back to the sponsoring organization and decision makers.

Chapter 19 develops the strategic implications of the scenarios and uncovers the many recommendation possibilities for the organization by rehearsing the future with the scenarios. By assuming the roles of decision makers in the different scenarios, the scenario team is able to identify a broad range of threats and opportunities the organization might face and is able to generate imaginative, powerful ideas about what the organization should do.

Scenario teams must always keep the decision focus in mind. Chapter 20 focuses on developing the decision recommendations from all the ideas and analyses generated. It highlights the different uses for scenarios in developing strategic recommendations and describes a structured methodology for developing the recommendations.

Recommendations derived from examining the uncertainties of the external environment will depend on a monitoring process to spot the early signals of change and alert the organization to possible changes in direction. When you know what to monitor, you're in a position to spot important signs of imminent threats and opportunities. Chapter 21 addresses identification of signposts and early warning indicators that are needed to execute the decision recommendations.

Communication of the outputs of the scenario-planning project to the decision makers and sponsors is of critical importance because only through effective communications can the scenario team be assured of success. The scenario planning may be over, but the decision making is not. Chapter 22 discusses how to plan and execute the communications effort.

CHAPTER 19

REHEARSING THE FUTURE WITH SCENARIOS (STEP 15)

With focused scenarios that cover the envelope of uncertainty and a scenario team armed with a common language about the world and its major issues, we now need to focus on what the organization should do to exploit change in the external environment and make us flexible in the face of new threats. We need to identify all our opportunities and options and develop decision criteria for when we should execute those options. This typically is a major challenge facing organizations—to identify strategies that can succeed in the future, understand their risks and rewards, and know when to implement them—but now we have developed the tools to meet that challenge in a straightforward but powerful way.

In this chapter we explain the immersion of the scenario team in the different scenarios as if each were to occur, forcing each participant to think of the important opportunities and threats the organization might face, the strategies it might use, and the competitive responses it might execute. Through this process we identify the different decision-making situations in which the organization could find itself and push ourselves to rehearse how the organization should act.

What Does "Rehearsing the Future" Involve?

Scenarios are realistic descriptions of the organization's possible futures that allow the scenario team to set aside its individual and organizational assumptions about how the external environment will operate and explore new ones. This step involves placing the scenario team in decision-making roles in each of the scenarios so that team members can visualize the threats and opportunities that they might face and the strategic alternatives they could implement. By imagining themselves in decision-making roles in each scenario, scenario team members are able to ignore their current preoccupations with the external environment and appreciate the different dynamics they could face. Potential strategies appear very different when seen from different vantage points in time and under different conditions. When viewed through the lens of current assumptions, a strategy will often appear constrained, difficult, and limited. With scenarios, the scenario team can spot new strategies that could be important and lead to significant rewards.

This visualization of the strategic implications of the scenarios is guided by asking the team members to consider three questions:

- In your capacity as a decision maker, if you knew this scenario were going to occur, what opportunities and threats would you face?
- What strategies would you implement if you knew this scenario were going to occur in order to best take advantage of the opportunities and remove the threats?
- What signposts or leading indicators will alert you that this scenario and dynamics are going to occur?

Too often, decision makers move to a perceived solution without identifying and understanding all the threats and opportunities they might face or examining the innovative alternatives that they could implement to best realize all the value in the situation. The decision makers believe strongly in their strategy because they've successfully deployed it in the past, and at this stage in the planning process often want the group to move expeditiously to adopt it or a variation of it. The immersion step with scenarios effectively sidesteps that urge by forcing the decision makers, as part of the process, to face extreme yet plausible situations of the future that are probably very different from the decision makers' own views of the future. As they immerse themselves, the decision makers quickly see that many strategies won't work across all the scenarios and that it often takes a very focused strategy to get the most value out of any one scenario. The story line of a scenario allows the scenario team members to quickly immerse themselves in the dynamics and logic of the scenario and to assume their roles as decision makers. This is the power of scenarios: to be able to see important differences in how the future could play out.

Learning How to Succeed in the Future

Psychologist Karl E. Weick, a professor of organizational behavior and psychology at the University of Michigan, once commented, "In business, we tell ourselves stories in order to know more and compete better." A significant benefit of the immersion step is the learning that occurs from rehearsing the organization's actions and responses in the face of new and challenging situations. This learning occurs at both the individual and organizational levels. Each scenario team member experiences the pressures and stakes involved in assuming the senior decision maker's role in each scenario. Team members see the threats posed by the changing market dynamics, crises, and competitor strategies and experience the discovery of new opportunities. Later as the reality unfolds, they often perceive that they've already experienced something like it because of the scenario immersions. Because of this, they're motivated and able to act more decisively than the competitors.

At the organizational level, the immersion process forces the cross-functional team to see the new threats and opportunities together, to consider alternative strategies, and to reach conclusions about high payoff, robust, low payoff, and risky strategies. As a group, the team sees the benefits of maintaining flexibility in the face of uncertainty, of avoiding large investments that can't be undone, of keeping one's options open, and of monitoring continuously the external environment for new trends and signals of change.

By assuming the same decision-making roles in several different scenarios, team members also see the benefits of creating an organization and strategy that allow the company to change direction effectively in response to emerging trends and disruptive events. Companies that develop their decision-making capabilities using scenarios will find themselves better able to reach a decision with incomplete information, act without a complete plan, adjust rapidly to changes in the marketplace, and realign organization priorities in a short period of time. That is the essence of a resilient organization: It thrives in environments of high uncertainty and is able to make better decisions in those situations than others.

How to Conduct the Rehearsals Workshop

We've found the immersion process and the identification of the strategic implications works best in a workshop environment. It usually requires two to three hours to immerse a team into each scenario and develop team members' thoughts about the threats and opportunities in the scenario and possible actions or strategies. With three to four scenarios to rehearse, a two-day workshop is often required to complete the step.

The first activity of the workshop is for the facilitator to explain that the goal of the workshop is to identify as many ideas as possible about what the organization should do in the future. The scenario team will largely be operating in an expansive-thinking mode, and criticism and debates about the merits of one idea versus another need to be discouraged. After the workshop is over, the next step in the scenario-planning process will be to develop the recommendations for the strategy or decision. A structured process for analyzing the strengths and weaknesses of the strategy alternatives, and debating their merits, will then be used.

The purpose of the immersion activity is to tap the skills, experience, and knowledge of the scenario team members to identify the full range of opportunities and threats that the organization might face in the future and to develop an assortment of innovative and incremental strategic options and alternatives for addressing those opportunities and threats. This is why it's important to include decision makers and experienced managers on the scenario team.

The activities are organized so that individuals in the workshop are forced to reach conclusions about what they think would be the most important threats and opportunities in each scenario, and what strategy they would implement to realize the most value in that scenario. Because each member is stimulated to develop ideas and then share them with the group, a very rich set of ideas and concepts is generated. The sharing part of the workshop process is important because it generates competition among the members to come up with the most compelling strategy for each scenario. As the workshop moves from the first scenario to the second, and from the second to the third, the competition continues for participants to be innovative with ideas being generated. Often elements of strategies described for the first scenario are incorporated in strategies suggested later.

The immersion process starts with the facilitator or one of the scenario team members reviewing the key causal dynamics of the scenario, important events, and outcomes. Since each scenario was written as a story, it's relatively straightforward to get the listeners to immerse themselves in the atmosphere of the scenario. The team members have already read the scenarios—they are their scenarios—so they don't need to be reminded of every little detail, but they do need the basic features and distinguishing dynamics to begin visualizing the threats and opportunities the organization could face. It usually takes five to ten minutes to complete the immersion.

Then the facilitator asks the scenario team members to assume the role of the decision maker in the scenario just described, with the task of identifying the threats and opportunities that they will face in the scenario and the strategies they would implement if they knew that scenario were to occur. The facilitator then asks each member of the scenario team to respond to the question, "What are the most important threats and opportunities that the organization will face in this scenario?" The facilitator requests each participant to identify three to five threats and several opportunities, referring, if necessary, to the detailed scenario descriptions that participants should have in front of them. Some threats or opportunities are written directly into the description of the scenario, while others will be implied by the scenario's dynamics.

Depending on the recording process being used, the facilitator may ask the participants to write the threats and opportunities on 5" $\times$ 8" cards, one per card. After 10 to 20 minutes for thinking and writing, the facilitator goes around the room asking each participant to nominate one threat and one opportunity. The facilitator continues around the room until there are no more responses. Extensive debate on whether a threat or opportunity would be real in the scenario should be discouraged. This is a brainstorming task with the goal of identifying a full spectrum of ideas.

The next activity is for scenario participants, while remaining immersed in the scenario, to individually develop a strategy that they think would contribute the most value for the organization, if that scenario were to occur. It's important that the participants understand that, for the purposes of this task, they're omniscient in knowing exactly how the future will play out. With this knowledge, what strategy or decision would they implement at the beginning of the scenario?

So that the strategy descriptions contain the necessary information, participants are asked to write down their ideas in a strategy template before presenting them to the rest of the group. Box 19-1 provides an overview of what is included in a strategy description.

BOX 19-1
Elements of a Strategy Alternative

Strategy Description:

We define a strategy as the means for reaching an overall objective by the end of a period. In our process, the overall objective is developed as part of the decision focus: Where do we want to be at the end of a certain period of time? A strategy description will include five elements:

- **Concept.** The concept describes how the organization should achieve its overall objectives, how progress toward the objectives should unfold, and how the resources of the organization should generally be developed and used. The concept is the focus of the strategy.

- **Programs.** The programs are the means for succeeding in the current environment and being ready for future environments. For companies, programs are the specific products and services and markets they will develop. Measurable targets can be developed for each program, and plans and roadmaps are the means for communicating what the recommended programs are and when they should be implemented. Programs defined for a scenario-based strategy are typically overlapping and are a mixture of major programs, new programs, and options. The options provide the means to respond as reality unfolds.

• **Resources.** The strategy recommendations must include how people, money, and time will be used, as well as how the capabilities of the organization will be developed and applied to some unique advantage. Advantages can include speed of execution, scale of operation, costs, product or service quality, technological innovation, and so on. Competitive advantage and key success factors are usually defined by the resource element. For scenario-based strategy, speed, flexibility, and versatility are often specifically developed capabilities.

• **Monitoring and Response.** A scenario-based strategy must describe how the environment will be monitored and how program decisions will be made so that the right actions are taken at the right time. Those decisions include which options to implement, what new options to invest in, and which resources to redirect. Often the timing of the decisions is based on the monitoring of key forces and drives and expectations of seeing specific indicators and signposts of imminent threats or opportunities. The most obvious things to monitor are the forces and drivers related to the major axes of uncertainty of the scenarios, but they also will include indicators related to the recommended programs.

• **Next Steps.** The first four elements describe the overall strategy, but organizations need a short-term list of priorities to initiate the strategy and to outline how an effective transition will be made from the current state and capability to more flexible ones. This element also becomes a critical part of the decision communications that will occur.

Source: Concepts developed from author project experiences and from *Hope Is Not a Method*, by Gordon R. Sullivan and Michael V. Harper. Times Books, 1996.

Given these elements, a typical strategy idea will include responses to the following questions:

- Concept: What is the concept or focus of the strategy?
- Programs: What products and services will be developed and sold?
  What markets and customer needs will be served?
  What geographies will be served?
- Resources: What strategy model will be used to integrate all these elements and compete successfully as reality unfolds?
  What will be the key success factors?
  What investments in plants, technology, people, and organizational processes will be made?
- Monitoring, Response, and Next Steps: What do we want to do when?

Figure 19-1 shows a strategy idea template to be filled in, used in a recent project. During a workshop, it takes 15 to 20 minutes for everyone to fill in one template with an idea.

After participants fill in the idea templates, it's important to take the time for participants to share their ideas with the rest of the team. We ask participants to stand up in front of the group, one at a time, and read their ideas. We set a time limit, usually no more than five minutes per idea, and ask everyone to stay within that limit. Listening to 15 persons read their strategies can be tedious and requires a lot of concentration, but we find this to be one of

---

Title of Strategy: _____   Scenario: _____

Overall Concept:

Key Success Factors:

Products and Services:

Markets:

Geographic Coverage:

Technology Development Priorities:

Organizational Skills, Capabilities:

Key Partners or Suppliers:

Your Name: _____

Figure 19-1   Example of Template for a Strategy Alternative

the most important activities of the entire process. Each person is exposed to a series of innovative perspectives on how to create value in a challenging environment. Participants always comment afterward about how impressed they were with the quality of the strategies presented and the lessons they took away on how to address various challenging circumstances. The process is frequently entertaining, too, as one proxy CEO after another says what he or she would do.

The threats and opportunities for a scenario are displayed together in front of the group, using 5" × 8" cards or on easel paper. The strategy ideas are then arrayed next to those threats and opportunities.

After the two questions, what would be the major threats and opportunities and what would be the best strategy or course of action, are answered for the first scenario, the team then proceeds to immerse itself in the second scenario, answer the same questions, and so on, until each scenario has been explored.

With the scenario immersions completed, the scenario team is now primed to identify strategies that could work in all scenarios. It does this by looking at all the strategy ideas that have been generated to spot those that show up in more than one scenario, and by reflecting on strategies that could be resilient under a number of conditions. A low cost strategy can often work regardless of the scenario, although it may not generate any exceptional returns. But that's often the tradeoff among strategies: Do I select a high risk, high reward strategy or a low risk, low reward one? Again, the facilitator leverages participants' ability to think creatively by asking them to fill in a template individually and then stand up and outline their ideas to the group.

Once the robust or resilient strategies have been described, the main activities of the workshop are complete. To generate a sense of closure with the step, the facilitator should ask the group for its comments on lessons learned and overall conclusions about the ideas generated. At this stage, the participants are generally quite excited by the results, having been energized by the display of ideas for all the scenarios. A new set of evangelists for scenario planning has often been created.

The facilitator concludes the workshop by outlining how the results of the workshop will be captured and distributed to everyone and by describing the next step in the scenario-planning process for using the results to develop decision recommendations.

CHAPTER 20

GETTING TO THE DECISION RECOMMENDATIONS (STEP 16)

For the scenario team to develop recommendations for the decision under consideration, it must identify what the organization should do but also must integrate flexibility and capability into the recommendations so that when the organization later sees specific signposts, it can quickly and effectively tailor a response to address the opportunities and threats. The scenarios represent the organization's knowledge and best thinking about the marketplace's forces and drivers and possible outcomes and provide the team with a common language and context for evaluating strategy alternatives and selecting the best one. Instead of working with one forecast and set of assumptions about the future, we now have the means to make the decision in the full awareness of the uncertain environment.

Given that multiple scenarios of the future are plausible, there can be no perfect choice. Instead, the team must develop recommendations for a decision that has a focus but pushes multiple, overlapping agendas, so that the organization is constantly preparing for new investments, products, and markets; incorporating new technology; and changing the capabilities of the organization in response to changing circumstances.

Developing recommendations for the decision, then, is a matter of selecting among a set of defined alternatives, each of which has its own potential consequences. The objective is to select the alternative whose consequences are preferred, based on the organization's goals and interests, which could include levels of profitability, market position, leadership, resilience, and so on. In an uncertain world, the organization can only estimate possible consequences (for example, a competitor's behavior).

But the team must do more than identify the alternative with the best potential consequences; it must also select the alternative that is best suited to the skills, capabilities, and experience of the organization.

In this chapter, we show how to develop the strategy or decision recommendations using scenarios. We start with a discussion of different types of strategic decisions that we may have been asked to address, because the nature of the decision often determines the activities and level of analysis required.

We then proceed with describing the activities and analysis to develop recommendations for the more sophisticated decision, selecting a new strategy. Those activities include:

- Developing a set of alternatives that we might be able to execute from the ideas generated by the scenario-immersions step
- Defining the relevant preference and organizational criteria for selecting the best alternative, based on preferences of the organization for profits or market position and the capabilities or limitations of the organization in executing the decision
- Describing the process for evaluating the alternatives using the criteria and scenarios
- Developing the recommendations for the best strategy

Tailoring the Process to the Type of Decision

Any organization using scenario planning has to have some sort of a process, a template, for moving from scenarios to strategy. Some critics will protest that this approach trivializes strategy development, substituting analytical structure for intuitive and informed insight. But the scenario player needs to apply some basic techniques to integrate all the information and insights generated and bridge the gap between scenarios and strategy.

Since scenario planning can be applied to many types of strategic decisions, we offer five roadmaps, ranging from the most elemental to the more sophisticated, for how to move from scenarios to strategy.

Sensitivity/Risk Assessment for a Go/No Go Decision

This approach can be used to evaluate a specific strategic decision such as a major plant investment, entry into a new market, or development of a new technology. Here, the need for the decision is known beforehand: The question, therefore, is simply whether or not to proceed, after assessing the strategy's resilience or vulnerability in different conditions.

A step-by-step approach first identifies the key conditions (such as market growth rate, changes in regulatory climate, technological development) that the future market or industry would have to meet to justify a "go" decision and then assess the state of these conditions in each scenario. It is then possible to compare the scenario conditions with those needed to justify proceeding with the decision and to assess how successful, and how resilient and vulnerable, a "go" decision would be in each scenario. Finally, it is possible to assess the overall resilience of a decision to proceed with the proposed strategy and to consider the need or desirability of "hedging" or modifying the original decision in some way to increase its resilience.

This approach provides a relatively straightforward application of scenarios to decision making, using a series of descriptive and judgmental steps. However, it depends on having a very clear and specific decision, one that lends itself to a "go/no go" decision.

An illustration of this approach was provided by a paper company confronted with a decision about whether or not to invest $600 million in a new paper-making plant. The company did not normally use scenarios in its strategic planning but decided that they would be useful here, given the long life span (30–35 years) of the plant and the corresponding range of uncertainties regarding future electronic technology development, consumer values and time use, prospects for advertising, and general economic conditions.

The scenarios showed, as one would expect, vastly different levels of demand growth but similar patterns of eventual decline, with the timing of key threats remaining a critical uncertainty. Playing out the investment decision in these different environments suggested that only in the most optimistic conditions would the company meet its "hurdle rate" for return on investment. As a result, the executives decided on a more incremental approach to the investment, significantly scaling down the initial plant size.

Evaluation of an Existing Strategy

Another relatively straightforward role for scenarios is to act as "test beds" to evaluate the viability of an existing strategy, usually one that derives from traditional single-point forecasting. By playing a company-wide or business-unit strategy against the scenarios, it is possible to gain some insight into the strategy's effectiveness in a range of business conditions, and so to identify modifications and/or contingency plans that require attention.

First, it is necessary to disaggregate the strategy into its specific program thrusts (e.g., "Focus on upscale consumer market segments," "Diversify into related services areas") and spell out their goals and objectives. Then it is possible to assess the relevance and likely success (in terms of meeting the desired objectives) of these thrusts in the diverse conditions presented by the scenarios. Assessing the results of this impact analysis should then enable the management team to identify:

- Opportunities that the strategy addresses and those that it misses
- Threats/risks that the analysis has foreseen or overlooked
- Comparative competitive success or failure

At this point it is possible to identify options for possible changes to the strategy and the need for contingency planning.

This approach offers a natural and relatively simple first use of scenarios in a corporate strategic planning system. Assessing an existing strategy requires less sophistication than developing a new strategy. Nevertheless, this assessment approach provides a relatively effective demonstration of the utility of scenarios in executive decision making by identifying important bottom-line issues that require immediate attention.

A large department store chain introduced scenarios this way into its strategic exploration of future patterns of change in the economy, consumer values, lifestyles, as well as the structure and operations of the retail industry. The company used these scenarios in three distinct ways:

1. To evaluate the likely payoff from its current strategy;
2. To assess and compare the strategies of key competitors (Note: This was an interesting and useful application of scenario planning—assessing competitors' as well as one's own strategy); and
3. To analyze retail strategy options for possible inclusion in the company's strategy. The company did, in fact, expand greatly into speciality stores as a result of this exercise.

Strategy Development (Using a "Planning-Focus" Scenario)

This approach is an attempt to bridge the "culture gap" between traditional planning that relies on single-point forecasting and "pure" scenario planning. Basically, it consists of selecting one of the scenarios as a starting point and focus for strategy development and then using the other scenarios to test this strategy's resilience and assess the need for modification, "hedging," or contingency planning.

The steps involved in this approach are as follows:

• Review each of the scenarios to identify the key opportunities and threats for the business, looking at each scenario in turn, and then looking across all scenarios to identify common opportunities and threats.

• Determine, based on this review, what the company should do, and should not do, in any case.

• Select a "planning focus" scenario—usually the one judged to be "most probable."

• Integrate the strategic elements of what should be done/not done in any case into a coherent strategy for the "planning focus" scenario.

- Test this strategy against the remaining scenarios to assess its resilience or vulnerability.

- Review the results of this test to determine the need for strategy modification, "hedging," and contingency planning.

It should be obvious that this approach flies in the face of our earlier assertion that scenarios should not deal in probabilities. And, while the other scenarios are not discarded, there is still the danger that this approach may close minds to "unlikely" (which often means "unpleasant" or "threatening") scenarios and so limit the search for strategy options. However, the approach can be justified as a useful intermediate step between traditional and scenario planning, one that helps to wean executives away from their reliance on single-point forecasting. It does not commit the ultimate sin of disregarding the other scenarios entirely; and, in its step-by-step process, it does address many of the key questions that scenario-based strategy should ask.

Shell Canada used this approach when it introduced scenarios into its strategic-planning system. Because it is a member of the Royal Dutch Shell Group, its executives were well aware of the strict interpretation of scenario-based planning but felt that this modified approach would help the company ease into the new process by making this concession to traditional thinking. In fact, the discussion of probabilities revealed so much uncertainty about future trends that there was no agreement as to what was the "most probable," and two scenarios—each with dramatically different drivers—were selected as the "planning focus." The company then proceeded to structure its strategic positioning in response to three questions:

1. What strategies should we pursue no matter which scenario materializes?
2. What strategies should we pursue if either of the "planning focus" scenarios materializes? and
3. How sensitive are base strategies to variations in assumptions under contingent conditions?

Growth Opportunities Identification

Developing growth opportunities is the biggest challenge facing many large companies today, requiring activities and thinking that cut across virtually every function and organization in the company. Scenarios help participants to envision what the company could be and conduct the "out of the box" strategic thinking to identify, assess, and value potential opportunities.

In the growth-opportunities identification approach, the organization identifies new directions that leverage and enhance what the organization can do now to redefine the future of the organization and—most significantly—the industry itself. Typically, at the heart of discovering new opportunities are new relationships between the company and both new and existing customers and new ways to compete in providing value to those customers—all of which change the rules of the game and can redefine an industry. As Apple's entry into music distribution, eBay's entry into telecommunications, and Google's entry into wireless all suggest, new technologies and new applications and cross-linkages among technologies provide major paths for such innovation, but other routes are also possible, including mergers and acquisitions, new markets, and the invention of new businesses with existing technologies.

Developing new opportunities requires portfolio investments, taking risks, and responding quickly to new events and circumstances not unlike those actions needed to develop a new strategy, except that the company must sustain these actions in the face of pressure to support and maintain the main business. The opportunity-identification activities using scenarios include:

- Identifying the key technologies or capabilities to leverage, or the market arenas or areas of change to focus on
- Analyzing each scenario to determine the the major threats and opportunities for the organization (e.g., what consumer demand will grow rapidly in Scenario A? for Scenario B? what technologies will be commercially available in Scenario A? in Scenario B?, etc.)
- Reviewing these scenario-specific opportunities and threats to identify the most attractive ones to the organization
- Evaluating the most attractive ones against multiple criteria, and selecting a portfolio of opportunities to pursue

Strategy Development (Without Using a Planning-Focus Scenario)

In this approach, the scenario team takes all scenarios at face value without judging probabilities and aims for development of a resilient strategy that can deal with wide variations in business conditions yet meet profitability and growth goals. The step-by-step process in this approach considers:

- Identifying the key elements of a successful strategy (such as geographic scope, market focus, product range, basis of competition)
- Analyzing each scenario to determine the optimal setting for each strategy element (e.g., what would be the best strategy for Scenario A? for Scenario B?, etc.)

- Reviewing the scenario-specific settings and evaluating the different alternatives against multiple decision criteria
- Combining the most attractive strategy alternatives into an overall, resilient, coordinated strategy

Without doubt, this is the most sophisticated—and demanding—approach, one that most closely approximates the goal of strategizing within the scenarios framework and that makes optimal use of the scenarios in strategy development. It provides management with the maximum feasible range of choice and forces careful evaluation of these options against differing assumptions about the futures. It does, however, demand effort, patience, and sophistication and works best when the decision makers participate directly in the whole process.

This was the case, for instance, with a large European bank in which the senior management team was, in effect, both the scenario team and the strategy-development team. After structuring scenarios around their perceptions of the critical uncertainties facing the business, team members first identified the strategic opportunities and threats arising from these scenarios. They then used this framework to assess the company's current competitive position and prospective vulnerability. Their approach to strategy development then led them to the following steps:

- First, to single out 11 key elements of a well-rounded strategy (e.g., product scope, alliances, distribution/delivery, technology)
- Second, to identify the optimal strategic option for each of these 11 elements in each of the four scenarios
- Finally, to select the most resilient option for each element, and integrate these options into a coherent strategy for the company

Conducting the Activities to Move from Scenarios to Strategy

Given our new-found appreciation of the uncertainties of the external environment and the potential for sudden change and discontinuity, the strategy-development process must provide the organization options and position it to respond to change. The organization's goal is not to be surprised, and in fact be able to find the opportunities and threats and act on them faster than anyone else.

To accomplish this, we need to conduct activities that generate a strategy that is inherently flexible, focused on an objective or set of objectives with time frames, and organized as a series of overlapping programs and initiatives. We need to balance the need for focus with the need to accommodate uncertainty; we need to balance the need to compete in today's markets yet be able to adjust to future markets. Because we don't know how future markets will change, we need a resilient or robust choice, one that can succeed regardless of how reality unfolds. At the same time, we recognize that we can't be overly sensitive to changes in the external environment and constantly jump from one course of action to another. So, we need a decision-making process that is measured yet allows for bold acts.

The basic activities of the process are as follows:

• **Activity 1: Developing the alternatives to evaluate.** The immersion process probably generated from 30 to 50 strategy alternatives, along with many individual ideas of programs, business models, and resource investments. The first activity is to address this complexity by developing a more manageable set of coherent alternatives from all the ideas.

• **Activity 2: Defining the evaluation criteria.** Criteria are defined for evaluating the alternatives so that we can compare and contrast the possibilities on the basis of the organization's interests, objectives, and capabilities. Typically, multiple criteria and scenarios are used to develop the necessary insights about the strengths and weaknesses of the alternatives.

• **Activity 3: Conducting the evaluations.** Each alternative is evaluated under the conditions of each scenario using the criteria.

• **Activity 4: Selecting the best strategy.** The alternative evaluations are compared, and a set of recommendations on the best approach is then crafted through structured discussion and debate.

Agreeing that the usefulness of scenarios depends upon their ability to influence our strategy recommendation(s), we should stress that we need to avoid too much detailed analysis early in process, or else we will be overwhelmed by all the analyses and information. We should *not* develop a complete strategy for each of the scenarios, and then by some means—maybe by applying the test of discounted cash flow to each of the alternatives—select the one that appears to give the greatest promise of success and profitability. No management team would willingly undertake to go through a full-blown strategy development exercise two or three or four times (once for each of the scenarios that have been developed). Such a course of action would more likely lead to "paralysis by analysis" than to constructive action. And, in any case, it would be based on a further misunderstanding of scenario planning: The real aim is to develop a resilient strategy within the framework of alternative futures provided by the scenarios.

Another word of explanation—and caution—is needed. In a number of places, we have referred to a major objective of scenario planning as the development of a resilient or robust strategy. Now, it should be obvious that these are not the only qualities to be sought in a strategy; and, taken to an extreme, they could mean little more than adopting the lowest common denominator of scenario-specific strategies. At a time that calls for bold, even radical, action in many markets, such an interpretation would be a prescription for mediocrity at best, extinction at worst. Our point is rather that, before taking bold steps, we should test the strategy against a variety of scenarios so that the management team is forewarned about potential vulnerabilities. Resilience or robustness can then be built into the strategy, *not* by reducing its force or boldness but rather by "hedging" or contingency planning.

Activity 1: Developing the Alternatives to Evaluate

In the previous chapter, we used the scenarios to identify a number of possible strategies for the organization. But the array of strategies can be overwhelming because the diversity and number of strategies were only limited by the imagination of the team members. The immersion process probably generated from 30 to 50 strategy alternatives, along with many individual ideas for programs, business models, and resource investments. Moreover, comparing the alternatives can be difficult or confusing if they are not defined or articulated in a consistent fashion that facilitates easy comparison and contrasts.

We deal with this complexity by developing a more manageable set of coherent alternatives from all the ideas. The target number of manageable alternatives will vary by decision circumstance, but generally one should expect to develop from three to ten alternatives, each having a focus, market, and product and service programs, and resource priorities and plans. (See Box 19-1 for the definition of a strategy.)

A three-step process can be used to accomplish this. In the first step, the facilitator asks the scenario team to look at the different alternative ideas from the rehearsals and quickly identify a target number of ideas to carry forward for evaluation. The criteria for selecting the ideas are the idea's potential to succeed in the marketplace and the organization's ability to implement it. During the task, the team will combine similar or duplicate ideas. It's important at this point to also include the current strategy as an alternative if it wasn't already described and selected.

The next task is to refine the alternative descriptions so that they are clear, complete, and unique. This will involve taking time to analyze the original description of the alternative and then adding or deleting items to make each alternative distinct from the others and possible to evaluate and compare against other alternatives. We want each alternative to be complete with the same strategy elements as the other alternatives. Often this work is done in small breakout groups that are formed with the appropriate expertise to make the adjustments. The breakout groups can be part of a workshop process or the work can be done between workshops.

The final task in the development of the alternatives is to review the work of the breakout groups and make the final selection of alternatives as a team. If the number of alternatives is close to the desired number, then the team can simply discuss the changes to the alternatives, make any additional adjustments, and go on to the next activity. If there are still too many alternatives to carry forward, then the team members can reach some agreement by ranking or voting on the alternatives and then taking the highest ranked or most popular ones.

An additional task to help in developing alternatives is to organize and arrange all the strategy ideas that came out of the rehearsals into strategy-element categories. These categories, or strategy levers, represent arenas of action and choices that the organization can employ to achieve its overall strategic objective. The concept of strategy levers is similar to a control panel with a mix of levers. The levers are the tools or means of the organization to get something done. Marketing, sales, and manufacturing are all strategy levers. They are elements of the business or environment that the organization can control. External elements, such as competitors, cannot be strategy levers. In a strategic plan, we describe how we're going to use the strategy levers to achieve an overall objective.

The strategy levers often carry familiar organizational function and activity names, including:

- Product Development
- Marketing Communications
- Marketing Channels
- Customer Service
- Distribution Channels
- Sales
- Geographic Emphases
- Customer Markets
- Alliances and Partnerships
- Vendors and Consultants
- Information Technology

- Regulatory Approaches
- Production/Manufacturing Emphasis
- Technology Investments
- Employee Skills or Competencies
- Corporate Affairs/Legal Specialties
- Core Values and Culture
- Intellectual Property and Trade Secrets

The ideas are placed into strategy-lever categories where duplicates are eliminated and similar items are combined. The result is the integration of all the ideas from the rehearsals into what we call a strategy table. The table has potentially several functions. One function would be to help generate new strategy alternatives by combining items from the different levers in new ways. Another function would be to highlight the differences among alternatives by showing which elements are and are not included in each. (see Figure 20-1).

Organizing the ideas into levers is not usually a workshop activity because developing the lever categories, eliminating duplicates, combining items, and so on often requires several hours. It should be done offline by a member or subgroup of the team.

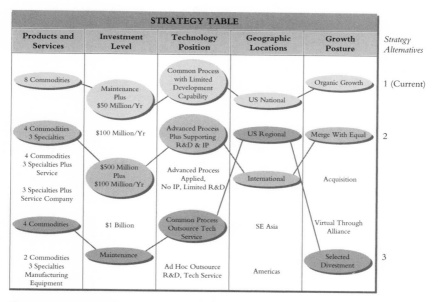

Figure 20-1   Development and Comparison of Strategy Alternatives Using a Strategy Table

Activity 2: Defining Our Evaluation Criteria

Evaluation criteria are measures of risk or value, or both, reflecting the interests, strategic objectives, and capabilities of the organization that we use to evaluate and compare the strategy alternatives. Typical criteria include:

- Capital required
- Cost
- Financial returns (return on investment, return on net assets, net present value, etc.)
- Alignment with corporate strategy, mission, vision
- Market share and position
- Technology/product risk
- Commercial risk
- Potential for unintended consequences or ancillary effects
- New product, service, technology leadership
- Ability of organization to execute

Key factors in the selection of which criteria to use is whether criteria information can be generated or estimated for each alternative, whether the organization's decision makers will understand and appreciate the criteria's value, and whether the criteria will help differentiate among the alternatives. We need to be able to clearly and accurately define the criteria to ensure that all the evaluations are conducted uniformly. And we can't use criteria where all the alternatives have the same value. If each alternative requires the same amount of capital, then capital required would not be a good criterion.

A criterion definition will have three elements:

- Criterion name: A meaningful title for the criterion
- Key question: The key question or issue that the criterion seeks to address
- Measures: Definitions of scores on a three- or five-point scale, "one" being the least desirable and "five" being the most desirable

Typically, we try to limit the number of criteria to no more than six. We have found that we don't create substantive, additional insight with more than six criteria, and often need only three or four for the rough-cut type of analysis that we're conducting. We need to be careful to not overanalyze strategy alternatives too early and get bogged down in unnecessary detail.

Once the criteria are selected, we need to define the range of possible outcomes for the alternatives. We often use an index system of one to five,

Figure 20-2   Example of Set of Evaluation Criteria

Evaluation Criteria	Worst 1	Average 3	Best 5
Market Growth	**Small** Less than 5%	**Medium** 5% to 10%	**High** More than 15%
Financial Returns	**Worst** Below New York Stock Exchange average returns	**Average** Provides medium growth short of goals	**Best** Meets or surpasses financial goals
Investment/ Resource Requirements	**High** Exceeds a billion dollars	**Medium** $500 million	**Low** No investment requirement
Current Ability to Execute	**Weak** Extremely hard to execute from current position	**Moderate** Difficult, but implementation is manageable and required competencies are attainable	**Strong** Straightforward and easy to implement in terms of skills and competencies
Unintended Consequences	**High Potential** Many repercussions are possible, some of them quite severe	**Medium** Some unexpected reactions could occur	**Low Potential** Expected reactions are understood; none is severe
Risk	**High** Likelihood of success is uncertain and the cost of failure is high	**Medium** Some likelihood of success and acceptable cost of failure	**Low** Likelihood of success is high and cost of failure is low

or one to three, where a number is assigned to represent a portion of each range, to help us in using multiple criteria. See Figure 20-2.

The scenarios are important criteria in the process and play a special role. We would not expect an alternative to generate the same return on investment, obtain the same market share, or experience the same commercial risk for every scenario. In fact, the scenarios will be likely to have a major impact on the performance of the alternatives, according to the criteria, and we need to have an evaluation process that allows the scenarios to be taken into account. We do this by essentially applying the criteria to each alternative under each scenario. Figure 20-3 shows a standard template for recording the results of an alternative evaluation using scenarios.

Strategy Alternative _____

	Scenarios			Rationale
	A	B	C	
Market Growth				
Financial Returns				
Resource Requirements				
Ability to Execute				
Unintended Consequences				
Risk				

Figure 20-3   Template for Recording Evaluation Results Using Scenarios

Activity 3: Conducting the Evaluations

Alternative evaluation is the key activity for learning the strengths and weaknesses of an alternative and being able to develop a robust recommendation for the organization. It's important for the team to explore those variations and document the results before developing the recommendations of what to do in the face of an uncertain future.

Before the evaluation is conducted, some information about each alternative often needs to be developed. This is because market share forecasts, technology commercialization estimates, and financial return estimates by scenario don't normally exist, even at the back-of-the-envelope level of detail needed, in the minds of the scenario team members. So analysts or team members are asked to create the background market, technology, and financial information and some of the estimates needed for the evaluation and then present that information to the team.

One objective of the evaluations is to generate the rationale for selecting an alternative and developing the recommendations. The criteria are systematically applied by scenario to each alternative, and the rationale—assumptions, conditions, and logic—for the values of the criteria are recorded.

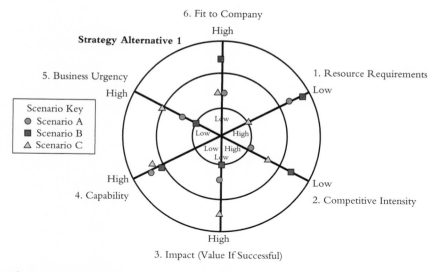

Figure 20-4   Graphical Display of Evaluation

The evaluations of alternatives can be done in a facilitated workshop discussion. This can take place in one room with a facilitator, or in breakout groups. Using workshops and breakout groups has the advantage of building consensus and common understandings of the evaluations in the team and avoids the need to explain the assessments to the whole team at a later date.

Once the evaluations are complete, the results can be shown easily with spreadsheets or graphical displays. See Figure 20-4.

Activity 4: Selecting the Best Strategy

The final activity is to select the concept, set of programs, and resources to best position and move the organization forward in the future. This activity—which typically occurs in a facilitated workshop—involves mixing and combining elements of the alternatives until the best combination is found.

The first task is to compare the alternatives using the evaluations. This often results in one or two alternatives being identified as superior based on the criteria, although given the multiple criteria, multiple scenarios, and the uncertainty of the estimates, this will always be a rough judgment. In addition to the identification of the better alternative(s), the comparison will generate considerable insight about the conditions in which the alternative will be likely to succeed, the conditions in which it will be likely to fail, as well as key success factors in implementation, and so on.

The team works together—through structured debate—to develop find-ings and conclusions from the evaluations and comparison and then selects the best solution for the organization. It's important in organizing the dis-cussion to hear what every member of the team thinks. When facilitating these discussions, we often structure the agenda around a series of questions that we want the team to answer:

- What alternative(s) are the most attractive based on the evaluations?
- What alternative could generate the most value for the organization in each scenario? (What are the high payoff strategies?)
- What contingencies could be added to protect the high payoff alternative(s) against the scenarios in which they're weak?
- What alternative could generate the most value across all the scenarios?
- What steps are needed to move from the current strategy to the higher value added ones?
- How could any of the alternatives be combined to increase the value across the scenarios, and reduce initial investment?
- What should be the recommended strategy?

Key Success Factors in Developing the Decision Recommendations

The major benefits of creating the scenarios will be missed if the team can't develop and defend a set of decision recommendations. In this chapter, we've described a structured process for driving toward this ultimate goal, leverag-ing the scenarios and the diverse talents of the scenario team. The key suc-cess factors for developing good recommendations include:

- Use multiple criteria, which permits consideration of several measures of value and risk rather than estimated financial returns and capabilities alone. The evaluation process should not be thought of as an algorithm for auto-matically selecting the alternative with the highest rating. Criteria ratings do not add well, and the team should consider the individual criteria, and com-binations of criteria, separately in developing the recommendations.
- Use criteria that are easily understood. The more subtleties and vari-ables involved, the less uniform and more subjective the evaluations will become.
- Allow ample time. Time pressure might result in hasty decisions. The outcomes from a hasty process will be obvious to others down the road.
- Stay disciplined and focused in doing the evaluations. It is easy to fall into the habit of assessing things haphazardly, especially when fatigue sets in.

• Strive for objectivity. Try to include known facts and research findings to support the evaluations.

• Ensure consensus on criteria and criteria ratings before developing the final recommendations.

• Remember to circle back to the original decision focus and question whether the selected recommendations, if executed, will achieve the desired results.

• Near the end, ask how prepared we will be for surprises or disruptions in the external environment. Can we survive a major surprise? What are the contingency plans?

Outputs of This Step

The outputs of this step represent the real payoff from the whole scenario process: detailed evaluation and guidance for strategy in general, and for the decision that has been the focus of this exercise. Specifically, the outputs include:

• A carefully crafted and detailed analysis of the major opportunities and threats posed by the scenarios
• A comprehensive database of strategic options that the organization should consider
• Comparable evaluations of strategic alternatives, providing the foundation for future contingency planning and crisis management
• Final recommendations of the scenario team

CHAPTER 21

IDENTIFYING THE SIGNPOSTS TO MONITOR (STEP 17)

Scenario planning will raise an organization's watchfulness and compel managers and staff to monitor forces that fall within a traditional industry analysis as well as those that fall outside. The scenarios and the strategic rehearsals also help them to appreciate the potential dynamics that the forces are signaling, and related opportunities and threats.

That heightened sense of awareness is needed because we want to act before unambiguous evidence on the importance of new developments is available. Therefore, as part of the scenario-planning process, we must prepare for this watch-and-respond system and identify the signs that could indicate an important shift or discontinuity.

The major barrier in accomplishing all of this is the voluminous amount of information that is available, much of it low quality. It's impossible to monitor everything, and at the same time it's very difficult to make sense of what information is being gathered. Organizations need a prioritization process that helps them select what information should be collected, so that the task is doable, yet helps them interpret the weak, sometimes conflicting signals, so that they can act ahead of others.

In this chapter we describe the selection of indicators or signs of future external developments based on their early-warning capacity and the availability of information for them. In Chapter 23, we discuss the design and setup of the ongoing monitoring process that uses those indicators and signposts.

What Are Indicators and Signs?

A road metaphor explains indicators and signs. Let's assume we were traveling by car to a destination 300 miles away but heard on the radio, just as we were starting out, that there was an accident on an important bridge still 200 miles away. We would immediately begin thinking about what signs would indicate that the bridge would still be closed when we arrived so that we could potentially take an alternate, but longer, route. Some signs, like the advisories on the radio, would be important because they could give us very early warning. As we got much closer to the bridge, we would begin looking for other signs, like very few cars coming in the opposite direction, or drivers in the opposite direction blinking their lights, and so on. As we saw or heard more and more signs, we would make a decision about whether or not to take an alternate route.

Signs or signposts play the same role with strategy. We've planned to execute a strategic action in the future, if or when we see the right signs. When we see signs that we're looking for, we prepare ourselves to act.

A sign or signpost, then, is a specific value or outcome of an important force or driver. Figure 21-1 provides some examples, from a recent project, of forces to monitor and signs to look for.

We identify the signs we should monitor by reviewing the forces and drivers of the scenarios and the decision recommendations. We would like to identify early warning indicators of new developments to help us foresee what scenario the world might be moving toward and strategic options that are increasing in value.

How to Identify What to Monitor

The process of identifying the indicators or signs starts with the scenario axes of uncertainty and the strategic recommendations. We should only monitor forces and look for signs for things on which we can act. There is much too much information available to monitor all of it, and we need to focus on monitoring only forces that can provide early warning indications.

Research analysts, experts, and specialists in the areas of interest should be asked to identify the forces, indicators, and signs that would give early warning of the scenario outcomes or the need to make a decision about a particular strategy. Those individuals should work directly with scenario team members to develop the portfolio of forces to monitor.

Key criteria that the team should apply in selecting the forces and signs include:

- **Early warning indicator?** Does the sign provide an early warning of the future? What does the sign indicate? What is the time window for making a decision?
- **Information available?** Is information available about potential outcomes for the force? How difficult is it to gather that information? How reliable is it?
- **Cost?** What does it cost to obtain the information?
- **Trustworthiness of information?** How believable are the signs? Will decision makers act on the sign information?

The table of forces selected and signs to look for become the basis for planning the monitoring activities. Individuals or groups will be assigned responsibility for monitoring the forces and periodically reporting on the findings.

Figure 21-1 Signpost Example

Forces (Important forces and dynamics to watch)	Indicators (Direction or condition of forces consistent with a given scenario)	Measures (Events, data, information that define direction or condition of indicators)	Signposts (Significant threshold measures that are judged to be clear indications)
Geopolitics, demographics, and economics	Elimination of trading blocks	China joins WTO	China abides by WTO rules and there are no sanction against that country
		Tariff reductions	India, Brazil reduce chemical product duties below $_/T
Regulatory/eco-factors	Increasingly harmonized and stricter environmental regulations	Global treaties implemented	Global CO_2 reduction treaty implemented by 2010
		EU directives on fuel quality are improved and spread	EU fuel quality directives are adopted by other regions, e.g., Eastern Europe, Russia
		Increasing use of lists (to identify bad products)	Number of chemical products on toxics lists increase by _%
		Government support of environment	Large government/corporate programs (like PNGV or FreedomCAR) funded
Feedstocks	Shift to low cost feedstocks	Commodities production moves to energy-rich countries	Petrochemicals construction projects and production in energy-rich countries increases from _ to _% of total
Technology advances	Technology advances rapidly	Technology evolves rapidly across large companies	Number and % of patents issued to large companies increases from _ to _; large companies carve out big new IP areas
		Government funding available for technology development	Government R&D funding increases by _%
	Broad IP protection	Shift toward effective worldwide patent system	Patent disputes/claims between countries decrease from _ to _ per year
Products	Product harmonization	Shift toward global specifications	Multinational companies require suppliers to meet global specs
		Deselection of flexible PVC and phthalate plasticizers	Major companies switch to alternatives
Industry/competitors	Industry consolidation	Number of commodity producers decreases	High profile chemical companies merge, e.g., SABIC buys Enichem
		High profile mergers increase	Number of high profile chemical companies mergers, e.g., SABIC buys Enichem, increases from _ to _

CHAPTER 22

COMMUNICATING THE RESULTS TO THE ORGANIZATION (STEP 18)

Communicating the findings, conclusions, and recommendations of scenario planning is the key last step of the project. Every project team will engage in communication or transfer of the results using reports, presentations, meetings, workshops, and one-on-one interactions. Sometimes scenario team members are described as evangelists as they attempt to communicate the information absorbed, insights gained, and decision recommendations. But the communication doesn't have to be such a large barrier to transferring the results back to the organization. If you understand that it's going to be an important step, you can plan for it.

Recognizing the difference between making a presentation of the results and engaging the organization in a meaningful dialogue of the results is a key factor. It's possible for a scenario-planning project to fail simply because of a weak presentation of the results. In this chapter, we address what the communications need to accomplish, what kinds of problems we could have, and what some of the best communication practices are.

Communication Is the Means for Engaging the Organization

Why is communication needed? Essentially, scenario planning occurs via projects that have beginnings and ends and in which the primary results or outputs are insights and recommendations for senior management and the organization. This temporary program of work requires the means for getting a focus at the beginning, dedicated resources to complete the program activities, and the means for transferring the results back to the organization at the end. Communication is the means for conducting that transfer of results at the end and ensuring the resources used in creating the results were well invested.

In a typical project, communication will include progress reports by the team to the organizational sponsor and reports by individual members to their respective business units; the briefings held during the course of the project on key findings and conclusions to date; final written reports of the project's results and recommendations; and final briefings or presentations, to persons or groups in the organization, of the results and recommendations.

What Must the Communication Accomplish?

The communication of scenario planning results is often difficult because the team is trying to change how decision makers in the organization—who were not part of the scenario planning project—think about a complex situation and influence the solutions and factors they might use in making a decision. On top of this challenge, the scenario team will probably only have a few chances to communicate the results and change or influence minds.

The communication step must convince the decision makers that the scenario and strategy analyses were thorough and complete, provide compelling insights on important issues, and transmit the scenario team's recommendations. The ultimate metric of a successful communications step is that decision makers who were not part of the scenario team make the decision and then communicate that decision and its rationale using the scenario-planning project's findings and conclusions.

Factors in Designing the Communication

Given that decision making in any organization is typically complex, involving many organizational and interpersonal factors, the planning for the communication activity needs to begin at project initiation and continue throughout the scenario-planning project. Key factors that will affect the planning and execution of the communication include:

• Decision focus of the project. The decision focus defines the purpose of the work, the intended recipients for the results, and the expected action to be taken by the organization with the results. Sometimes the purpose of the project is simply to influence the organization—to change minds—rather than to provide a solution. Sometimes the decision makers or intended recipients for the results are few; sometimes they are many.

• Decision readiness of organization. The communication activity will be affected significantly by how ready the organization is to make the decision. Often the organization isn't ready at all, and the scenario planning is being used to challenge the decision makers and make them aware of the need to do something. Other times, the decision makers are already close to a decision, and the scenario planning work is in a race to have results complete before the decision—potentially a very wrong one—is made. The communication process needs to fit the expectations and needs of the situation.

• Urgency of the situation. If most of the decision makers are not on the scenario team, then some amount of "soak" time will be needed to bring the decision makers up to speed on the project, to get them engaged with the alternative scenarios and the pros and cons of the strategic recommendations, and to have them make a decision that the recommendations will support. If the need to act is urgent, then measures will be needed to expedite the transfer process. The most important measures are to interview the decision makers at the beginning of the project to obtain their views of external developments and alternative strategies, provide interim briefings throughout the project, and stage a half-day to one-day workshop discussion of the final results with the decision makers at the very end.

• Representation of management and key stakeholder groups on the scenario team. The most important communication lever for the scenario team is the decision maker(s) on the scenario team. The credibility and the trust of the decision makers on the team will help overcome many of the communication barriers that will exist between the project and the rest of the organization.

• Norms and practices for disseminating results in the organization. Most organizations have well-established norms and practices for how presentations are made and meetings are conducted. Even though scenario-planning results lend themselves to multimedia events and out-of-the-norm types of presentations, it often works better in getting the messages across to use the standard formats, templates, and applications of the organization. We want the audience to focus on the results and not be distracted by new methods of communication. On the other hand, we often have to challenge the comfort zones of the decision makers and need to use compelling pictures of the future and descriptions of possible outcomes—both positive and negative—to get and maintain their attention.

How Do We Conduct the Step?

The tasks in conducting the communication step include:

1. Establish the communication objectives and constraints at the beginning of the project. What do we need to accomplish? What decisions or behavior are we trying to achieve? What are the biggest obstacles to achieving the objectives? What levers should we use to overcome the obstacles and achieve the objectives? How much time do we have? What resources will we have? What forum or methods can we use or not use?

2. Develop the initial communication plan. The communication plan highlights the communication activities that will occur, who will be responsible for carrying them out, and the schedule. The plan will largely be

oriented around the transfer of the final results to the organization. But often the plan has activities throughout the project, even immediately after the project starts, because to get decision makers to act on the results of the scenario planning project, it is often necessary to educate and advise them on a number of issues first.

3. Begin execution of the plan.

4. Develop the end-of-project communication plan. Near the end of the project, the team rethinks its final communication activities, based on the project's results and progress to date in educating the key stakeholders who have not been part of the project.

5. Execute the end-of-project plan.

The scenario-team leader and one or two others typically perform the first two tasks because most of the scenario team is not ready yet to communicate the project's purpose, process, and results to those not on the team. Once work has begun, though, all of the scenario team should be involved.

The basic communication options for the scenario team include:

• Formal briefings, by the scenario team, of decision makers and key stakeholders. Formal presentation briefings are the standard approach for transmitting project results to a group. PowerPoint™ presentation formats are often used, but a number of presentation applications and formats are available.

• Informal briefings by the team members to their business groups. A responsibility often of scenario team members is to keep their home organizations informed of the progress and results of the project. This occurs through meetings with their managers, through regularly scheduled meetings of their home organizations, and through informal interactions with colleagues.

• Written reports of the results by the scenario team. A scenario-planning project will generate several volumes of research, analyses, and results that are summarized by the scenario team in a written report. The contents, form, and format of that report are often specified at the beginning of the project.

• Structured workshop discussions. An effective means for communicating the details of the scenarios and key management insights is to stage an interactive discussion. The results of the scenario-planning project provide background information and discussion hypotheses for the workshop group. Sometimes audience members are asked to immerse themselves in a particular scenario of the future to have them identify possible threats and opportunities and imagine the decision-making circumstances. An extreme version of this option is conducting a "war-game" exercise, using one or two of the scenarios.

A key issue in the communication design is what to communicate. How much effort should be focused on describing the scenarios and convincing the audience of their value compared to outlining the decision alternatives, discussing their pros and cons, and laying out the final recommendations? The scenario team has invested a significant amount of time in both the scenarios development and the strategic implications of the uncertain environment and has developed a lot of valuable knowledge and insight about the future dynamics and what the organization should do. The scenario team rightly feels quite passionate about the results and wants to transmit as much as it can, as fast as it can, to those who weren't part of the effort.

But we've seen a lot of projects fail in the communication step because the team presented the wrong things to the audience or tried to do too much. While the scenarios can be very compelling and interesting, it often takes valuable time to introduce them and describe them in sufficient detail so that someone outside the team can fully appreciate them. If the team has only one opportunity to engage the key decision makers about the results— which is typical—then we suggest that the team focus on the final recommendations and not the scenarios. The agenda for the final presentation should start with recommendation(s), explain the major axes of uncertainty, outline the best strategic alternatives for addressing the uncertainties, and then describe the rationale for the recommendations.

If the team has two windows in which to engage the decision makers, then the scenarios can be introduced. We recommend the first window be used to describe the major axes of uncertainty, the scenarios of the future, and then the major strategic threats and opportunities. In the second window, the strategic alternatives, the pros and cons of the alternatives, recommendations, and next steps should be outlined.

In Box 22-1, we describe the formal briefing conducted at the end of a scenario-planning project for a consumer products company. The scenario team presented its recommendations for a new marketing strategy to the executive team in a full-day session. Most of the time in the presentation was spent discussing the strategy recommendations. Since the strategy included several possible pathways to take in the future, a fair amount of time was spent discussing the major uncertainties that would directly influence the choice of alternatives.

BOX 22-1
A Full-Engagement Briefing of the Executive Team

At the end of a major, five-month scenario-planning effort to develop a new marketing strategy for a major consumer products company, a group of five persons from the cross-functional scenario team assumed responsibility for delivering the final report briefing to the executive team. Much was expected from the scenario-planning effort, and the project team wanted to orchestrate an intensive discussion of the project's recommendations with the executives. The preparation for the recommendations briefing became a project in itself. Several working sessions were required by the core group to design the agenda, create briefing assignments, and review the material as it was coming together. In addition, a one-day dry run was conducted with the full scenario team to judge the potential effectiveness of the agenda and briefing material in communicating the major findings and recommendations and moving the executive team toward a decision. Each person on the scenario team was given a preparation role for the briefing. Some were required to conduct informal meetings with executive team members prior to the briefing; others were assigned to help the core group prepare the presentation materials.

The briefing was scheduled to coincide with a regular executive-team meeting—that was mandatory—but held in a larger conference room to accommodate both the scenario team and the executives. Five different scenario-team members, each of whom was senior manager in a different function of the organization, presented the material. Two members of the executive team, including the head of marketing, were part of the scenario team, but neither presented. The standard PowerPoint template for executive briefings was used. Video clips and a graphical artist were employed to spice up the content. The agenda was planned so discussion would take place throughout the day. The agenda contents and timetable are as follows:

8:30 am   **Getting Started.** The objectives of the presentation, the planned format for the day, and the agenda are presented

8:45 am	**Summary of Recommendations and Key Issues.** The executives were given a quick review of the recommendations and the issues that the team struggled with before the process, research, and key findings were discussed. Only questions of clarification were taken.
9:30 am	**Review of the Structured Process to Conduct the Analysis and Generate the Recommendations.** The executives were already familiar with the process, but a reminder was needed.
10:00 am	**Break.**
10:30 am	**Major Axes of Uncertainty Facing the Organization and the Scenarios Used.** The focus of this section of the briefing was on the different marketplace dynamics. The scenarios were highlighted simply to show that the dynamics were thoroughly probed and tested.
11:30 am	**Strategic Issues for Organization.** The major threats and opportunities were highlighted, along with the conclusions about which strategy alternatives were selected.
12:00 pm	**Lunch.**
1:00 pm	**Pros and Cons of the Strategy Alternatives.** The decision criteria were reviewed, and the pros and cons of the different altternatives were presented.
2:00 pm	**Strategy Recommendations.** The overall approach, the main pillars of that aproach, and main management challenges in its implementation were presented. Discussion.
3:00 pm	**Break.**
3:30 pm	**Closed Executive Team Discussion.** The scenario team, except for its executive team members, was excused.
4:45 pm	**Close.**

PART 6

CREATING A CHANGE-ORIENTED CULTURE

Scenarios are more than a new methodology: They entail a new way of thinking about the future, a new approach to strategic planning and decision making, and a pronounced shift in the prevailing management culture. Left to itself, the "old order" will always seek to reassert itself and relegate scenarios to, at best, a position of merely "interesting studies" of the future. We need, at the outset, to recognize the barriers to change and to the effective use of scenarios, and devise programs to surmount them.

Changing the planning and decision-making processes of an organization to make them fully compatible with scenarios thinking is clearly a more complex and demanding problem than linking scenarios to specific strategic decisions. Royal Dutch Shell is a premier corporate example in the world of the successful integration of scenarios into planning processes and executive thinking, but the company achieved this happy state only with effort and over time. As the current chief executive of Royal Dutch Shell, Jeroen van der Veer, states, "Within Shell, I think the imperative is to use this tool [the Global Scenarios to 2025] to gain deeper insights into our global business environment and to achieve the cultural change that is at the heart of our Group strategy." That is why we need more than a careful adherence to this step-by-step approach to developing scenarios. If scenarios are to take root and be used, we need to develop the appropriate change-oriented culture and undertake a comprehensive program of organizational development.

Consistently making better strategic decisions in an environment of uncertainty is a difficult proposition. A number of organizations accomplish it. Most do not. What do the better-performing organizations do that the rest do not? They turn their organizations into adaptive organizations, where continuous thinking and preparation for the future is a priority and where strategic decision making in the midst of change and uncertainty is a real competence. Thinking about the forces of change some of the time, and deciding what to do after the change is upon you, just won't work.

Microsoft has understood this and for years has reacted decisively in response to emerging trends and discontinuities. That's why it has managed to succeed in so many of the new markets that have opened up because of information technology innovation. Many observers see only Microsoft's dominance of the personal computer operating system market, and they miss the fact that Microsoft is a great adaptive organization. Microsoft and other successful adaptive organizations have a change-oriented culture that continuously examines the signals of change in the external environment and systematically prepares to implement strategies for pursuing new opportunities and addressing new threats. These adaptive organizations believe that the innovations of the marketplace will overwhelm them if they stand still, and that they will need to transform themselves in significant ways in order to survive and prosper. So they make sure that they're systematically trying to understand how the environment is changing and constantly developing new capabilities, products, and services with which to compete. And they build the organization, skills, and processes to support that market awareness and rapid-response execution.

This systematic approach to developing and executing strategy under uncertainty, and to preparing the organization to effectively use scenario planning, is based on four main elements:

- Developing in the executives, managers, and staff of the organization a set of **values and beliefs** that long-term, superior performance of the organization will depend on anticipating and responding to future events, discontinuities, innovations, and trends better than the competition
- Building an **organization** where information about internal and external developments flows freely and where seeds of new businesses can grow as existing businesses compete aggressively for market share
- Developing **competencies** in external-environment intelligence, technology innovation, planning under uncertainty, experimenting with new products and services, and executing change
- Designing and implementing **processes** for scanning and monitoring, scenario planning, technology innnovation, and decision making under uncertainty

Together these elements create the change-oriented culture to complement the scenario-planning capability in order to create an adaptive organization, giving better-performing companies their edge. Developing this culture requires hard work and involves a series of activities in order to move an inflexible organization that is focused on the present to an adaptive organization that is poised for the future.

It's not a transformation that happens overnight. Organizations must first create the awareness and commitment in the organization to have an open, change-oriented culture. Some scenario-planning successes and widespread communication of the scenarios and their strategic implications will go a long way toward building that awareness. But much more work is required to increase the number of individuals in the organization joining in to explore continually for new opportunities and threats and taking responsibility for the decisions under uncertainty. Through communications, case studies, and learning opportunities, the organization needs to enlist more and more people to adopt the belief that better performance will be a function of the organization's decision-making capabilities in a rapidly changing and uncertain environment.

Organizations can create this new sense of individual responsibility to be ready for the future by helping individuals connect their work and contributions to the overall adaptive strategy and by putting them in a position to learn new skills and decision-making capabilities through real exposure and experience.

As a foundation for the change-oriented culture, organizations must create a vibrant, ongoing exchange and sharing of information about the external environment, the key uncertainties, and future prospects of the organization's many business endeavors. People cannot make difficult decisions without knowledge and awareness, and organizations must develop the processes and capabilities to gather and analyze external information, anticipate future developments, share insights, and transmit those insights broadly throughout the organization.

Organizations must also invest in developing opportunity-development and strategic-thinking capabilities for situations in which the future is highly uncertain. Managers and executives need to acquire new skills so that they can lead and make decisions when the information is imperfect but the need is there.

Finally, the organizations must recast work processes and practices so that a new balance is developed between managing today's business plans and preparing for future ones. A number of cross-organizational processes for human resources management, operations management, strategy development, and intelligence must be aligned and coordinated for the entire integrated effort to work.

Implementing Scenario Planning at Statoil

The experience of Statoil, a Norwegian based integrated oil and gas company with operations in 32 countries, provides a good illustration of the extent of the effort needed to develop a change-oriented culture and a scenario-based approach to strategic planning in any large organization. Statoil was no exception to this rule. Indeed the company's earlier contacts and experiences with scenarios had left some negative impressions of the process.

However, in 2004 the company's corporate strategy group initiated a broad-based effort to introduce scenario planning throughout the company, and make it a basic tool for dealing with the dynamics and uncertainties of the company's external environment. By 2006, the organization had made significant progress in establishing the process as an integral part of strategy development at the corporate level, and made important inroads in getting some of the business units to use this process.

The progress this time was due to several important steps that were taken to ensure the success of this effort. First, and most important, was assigning the development of the corporate scenarios and the implementation of the overall process to a team from the corporate strategy group. Introducing an important new process such as scenario planning is best accomplished by starting at the top. A successful pilot project in a business unit will produce positive results for that unit, but it will not have the energy and means to push the process into other parts of the organization. To succeed on a company-wide basis, it is best to start at the top, using the authority, resources and expertise of the corporate strategy group.

The second step was to get senior corporate management involved in the initial development and use of scenarios. To begin with, the scenarios were based on input from senior Statoil executives, and then discussed thoroughly with them, before the scenarios were introduced to key stakeholders in the organization.

Third, it was important to leverage those corporate scenarios as much as possible throughout the organization. It would be virtually impossible for the corporate-level scenarios to be sufficiently focused and detailed to serve the planning needs of each of the business units. So a series of workshops, facilitated by the scenario team from the corporate strategy group, was held for different parts of the organization to discuss the implications of the corporate scenarios. Further, assistance was given to develop more focused scenarios for the business units when it was appropriate. Key to getting the business units to use the scenarios in their own planning and strategy development is their recognition that the corporate scenarios need to be amplified and modified to create, in effect, distinct business unit scenarios. With this in mind, the scenario team facilitated the development of "quick-and-dirty" business unit scenarios, country scenarios, etc. to make the scenarios relevant to each group. The objective has been to involve key decision makers and decision influencers in the scenario development process–often a challenge because of the intense focus of business units on operational matters–to increase their understanding and use of the scenarios in their own planning.

Finally, the success in Statoil's current scenarios effort stems from the decision to position scenario planning, not as a "grand solution" for all strategic planning problems, but as a tool that can help create insight into possible key developments that the business will have to deal with. Heavy scenario users are often passionate about the extraordinary learning, preparation and support for decision making that scenarios can provide. However, that passion and learning take years to develop, and many very capable individuals never succeed in developing it. It is critical, therefore, not to oversell the process at the outset, but to call it a tool—an invaluable tool, but a tool nonetheless—for integrating, and making sense of, the voluminous, disparate information about the external environment, and identifying the range of possible outcomes in the future.

As Statoil moves forward with its scenario planning efforts, the task will be to increase corporate and business unit executives' familiarity and experience with this tool. One next step that will solidify the use of scenarios at all levels is the development of a scanning and monitoring system tied to the scenarios. The more that scenarios are used on a continuous basis to help in decision-making, rather than as an interesting but episodic exercise, the more change-oriented the culture will be.

Developing an Implementation Roadmap

In the end, the transformation to a change-oriented organization will not be smooth, and many issues and obstacles will need to be addressed. Many of today's practices, beliefs, capabilities, products, and services will come into question, and a well-thought-out roadmap and a process for addressing issues as they arise will be needed to avoid the entire effort becoming stuck. Figure Part 6-1 highlights a three-phase implementation for an organization to become change oriented and to be able to leverage all the benefits of scenario planning. The initial phase is focused on developing an awareness and commitment in the organization to the new culture and creating some early successes. The second phase addresses development of needed competencies and infrastructure. The third phase aligns processes, capabilities, and commitment so the organization can produce ongoing results with its new adaptive manner.

Because this book is about how to get started with scenario planning, in Part 6 we will focus primarily on the first phase of the transformation,

Figure Part 6-1 Program for Developing a Change-Oriented Culture

Phase I Awareness	Phase II Competence Development	Phase III Work Alignment	Culture Elements
• Develop communication program • Re-orient manager education • Conduct an organizational values assessment	• Create stories and build values	• Develop vision of future • Revise communication program	Values and beliefs
	• Set up central intelligence group • Create seats at the table for senior strategy and innovation leaders • Create strategic issues groups in businesses and at corporate level	• Develop human resource development criteria and performance metrics • Develop rapid-response capacity • Engage partners, suppliers, and customers with the new approach	Organization
	• Involve individuals throughout organization in scenario planning efforts • Train executives in strategy under uncertainty and the language of scenario planning • Develop facilitation skills	• Establish individual and organizational expectations • Rehearse for rapid response decision making • Develop an after-action review capability	Competencies
• Develop environmental-analysis capability • Fine-tune and update scenarios • Target and tailor scenarios to organizational needs	• Design decision-making methods for executing strategy under uncertainty • Establish annual review discussion of external issues • Fund new scenario-planning efforts • Develop IT infrastructure to support	• Align planning and resource allocations • Set agendas for senior management meetings • Develop corporate scenarios • Develop adaptive strategy with options for organization • Set new business development portfolio	Processes

Phase I Awareness. For the results of the scenario-planning project to have an impact on the organization and not just be an interesting thinking exercise, the organization must first develop a belief throughout the organization that making better strategic choices in dynamic environments means having a change-oriented culture and a commitment to changing things for the better. The organization must value having superior insights about how the future could evolve and being prepared to act ahead of the competition.

To develop that belief and heighten the organization's receptivity to change, Phase I activities focus on making individuals throughout organization, starting with the executives, aware of the uncertainties, threats, and opportunities of the external environment, the implications of not being prepared for change, and the benefits of being prepared. As part of this awareness development, the organization must develop the information flow about the critical forces and drivers affecting the organization and leverage the results of the scenario project to demonstrate the potential of the new culture and help everyone learn.

Change-oriented companies must have superior intelligence about the external environment. It's that simple. Chapter 23 outlines the basic elements of an environmental analysis system that will provide the continuous flow of signpost information, signals of change, and focused analyses needed to think about the need to change and then act on it.

Managers and employees in most large organizations are unfamiliar with the concepts and use of scenarios. And for the most part that's understandable, given the focus in many organizations on current operations and the common expectation that it's someone else's responsibility to think about and prepare for the future and long-term change. To address this issue, organizations need to differentiate between the tools and culture for competing today and those needed to do well in the future. There are, of course, many ways to communicate these things and develop a commitment to being superior at making adaptive strategic decisions. Chapter 24 describes the elements of an initial communications and education program to inform everyone about scenario planning, what it means to be future and change oriented, and how to use scenarios on an ongoing basis to make decisions.

The decision focus of the scenario-planning project is not the only important decision that must be made by the organization in the face of environmental uncertainty. In fact, most large organizations make strategic decisions under uncertainty all the time. Chapter 25 describes how to target and tailor the scenarios to other decision focuses and get some other immediate results for the organization. This allows the scenarios to spread to other parts of the organization and expose many more individuals to their use and benefits.

Because scenarios are projections of how the future might evolve, they begin to lose value as a means for testing strategy ideas over time as events unfold. The actions of competitors, customer behavior, technology commercialization activities, and overall performance of the economy are potential events that resolve how a number of the uncertainties that concerned the scenario team play out. Once those events occur, modified scenarios are needed to test future strategy options. Chapter 25 also addresses how to fine-tune and upgrade the original scenarios so that they can continue to act as test beds for strategy actions, without having to redo everything.

CHAPTER 23

DEVELOPING A COMPREHENSIVE ENVIRONMENTAL ANALYSIS CAPABILITY

Many organizations that have just finished a scenario-planning project may think they've already created a new environmental analysis (EA) system, but in fact they've only addressed one part of what's needed. A scenario-planning project essentially uses a snapshot of the external forces and drivers to develop scenarios of the future, but new information and learning are being produced all the time about the forces and drivers and how those forces and drivers could play out in the future. Making decisions in the future about alternative courses of action and developing contingencies will be very difficult using old information and understandings created for the scenario-planning effort. Also, old EA systems rarely look beyond the current competitors' capabilities, plans, and actions, even when those competitors are not the biggest factor in a strategy's success. And even in a particular business unit, the focus is usually on trying to understand the strategies of the current major competitors rather than on identifying the new entrants with different business models, the potential discontinuous innovations, or new customer segments.

Scenarios are a necessary but not completely sufficient response to the challenge that uncertainty poses to our decision making. To deal comprehensively and systematically with this challenge, we need to develop a multifaceted environmental analysis capability—what we might think of as a form of corporate "early warning system radar" to guide us through the uncharted waters ahead. This radar analogy is appropriate in at least three respects:

1. Radar scans the total environment, all 360 degrees of the horizon, not merely a segment of it (though it can focus on particular segments, when needed).

2. It engages in continuous, not intermittent, scanning.

3. It suggests, appropriately, the need for what we might term a "cybernetic pulsing through the future" (i.e., Sense . . . assess . . . act . . . measure . . . sense . . . assess . . . etc.).

Characteristics of an Environmental Analysis System

This analogy suggests, in turn, some of the essential characteristics that we should design into any EA system:

1. Integrative: It is vitally important that the environmental analysis system be an integral part of the strategic-planning and decision-making system of the corporation. Interpretation of the present and speculation about the future make no real contribution to corporate success if they result merely in "interesting" studies. To be effective, the linkage between the two systems must be tight and explicit.

Strategic planning must be designed with environmental analysis as its starting point and frame of reference. Organizationally, responsibility for the identification, analysis, and interpretation of environmental data should be located in the strategic-planning component; or, at a minimum, this component should be the focal point of the system, even if other corporate and operating components act as individual monitoring posts in an environmental network.

2. Relevant: The relevance that environmental analysis should have to strategic planning can best be defined as (a) a focus on strategic issues, and (b) assistance in making today's strategic decisions with greater environmental sensitivity and with a better sense of futurity. The first point is process oriented; the second deals more with managerial psychology. To be issue oriented in this sense, environmental analysis must be alert to both the social, economic, political, and technological trends impacting current strategic issues, as well as the emergence of new issues. To raise the level of managerial sensitivity and "futures consciousness," environmental analysis must constantly stress such factors as the past-present-future continuum, uncertainty, and the interconnectedness of all environmental trends.

3. Holistic: If for no other reason than the simple fact that "everything is related to everything else," environmental analysis must be comprehensive in its approach to the business environment, viewing trends "as a piece, not piecemeal." The corporate radar must scan the whole circumference of its environment in order to minimize the chance of surprises and maximize its utility as an early warning system.

4. Iterative (or continuous): Like radar, the environmental analysis system must operate continuously in order to keep track of the rapid pace of developments. In times such as these, it would be nonsensical to engage only in periodic operation of the system, to trust (implicitly) that the "blips" registered on the radar screen after a few sweeps of the horizon give a true and

lasting picture of the situation. Only continuous operation can sort out the true from the "ghost" images; define the nature, trajectory, and impact points of the incoming "missiles"; and pick up the inevitable new "blips" that will constantly be appearing on the screen.

At this point we should draw a distinction between the scanning and monitoring aspects of the system. General scanning of the horizon is essential to pick up new signals from the environment and to keep track of shifts in the overall pattern of developing trends. Monitoring, on the other hand, is designed to focus closely on the track of previously identified trends that have been analyzed and assessed as being of particular importance to the organization. This is not merely a semantic distinction. There is substantive difference in the focus and the content, and even in the talents required for the two operations. Monitoring requires meticulous aggregation and analysis of details, while scanning puts a high premium on intuition, "sixth sense," and pattern recognition. The two operations are equally important and, indeed, sufficiently different to merit separate attention, systems, and maybe staffing.

5. Heuristic or exploratory: While, admittedly, part of the system concerns itself with present developments, a large part of the environmental analysis seeks to explore unknown, and in a sense unknowable, terrain. As we have already pointed out, environmental analysis cannot forecast the future: What it can do—and it can do it very effectively—is to help clarify our assumptions about the future, speculate systematically about alternative outcomes, assess probabilities, and make more rational choices.

6. Qualitative: A large part of environmental input to strategic planning consists of what Igor Ansoff has termed "soft data." The EA system will, of course, use quantitative inputs when those are available, but it is not bound by the limits of what can be quantified. This does not mean that the methods are not systematic: quite to the contrary, a primary value of this technique is that it systematizes the process of looking at phenomena that are exceedingly slippery and elusive.

Key Elements of an EA System

To achieve these characteristics on a continuing and consistent basis, we need to develop a multifaceted EA system, based on these characteristics, and consisting of:

- Scenarios
- Monitoring
- Scanning
- Acting

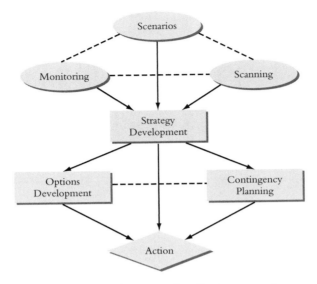

Figure 23-1   Key Elements of an Environmental
Analysis System

and forming an integral part of the organization's strategic planning
(Figure 23-1).

Scenarios are, as we have outlined, a key element in this system, providing detailed views of possible futures with which the organization should be
prepared to deal. As such, they set the tone and much of the agenda for the
other elements in this system.

Monitoring Process

While scenarios describe what *might* happen, **monitoring**—the careful
tracking of events as they occur and the watching for signposts—tells us what
is happening. This tracking of the course of events and looking for signposts
is, of course, a traditional and well-established form of intelligence gathering
practiced by most organizations. The introduction of scenarios into the system, however, requires some improvement and tailoring of the monitoring
effort. For example, as outlined in Chapter 21, the monitoring needs to include the new sets of key indicators and signposts from scenario projects.

The process of monitoring, as shown in Figure 23-2, begins with a
planning step that involves a survey of the environmental analysis and information needs of business decision makers. The planning results in the
organization having a clear idea of what analysis and information to search

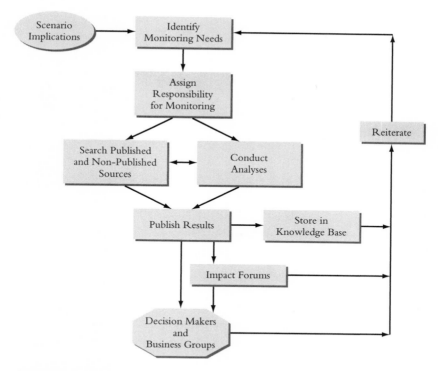

Figure 23-2   Monitoring Process

for, which in turn forms the foundation of the search of published and non-published sources.

Regular updates and ad-hoc analysis reports are published and stored online. The issues are sorted according to their impact and urgency. The ad-hoc reports are distributed immediately to members of the decision-making community and the business executive teams. Distribution is based on who is interested and/or needs to know a particular piece of information.

Regular semiannual or annual forums are held to review potential strategic actions and impacts resulting from the monitoring results and to set the stage for planning the upcoming monitoring activity.

The broadening of horizons that occurs in the course of developing scenarios often leads to identifying new sources of intelligence. For example, the actions and plans of the growing not-for-profit sector, which is often overlooked by corporate planners, are increasingly influential in shaping consumer behavior and public policy and so should be part of the monitoring effort.

Clearly, monitoring makes its major contribution to the system by supplying intelligence about current trends, which becomes the basis on which strategy and tactics are based. But monitoring also provides essential feedback into the scenario process, confirming, refuting, or modifying the logics that form the structure of the scenarios. It thus serves both a forward-looking and backward-looking role and is responsible for ensuring a continuous flow of intelligence into the planning and operating system, with special focus on the needs for "mid-course corrections" and exercising strategic options.

Scanning Process

Monitoring is, in most organizations, a traditional and well-established activity (along with forecasting): **Scanning** most definitely is not. Monitoring may need to be expanded, focused, and better coordinated: Scanning needs to be developed from the ground up.

The term "scanning" is derived from radar, and the analogy is apt. Scanning should serve as the organization's "early warning system," looking over the horizon, detecting and tracking new trends, the "blips on the horizon" that may turn out to be the incoming missiles of major change—or disappear and fade from the screen. In an era of radical change and uncertainty, developing such a capability is absolutely essential.

The aim of scanning is to detect discontinuities and inflection points, the first faint signals of impending change, and so to give the organization the opportunity to get a jump on events (and, hopefully, its competitors). And its aim should be to cover 360 degrees of the horizon, embracing and analyzing new developments in politics and economics, consumer behavior and social attitudes, culture, science, and technology.

Scanning may seem to overlap with monitoring, but there are two significant differences between the systems:

• Focus: Monitoring covers the well-established sources of information on a given subject (e.g., government and trade association statistics, published reports on known topics). Scanning develops its clues on new developments from any source (the press, professional journals, "off-beat" publications, leading-edge journals, the agenda of interest groups). The new developments are not predictable and could be anything.

• Personnel capabilities: Monitoring is best left in the hands of professional experts who have specialized expertise in the various arenas to be monitored. They are best equipped to identify and interpret the trends and developments in their specialized areas. Scanning has entirely different

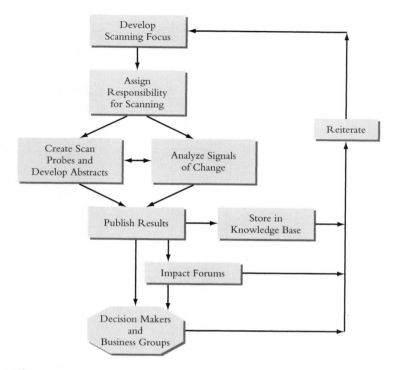

Figure 23-3   Scanning Process

requirements because what exactly it is looking for is not known in advance. Scanning therefore needs to be covered by people with acute but open minds who are adept at pattern recognition and at seeing connections between seemingly unrelated developments.

Figure 23-3 highlights the scanning process activities.

SRI Consulting Business Intelligence (SRIC-BI) has been managing a continuous scanning process for 25 years for its corporate and governmental clients. The Scan™ program and its key elements are further described in Appendix D.

Options Development

Options development is the fourth key element in a comprehensive environmental analysis system. In any strategy created from scenarios, there will be a number of actions that are reserved until more information is known about how the events will unfold. "If _____ happens, then we should do _____." "We can't do _____, until we know what happens to _____." Options development prepares for when more information is available.

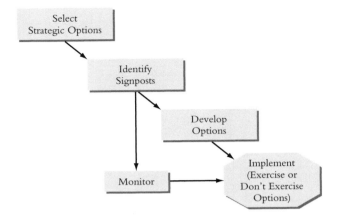

Figure 23-4   The Flow of Options Development

Since the strategy should be adaptive, there will usually be a set of actions that we have put off until their risks and rewards can be better understood. We then prepare ourselves to make future decisions about them along the following lines (see Figure 23-4):

- Select the strategic options for which some investment is worthwhile.
- Identify "signposts"—that is, the development of some trend, event, or development that indicates whether or not an option should be exercised.
- Invest in options—that is, make the small investments that prepare the organization to move quickly and take advantage of an emerging trend, event, or new development.
- Monitor events to identify the occurrence of the signposts that point to the need to move quickly with a strategic initiative or to terminate interest in an area.

Contingency Planning

Contingency planning is the last key element in a comprehensive environmental analysis system. As Figure 23-1 makes clear, the main value of scenarios, monitoring, and scanning lies in the contribution they make to organizational planning and strategy development. There is, however, always a residue of uncertainty about deviation from one or more of the assumptions on which the strategy is based: "What should we do if . . . ?" Contingency planning seeks to provide an answer to this question.

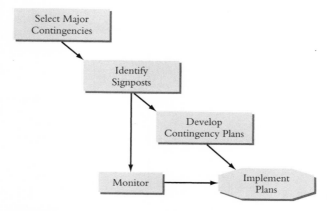

Figure 23-5   The Flow of Contingency Planning

While strategy should be resilient, and so capable of dealing with a range of market and/or competitive conditions, there will almost always be a set of developments that we have considered as possibilities but have, in the end, rated as falling outside the "envelope of uncertainty." Rather than omitting them entirely from our planning, we have the option of engaging in some "what if . . . " thinking along the following lines (see Figure 23-5):

• Select the major contingencies for which some preliminary planning is worthwhile.

• Assign responsibility for this contingency planning.

• Identify signposts or "precursor events"—that is, the development of some trend, event, or development that foreshadows the occurrence—or increase in probability—of the contingency.

• Develop plans to deal with the contingency should it occur, spelling out the preferred action to be taken; the alternative action, if the preferred action is not feasible; and the action to be taken "if all else fails."

• Monitor events to identify the occurrence of the signpost, that is, that point in the development of a contingency at which the previously prepared plans should be put into effect.

Organization and Responsibilities

The EA system is essentially management of the flow of information and analyses about the external environment throughout the organization and with external stakeholders such as customers, partners, and suppliers (see Figure 23-6). Sources of information and the expertise to conduct analyses

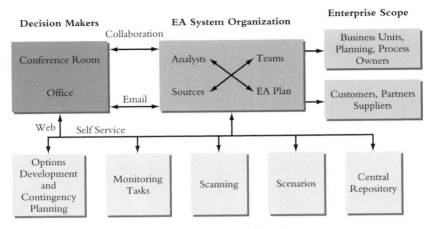

Figure 23-6 Schematic of an Environmental Analysis System

of that information exist all over. Decision makers who need the best intelligence are at all levels, in many functions, and in most locations.

The costs of gathering the information and conducting the analyses can be quite expensive. The costs of not sharing available information and analyses can also be quite expensive. As a result, important objectives for the system include minimizing duplication and overlap of information gathering and analysis as well as making sure those who need the information and analysis get it. To address these objectives, in our experience a central organizational unit is needed to coordinate EA process activities; to oversee the information technology infrastructure and applications for communicating, storing, and sharing the outputs; to conduct a portion of the monitoring tasks; and generally to make sure the information is flowing and serving the needs of strategic decision making. To ensure alignment with strategic decision making, that unit is often part of the corporate strategy-planning function.

Often the biggest challenge for the EA system is to get individuals throughout the organization who come in contact with the external environment to participate. Every day, many employees are interacting with the external environment, gathering or absorbing new information about new technology developments, competitor activities, customer needs, regulatory issues, business practices, and so on. The task for the EA system is to pick up the new, relevant information from those interactions when it is needed for upcoming decisions, without disrupting operations. To accomplish this, the organization must provide incentives and means for some, if not many, of the individuals who come in contact with the external environment to capture and forward the new information along when it's needed. The organization must ensure that any sensitive information that gets into the system is protected appropriately. And it must be vigilant against the creation of new barriers to the flow of the information or the use of filters. Some resources will be needed to maintain this network on a continuing basis, mostly for communications. A simple return message of acknowledgement or thank you to the sender can often be all the incentive he or she needs to continue participating the system.

Implementation of an EA System

Now that we see what an environmental analysis system is, how do we develop it? The key steps to take will be to conduct due diligence, develop a plan, create some pilots, and then with the pilot results implement the system throughout (see Figure 23-7). A challenge at the beginning is to find the right leader with the right knowledge and incentives to initiate the process and demonstrate the benefits of a new EA approach.

The next step is to take stock of current capabilities, information sources, alignment of environmental analysis activities and strategy decision making, and organizational, process, and resource needs in a new system. A set of goals for the system is defined along with key considerations in terms of resource availability, integration of the system with strategy processes, involvement of decision makers, and so on. A project plan for designing and implementing the new system is then developed, along with the recommended team to be responsible for the implementation.

Project resources are approved and implementation begins with the design step. The design leads to pilots of the different processes and their integration. Feedback from the pilots leads to a redesign and then a phased implementation of the processes. Continuous improvement activities are built into the system to ensure that the EA system always supports the desired culture and scenario planning.

Due Diligence: Making the Case

The most difficult step in developing a new EA system is getting started. Many organizational forces are typically aligned against a change, and it will take both a group of executives, including a strong leader who is determined to make EA a more essential element of strategic management, and a strong case for doing something to overcome those forces.

The EA system initiative needs some level of knowledge about the needs, alternatives, costs, and benefits of EA in order to develop an initial case for change. In the due diligence phase, a quick step is conducted to review the

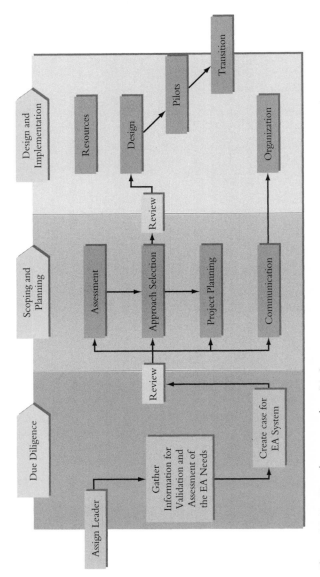

Figure 23-7 Development of an EA System

current situation, identify some of the possible process solutions, and analyze the potential costs and benefits. The case for evaluating the organization's current EA activities and upgrading them (to include the scenario, monitoring, scanning, and new strategy development processes) is then prepared for review by those in charge.

Often it's necessary for the case to describe a sense of urgency for a new system. "Flying blind" would seem to be a sufficient condition to create that sense of urgency, but decision makers are often lulled by the fact that they haven't hit anything yet. So we recommend finding some examples from within the organization where having timely, critical information and analyses about the external market was crucial to the organization making successful decisions.

Scoping and Planning

Once the case has been made and approval to proceed has been received, it's time to do the homework, analyze the specific needs and capabilities of the organization, develop the overall approach and goals for a new system, and create a plan for how it should be developed and implemented.

It's important to look at the entire organization for environmental analysis needs to support strategic decision making and for capabilities, skills, infrastructure, and resources to do the work. Our experience is that this internal assessment will uncover EA activities and skills in many parts of the organization but, at the same time, major gaps and needs.

Sometimes organizations view a new environmental analysis system as an effective way to satisfy executives or staff who always insist on having more information and analyses before making decisions. But if the system only serves those already inclined to look at environmental analysis information, then it won't contribute much value to the organization. Rather, the approach and scope of the system need to align with the entire organization's needs to be prepared for the future and make ongoing strategic decisions in dynamic circumstances.

Many organizations don't fully understand the communication challenge in developing and implementing a new system across the board, and they expect awareness, acceptance, and use of the new system to occur almost instantaneously. The reality is that communication about the new system often requires the most implementation resources and takes the most time. Careful, thoughtful planning is needed to devise a practical approach to make everyone aware of the system, help them learn how to use it, and get them to use it in their strategy making.

Design and Implementation: Getting It Done

One of the critical features of a change-oriented culture is being skilled at trying something, watching for the effects and impact, learning from the experience, adjusting the plan, and doing something again. The entire organization should be able to watch things—internally and externally—changing before its eyes. This should create a sense of flow in the organization and the momentum for change and quick response to new information.

To get the organization to implement an EA system throughout, it's necessary to show compelling evidence that it will work to those who will be expected to feed and use the system. But in most situations, that evidence doesn't exist, so what do you do? One approach is to implement a pilot or demonstration of the new system in one part of the organization and then focus the resources on communicating the results quickly and widely. Ideally, this pilot will be in a business unit where important business decisions need to be made in the face of highly uncertain external forces and drivers, and where the success or failure of those decisions won't be known for a few years. When the first results are available from the pilot, a presentation should be staged for potential future participants.

Consistent with a change-oriented culture, quick design and trial are expected. Don't spend months and months developing a perfect system. Instead, develop the design and pilots in a two- to four-week period, and then begin.

A Five-Year Commitment

While a few organizations can implement new strategic processes in a year or two, for the most part, the complete implementation of an EA system in an organization will require on the order of five years. This extended period is needed because new flows of information need to be established, new sources for that information developed, and new participants involved in the system. But, more importantly, a large number of business units and people, including all the key decision makers, must learn how to make sense of incomplete, voluminous, often incorrect information, spot new signals of change and be able to distinguish hype from a real trend. A significant amount of trial with the new processes—including some bad experiences— needs to occur before the majority begins to rely on the new processes and information to make strategic decisions. Real change and building a solid foundation take time.

CHAPTER 24

DEVELOPING A COMMUNICATION AND EDUCATION PROGRAM

Developing a Communication Program

Communication is an essential part of the changing-culture implementation blueprint. If we are to bring about such a major change in culture, we must define, clarify, and communicate both its nature and purpose. And communication must adapt to the needs of various internal (and some external) audiences.

Thus, "communicability" is a vital characteristic that we must build into the scenarios. To change the mind-set of executives and planners, the scenario process must first capture their attention. An excellent way to grab the attention of operating managers is to write imaginative but plausible scenarios about their markets. Then, to hold their attention, these "stories about the future" need to be both imaginative and logical, opening the corporate mind to new possibilities.

These stories need to have intriguing titles and captivating story lines. Story lines play an important role by presenting a dynamic rather than static picture of the future. And narratives describe not just an endpoint but how that endpoint will come to pass. Internalizing these story lines, so that they become part of what Pierre Wack called managers' "mental maps" of the future, is the ultimate objective of the communication program.

The most experienced scenario-planning organizations pay a great deal of attention to communication. They use the widest range of media available and rely heavily on workshops and seminars. Royal Dutch Shell, for instance, publishes its current set of detailed scenarios on its internet web site. But typically, the primary mode of communication is holding dozens of workshops throughout the organization, aiming to stimulate diverse groups within the company to consider the strategic implications of the scenarios for their businesses.

Most successful communication programs underscore the high value of hands-on work with scenarios. Initial presentations of the scenarios are followed by seminars for senior executives in which they can work through the implications of the scenarios for overall strategy. Some companies take a war room approach, bringing management teams into a large conference room and using many charts and descriptions of scenario elements for testing out their ideas about strategy options.

Most scenario planners also produce written descriptions of the scenarios and their implications, usually in long and short (executive summary) versions. But most scenario experts say that, though written materials are useful, they are not nearly as important as presentations and working discussions.

When organizations need to share results widely and get a number of groups, business units, and functions to think about the implications of the scenarios, they sometimes go beyond text and graphic presentations and use multimedia videos. While the investment is significant, running in the hundreds of thousands of dollars, the videos can be very effective in communicating the important features of the scenarios and explaining their differences. Audiences often have an easier time accepting the assumptions of scenarios when they can visualize the story lines, and as a result they can think about the implications more readily.

If the scenarios are truly to become part of the corporate culture, then communication about them has to occur at three levels:

• Communication from senior managers should clearly convey the seriousness of their commitment to this new way of planning. Senior managers can start by explaining how they intend to use scenarios in their own decision making and by being explicit about how they wish others to use scenarios.

• Members of the planning staff should provide step-by-step guidelines for constructing scenarios and putting them to best use.

• Individuals who need to use the scenarios should have easy access to them and should be encouraged, through open access, to use scenarios and know where to go to get them. Intranet portals that support environmental-analysis activities and strategic planning processes are an excellent means for providing that access.

Reorienting Manager Education

The current emphasis on becoming a "learning organization"—that is, one that senses and acts on change in its environment and that is quick to share knowledge across organizational boundaries—is particularly relevant to scenario-based planning. Indeed, we might say that scenarios are a form of "learning our way into the future."

There are, however, barriers to change that stand in the way of attaining these goals. Most particularly, we have found:

- There is in most organizations what we might term a "cultural bias" toward single-point forecasting that tends to reject the notion of alternative futures.

- Most organizations tend to be dominated by a "numbers culture," a pronounced preference for quantification and "hard" facts over "soft" data.

- There is widespread unwillingness to go beyond conventional views, a tendency to interpret the unknown future in terms of the known past.

- Autocratic leadership often has a tendency toward preordained decisions, and curtails discussion and rejects or downplays any evidence of new trends or disruptive events.

The only way to remove these barriers is through an extensive and sustained program of manager education. "Learning by doing" clearly is important. However, to achieve a culture shift of the sort that scenario planning entails, formal education programs must reinforce on-the-job learning.

First, institutionalizing scenario planning normally requires a broad review—and some revision—of the existing planning system. At a minimum, both planners and executives need to learn about the requirements of the new system, and guidelines must be developed for the use of scenarios.

Some of this education can occur through manuals and other written materials—but not much. Everything we know about adult education suggests that investing in seminars, group interaction, and hands-on experience pays off.

The core of a manager education program can be a one- or two-day seminar on the purpose, methodology, and applications of scenario planning. In such sessions, the most valuable lesson to teach managers is the need for, and role of, scenario planning, its proposed application in the strategic-planning system, and the changes in culture and decision-making processes that this new approach requires. However, beyond this message, the real aim of the education program should be to integrate the implications of scenario thinking into other programs, especially those that touch on management style and organizational culture. Scenario planning will not take root in a company whose education programs foster a culture of hierarchical thinking and "going by the numbers." Such an approach is at odds with the flexibility and innovative thinking that scenarios require. It is critically important, as Jack Welch is fond of pointing out, that managers should practice the values of the new culture as well as "meet the numbers." Without this, the new culture will stand little chance of surviving.

CHAPTER 25

FINE-TUNING, TAILORING, AND UPDATING SCENARIOS TO MEET ORGANIZATIONAL NEEDS

Targeting and Tailoring Scenarios

Scenario planning, like any new methodology, can succeed only if it meets the criterion of corporate relevance. Pierre Wack noted, in his *Harvard Business Review* articles, that scenarios must reflect management's central concerns. This is not to say that scenarios should uncritically accept managers' views of the future: indeed, they should aim to challenge conventional wisdom. But they must focus on what managers see as the critical uncertainties and key issues that they face.

This requirement is perhaps the most potent argument against using "off-the-shelf" scenarios and for involving senior managers in scenario development. Producing "cookie-cutter" scenarios for a company is counterproductive. Only by tailoring scenarios to planning needs, emphasizing a "decision focus," and actively involving decision makers in the process can a company assure a reasonable chance of gaining executive ownership of the final product—and so of effective use of the scenarios. As we have already noted, one of the most productive scenario projects we have undertaken—with a European bank—involved the CEO and his direct reports throughout the process. Because the senior executives formed the scenario team and actually developed the scenarios themselves, they understood and owned them fully and so were able to incorporate them more easily into their thinking and strategy development.

Multidivisional companies have a special need for tailored scenarios, because scenarios developed at the corporate level are not likely to be detailed enough to guide strategic business units. Indeed, planning needs will clearly vary from business unit to business unit. But these business unit-specific scenarios should fit under the umbrella of corporate macro-scenarios to ensure consistency in their common elements. The more focused scenarios should capture the details of each business unit's markets, competition, technology, and other key environmental variables. In addition, they also enhance business unit managers' understanding of the relevance of the scenarios to their particular business, which in turn helps to ensure their commitment to using the scenarios.

A key challenge in bringing about this culture shift is to jump-start the scenario process. Executives need time to develop the skills—and the attitude—to use scenarios universally, instinctively, and imaginatively. One way to ease the transition is to use scenarios, initially, one step at a time in targeted situations.

An important element in the culture-change plan is, therefore, selecting "targets of opportunity" for the use of scenarios. For example, a company might want to start using scenarios as a test bed for assessing the resilience, risks, and payoffs of major investment decisions. Such a target has at least two obvious advantages:

- These key, long-term decisions most readily lend themselves to scenario-based evaluation. Examples of such projects include determining the pace and timing of opening a new copper mine in Chile and assessing the long-term payoff and feasibility of a $600 million addition to a firm's paper-manufacturing capacity.

- Because the investment approval process involves both business-unit managers (the proposers) and corporate executives and the Board of Directors (the approvers), it promotes use at two levels. If a business-unit manager knows that corporate executives will use scenarios to evaluate requests for investment funds, he or she—and the business unit management team in general—is much more likely to use scenarios to help shape a proposal.

Two other targets for introducing scenarios are planning assumptions and contingency planning. Virtually every strategic plan contains a set of assumptions about future economic, market, competitive, and other trends. Typically, these assumptions are the product of traditional single-point forecasting. What better point of entry for scenarios, therefore, than in assessing the strategic significance of trends, uncertainties, and assumptions about the company's future business environment?

Similarly, every strategic plan should consider how the business would deal with contingencies—the divergences from planning assumptions that could batter corporate performance. The scenario process aims specifically to explore contingencies and their consequences. As a first step, corporate executives could use a contingency scenario to assess all current strategies and investment decisions. Encouraging this sort of "what if" thinking builds a constituency for full-fledged scenario-based strategy development.

Whatever target of opportunity managers may select, they should recognize the need for changes in the existing strategic-planning system. They should have a clear idea of what changes are necessary and establish a schedule for bringing them about. These targets should be steps in an overall implementation plan, not a random set of actions.

Fine-Tuning and Updating Scenarios

One good indicator of whether or not scenario planning has taken root in a company is how faithfully players update and revise the scenarios. If scenarios are to contribute fully and effectively to a company's strategic thinking, they must parallel actual events in order to maintain their relevance.

There are reciprocal relationships among scenarios, monitoring, and scanning that strengthen each of them individually and the foresight system as a whole. Thus, scenarios benefit from the input of new ideas and new trends from scanning, and new data for existing trends from monitoring; and, at the same time, they provide a broad contextual setting that gives guidance and focus to the other two systems. Scanning, in turn, gains perspective and focus from the scenarios and alerts the organization to the emergence of new trends that should perhaps be incorporated in the next cycle of scenario-building and/or scheduled for more detailed follow-up monitoring. And, finally, monitoring is strengthened by the perspective provided by scenarios and expanded by evidence of new trends from scanning, while its output serves to update the scenarios and to indicate which of the alternative scenarios is, in fact, apparently coming into play. The foresight system thus has the stability of a tripod formed by these three interlocking methodologies.

Experience points to three courses of action that are useful in keeping the scenario process lively and perceptive:

• First, organizations should schedule scenario-development sessions so that their output feeds naturally into the planning cycle. Without this synchronicity, scenarios are apt to develop as a separate activity, and their disconnection from strategic planning will, sooner or later, ensure their demise.

• Second, the more people with differing viewpoints participate in the process, the better. Certainly, restricting participation to members of the strategic planning department is not a good idea. Instead, management should seek the ideas and insights of marketers, technologists, public-policy analysts—from inside or outside the company—anyone whose expertise offers a useful perspective on the driving forces of the scenarios. Such broad-based involvement produces a double benefit: Both the scenarios and the participants gain from the process. But it has to be said that such broad-based cooperation does not come easily to most organizations: indeed, it is one of the culture changes that scenarios should help to foster.

• Third, establishing a provisional schedule for scenario revisions is helpful. Though annual fine-tuning is necessary, companies should engage in more radical rethinking and restructuring of the scenarios every three or four years. This revision schedule depends, of course, on the pace and course of events and on the foresight of the original scenarios.

Steps to Modify or Fine-Tune a Given Set of Scenarios

Modifying, tailoring, fine-tuning, or updating a set of scenarios requires an abbreviated process—thank goodness—compared to the original one. Some steps from the scenario-planning methodology are truncated, some are repeated, but generally the same sequence of steps is followed. The time to re-develop the scenarios will range from 20 to 50 percent of the time it originally took to develop a full set of scenarios.

For the most part, tailoring of the original scenarios can be done by using the structure of the original scenarios and adding details to reflect the different decision focus.

But when the decision focus is quite different, then tailoring of the scenarios can result in a different set of forces and drivers and a different set of story lines. Much of the information developed for the original effort will be useable, but a lot of new information will be needed. This means that changes will be most likely to occur in the composition of the high impact, high uncertainty forces, the axes of uncertainty, and the scenarios. The original scenarios may have to be completely rewritten. It all depends on how different the decision focuses are and how overarching the original scenarios were.

The fine-tuning of the scenarios with more recent information about key forces and drivers probably won't require new scenarios to be developed, but rather adjustments to the story lines and dynamics to reflect the latest information. Some sets of scenarios are useable, without any adjustment, up to five years after their original development, while others need fine-tuning almost immediately to accommodate significant events, like a presidential election. Figure 25-1 highlights the abbreviated process for updating the set of scenarios.

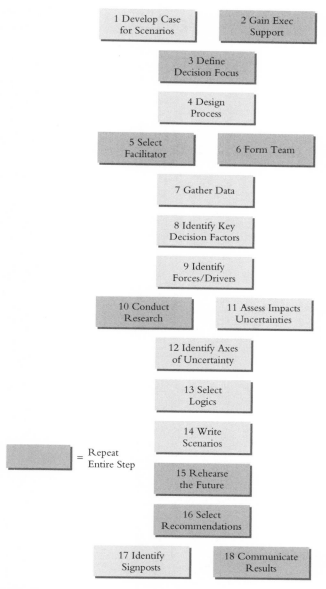

Figure 25-1   Steps to Update Scenarios

SUMMING UP

To sum up, then, if we want to get the best out of scenario planning and make it an integral part of the way we look at the future and—most importantly—make decisions, we have to face the fact that we are undertaking a change of major proportions in our planning and management. We need to change the way we develop strategy, recognizing that in conditions of extreme uncertainty, resilience becomes a key strategic objective. We need to reform the culture of our organizations to make them more flexible, open, and "boundaryless" (to use Jack Welch's term). We need to admit that we can never truly *know* the future: but we should not allow that fact to weaken our ability to take decisive action.

There are, indeed, other reasons for making these changes besides accommodating scenario planning. But we do know that, without these changes, scenario planning will, sooner or later, be rejected by the organization as surely as a transplant will be rejected by the body if it is not prepared to receive the new organ.

We know, too, that the task of changing the culture and the system is a formidable one that cannot be left to chance or to any one component. As the chart makes clear (see Figure Summing Up 1 Company-Wide Roles and Responsibilities in the Culture Change), responsibility for the efforts is widely diffused throughout the organization, at both the corporate and business unit level. We have already stressed the leadership that the CEO and senior corporate management must exert in initiating and sustaining these changes. But in the final analysis, each one of us in an organization must take responsibility for opening our minds to the broader, more imaginative thinking about the future that scenarios make possible.

In total, the changes required in re-perceiving strategy and reorienting the culture are massive, demanding, and time-consuming. But they are necessary not merely to ensure the flourishing of scenarios but to create an organization capable of succeeding in these demanding times. In terms of re-perceiving strategy development, we must move:

- From treating strategy as an annual ritual (Gary Hamel calls it an "annual rain dance"!) to a process of continuous adaptation to changing conditions

	Corporate Staff					Business-Unit Functions			
	Corporate Management	Planning	Finance	Human Resources	Other	Strategic-Business-Unit Management	Planning	Finance	Operations*
Communicating	●	●		○		◐	◐		
Tailoring		◐	○			◐	●	◐	◐
Using	●	◐	○	○	○	●	◐	○	○
Educating	○	◐		●		○	◐		
Updating		●					●		

Key: ● Primary or Lead Responsibility ◐ Secondary Responsibility ○ Supporting Responsibility

* Includes marketing, manufacturing, engineering, service, and other functions.

Figure Summing Up 1 Company-Wide Roles and Responsibilities in the Culture Change

- From selecting the "obvious" strategy (that is, the first one that meets our basic criteria) to generating true choice among differing options
- From a fixed strategy to one that possesses a high degree of flexibility and resilience

Simultaneously, we have to reorient the cultural values and practices of the organization:

- From our traditional reliance on "certainty" (our belief in the value of the single-point forecast) to generating a high comfort level in dealing with uncertainty
- From highly segmented knowledge, created behind functional barriers, to knowledge sharing and "boundarylessness"
- From financial factors to a more holistic view of strategy and the organization, one that sees the value of both the "hard" and "soft" factors needed for success

The turbulence of today's business environment is forcing companies to rethink both their short-term capabilities for flexibility and their longer-term strategic visions. In this latter context, an increasing number of firms are recognizing the value of scenario planning. The evidence provided by the growing literature on this subject indicates greater corporate receptivity to the need for a new approach to strategic planning in an environment of uncertain complexity.

Second, however, is the observation that developing and, most particularly, using scenarios effectively are demanding and challenging tasks. Scenario planning demands extensive knowledge, interdepartmental cooperation, commitment to individual and organizational learning, and blending of disciplined analysis with imaginative insights. It challenges organizations, managers, and planners to rethink their approaches to strategy and decision making, and it forces them to confront uncertainties about the future more realistically. Scenario planning is as much a culture change in business as it is a methodology.

Third, the rewards of successful scenario-based strategy development are considerable. Scenarios can result in better understanding of the dynamics of the business environment, more complete assessment of the full range of opportunities and threats, greater range in the strategy options that decision makers are prepared to consider, more robust and resilient strategies, and reduced vulnerability to being blindsided by surprises.

Fourth, there are a number of preconditions for the successful transplant of scenarios into a corporate planning culture, but two are preeminent:

• The scenarios must be grounded in real business choices—in our terminology, they must be decision focused.

• The process must involve decision makers intimately and continuously. The scenarios must encompass their perceptions of issues, uncertainties, and concerns. They are the ones who will use the scenarios: hence, their understanding, commitment, and ownership of the scenarios are essential.

Many of the failed ventures in scenario planning stem from a failure to assure these two preconditions.

Finally, we should note the critical importance of insight, imagination, and openness of mind not only in members of the scenario team but also in those who use the scenarios to develop strategy and guide actions. These are qualities that scenarios both require and foster. And in the process, they change the very character of the organizations they serve.

APPENDIX A

EXAMPLE SCENARIO WRITE-UPS

In 2001, the new venture group, Innovent, of Nokia conducted a scenario-planning project to explore for new investment ideas in the peer-to-peer networks space. Four scenarios were developed, using the SRI methodology, to cover the range of possible futures for the marketplace, technologies, consumer behavior, and regulatory issues involved, and are included in this appendix. They are stories written about the future, but they are not predictions. None of the story lines are actually expected to occur, but the four stories together as a set are intended to cover the alternative P2P network environments that Innovent and Nokia could encounter.

Scenario: Battle of the Brands

Axes of Uncertainty positions:

- Power and Money: Gorillas
- Nature of the Community: Individual
- Scope of the System: Fragmented

November 1, 2008, Commentary, *New York Times* (An Operating Division of AOL-Time-Warner-Viacom)

As we approach the final days of the Bush Administration's second term in office, we find ourselves looking back over the past eight years to weigh the economic effects of the Administration's policy. Today's economy is the child of regulatory change. As one senior Department of Justice official noted, "Times have been good for the U.S. economy and our citizens. The Administration brought rampant regulation under control—reducing burdensome constraints on growth, while strengthening protections for providers of digital content. These advances have kept us internationally competitive, particularly in the crucial services and content sectors of the economy." Witness the consolidation among content providers, for example Dreamworks SKG buying NBC-TV, to a handful of very large players who in turn have overtaken the powerful electronic distribution networks.

Consumer brands such as Disney, Nike, and Coca-Cola, already important in 2000, have assumed even greater power as the U.S. economy shifts further toward content and services, and as the United States increases its role as the world's largest developer and merchandiser of content. New technologies enabling easy discovery of content piracy, combined with strong and swift legal retribution, give corporations a virtually unshakeable control over content, and encourage U.S. businesses to invest even more in the area.

A major feature of the Bush Administration's regulatory policy is the scaling back of excessive regulations supporting consumer protection and individuals' rights to privacy. As a result, major corporations can protect their content while exploiting the vast databases of consumer buying information being compiled each year from the billions of individual transactions. A number of agile corporate giants take full advantage of their economies of scale and develop a sophisticated understanding of their consumer bases. Today, after a number of investments in the area, large merchandisers can analyze consumer behavior and predict buying patterns with astonishing accuracy, down to very small groups, and still take advantage of their buying power. Cross-selling across channels is rampant and highly evolved, and competition from smaller players is limited to niches.

Technology infrastructure choices largely followed geographic boundaries. The Sony, Microsoft, and AOL Time Warner keiretsus (groups of tightly owned and operated organizations) each chose different "standards" for wireless communications that are incompatible with those of their competitors. Consumers readily buy what the major brands offer, and respond positively to individually targeted electronic specials. Brand groups are broad enough to satisfy most, if not all, consumer needs. But with no strong sense of community, consumers tend to follow fashions, as determined by blockbuster movies, celebrities, and the like, without complaints about the Balkanization of offerings.

The growth of Internet penetration to the home has continued unabated since 2001 and has become the major distribution channel for digital content. P2P (or "distributed computing") technology allows the large content providers to distribute their products and services more efficiently, and is one of several approaches used, but certainly not the dominant one. Voice Over IP (VoIP), content delivery, merchandising, billing, and related services are largely provided over corporate P2P networks, which are essentially transparent to most consumers. The P2P exceptions to the corporate model are the result of avant-garde technologists who dabble in do-it-yourself P2P as a hobby (for instance, working on SETI at Home or its multiple follow-ons) or who build P2P-provided computer services that rival the cost-effectiveness of more centralized computational models.

Large content providers use whatever technology works best for a given investment. As always, their emphasis is to dominate the market in content production and distribution, not in technology-specific deployments.

Involvement by consumers in content development remains minimal. Consumers buy what entertainment is provided by the large brands, and on-line communities did not grow beyond what already existed in 2001. The online communities slowly migrated to systems provided, as a service, by the large content providers. Service providers keep close attention to ensure that what minimal content is developed by consumers does not impinge or reduce the value of their commercial properties. What passes for innovation is the development of new entertainment content that cross-sells the brands' multiple products.

Overall, the changes initiated by regulatory revisions and furthered by competitive and technological forces have created an economy of strong and highly competitive corporations, keiretsus separated by their slightly different technology infrastructures, and consumers who remain focused in brand awareness and passive experience. Times have been relatively good for the consumers, but particularly excellent for the global brands.

Scenario: Enlightenment

Axes of Uncertainty positions:

- Power and Money: Gorillas
- Nature of the Community: Social
- Scope of the System: Transparent

"The Resurgence of Telecommunication Operators"
November 1, 2008, *Wall Street Journal* Editorial

The first decade of the 21st century has been a telecommunications operator's dream, in spite of Wall Street's early concerns. After three years of economic problems and consolidation at the beginning of the scenario's time-frame, the telecommunications operators broke through from their bloated, uncompetitive positions by finally succeeding in developing viable business models for a broad array of value-added services. By 2004, they quickly began to build dramatic economies of scale using their now relatively efficient infrastructures and broad consumer access.

Of particular importance in the early part of the scenario's time-frame was the dramatic increase in social and community-based activities online, which took off in 2004 as a result of the availability of many, new inexpensive products and services online, and the resurgence of the U.S. economy. Consumers have come to appreciate and are willing to pay well for the billed-per-view, value-added services that started becoming readily available half way through the time-period of the scenario. Telecom firms have also made use of their infrastructures and consumer access to take over many billing and payment activities, particularly those online, originally handled by banks and credit card companies.

Today, in 2008, Telecom operators are at the heart of most, if not all, the important online activities of consumers, and are taking some financial cut from each transaction. They have become more innovative, devising and promoting activities that drive traffic, and are at the core of their own resurgence.

A significant development for society from the economic boom that began in 2004 is the reduction of the extended workweeks of the early 2000s. Now, individuals in all segments dedicate more time to individual and group pursuits of leisure and have generally shifted away from focus on the consumption of goods toward an emphasis on experiences, including travel (physical and virtual), and learning. Many former providers of career or job training have broadened their offerings to meet the demand for self-improvement and self-fulfillment.

E-learning is also now commonplace as a way for individuals to upgrade corporate careers and, after some fits and starts, as an add-on provider of secondary and tertiary-level education. Niche players, including domain experts, develop the E-learning content with the help of telecom firms.

A surprising development for many pundits is the rich content, being generated and distributed by new players and by the users, that is as important as the content from the traditional content providers such as Disney. The broadband infrastructure, available exclusively through the eight multinational telecoms that are left, is enabling the distribution of content previously inaccessible via narrowband. E-learners in Europe and the United States now study flower arrangement and origami interactively with their masters in Japan, and practice meditation with Buddhist monks in Tibet. In fact, the largest community online event of 2007 is the daily meditation at 10:00 pm GMT led by Tibetan monks in which often 50 million people participate.

Telecommunications companies, now involved with a large number of partners such as Microsoft, Sony, and AOL Time Warner, are flourishing financially and once again dominate the capital markets with their very large market capitalizations. They invest heavily in state-of-the-art equipment and the deployment of even more value-added services.

But this time, the telecoms operate with a lean and mean attitude toward profits, costs-of-service, and acquisitions, and seem poised to continue their growth into the next decade. Telecom operators use whatever works and is affordable, and all make good use of P2P technology to provide Voice Over IP and other services more efficiently (including content delivery, merchandising, billing, and the like). While P2P is essentially transparent to consumers and enables better distribution of computer power within corporate networks, it is not taken on by the masses. Corporations, including telecom service operators, use more or less centralized architectures, depending upon distance, quality of service, and the like. Regardless of their technology choice, the telecoms dominate the marketplace.

By the end of the time-frame of the scenario, telecom firms still don't operate seamlessly across applications and geographic boundaries. Connection and service are simpler within a keiretsu than across keiretsus. Nevertheless, affluent consumers consider the operators good enablers of their enlightened lifestyle, and don't complain.

Scenario: Tale of Two Cities Revisited

Axes of Uncertainty positions:

- Power & Money: Guerillas
- Nature of the Community: Social
- Scope of the System: Fragmented

"It was the best of times, it was the worst of times . . . " read a June 2008 *New York Times* article on the state of communications technology and business. The comparison is apt: In some cities and for a few people, it is the best of times, with free bandwidth and open access to services. For most other people in other parts of the country, it is the worst of times, with limited, costly communications and very few relevant services. What brought about this conflicted state of affairs? The Open Communications (OC) movement, which promised universal free bandwidth, fell prey to the combination of a successful counter movement by the large communications companies, unanticipated technological complexities, and the inability to fix on a universal set of standards. The result has been a mishmash of open and de facto standards, with a very few cities near universities having essentially free OC bandwidth (Berkeley, Santa Cruz, and Cambridge), and the rest of the country purchasing costly bandwidth from large telecom operators. The financial power and lobbying ability of big business proved too strong for the zealous but disorganized OC movement, which has fallen back into specialty niches, somewhat like CB-radio or ham radio operators in the 20th century.

On the other hand, it's not so great for the telecom firms either. The telecom companies that survived the financial downturn and capital problems of 2001 through 2004 are doing reasonably well in their existing markets, but they are not growing. Locally entrenched providers will not give up control of their environment by supporting open standards that would bring competition. Instead, they each have allied themselves with some content providers to offer a set of benefits within their milieu. But it is a time of segmentation into relatively large but slow-growing markets and stagnant innovation, and the financial markets continue to discount the equity of telecom firms because they see no growth, although the cash flows are strong.

The OC community can't seem to grow beyond the 2 to 3% of consumers it had in 2001, and remains highly fragmented with a few replicas overseas. Inhabitants of these free-bandwidth islands enjoy good access to bandwidth and services, with little or no overhead costs, and low barriers to switching—but only as long as they remain within their community, or venture to one equally isolated.

Consumers in non-OC communities, with limited access to broad bandwidth, are the masses but they remain segregated by their partially-regulated major telecom providers. Within these communities, services such as payments and billing are reasonably consistent, but the barriers to entry and switching are high. Consumers who switch providers, perhaps by moving to a new location, most likely must buy expensive new equipment to access broadband. Although consumers are upset about their relative captivity, they do not have the organization or wherewithal to rebel.

In respect to content, the situation is similar to that of the Battle of the Brands scenario but more fragmented and less rewarding financially. Involvement by consumers in content development is limited. Some consumers develop narrowly defined content for their niche groups, while online communities have remained about the same as in 2001: the domain of techno-geeks, college students, and a few other groups. Content is largely provided by large developers who work in conjunction with the telecom firms. Disney's keiretsu has done well, but not as well as in Battle of the Brands scenario.

All in all, the current situation has few real winners and too many losers—truly the best and the worst of times for communications. Innovation is relatively limited, and there are no clear leaders.

Scenario: Community Coup

Axes of Uncertainty positions:

- Power and Money: Guerillas
- Nature of the Community: Social
- Scope of the System: Transparent

Tim O'Reilly and his Open Source supporters are ecstatic at the 2008 Open Communications Summer Conference over the filling of Moscone Center in San Francisco with tens of thousands of participants. The sold-out event is the latest affirmation of the significant changes that have occurred in computing and communications since the beginning of the 21st century.

A revolution in communications has resulted in consumers tapping into the free bandwidth network, via Open Communications—the digital communications counterpart to Open Source software—rather than having to buy access from a few large providers like they did in the early 2000s. Leading users in some of the most densely populated and better-educated areas of the United States, some 10% of the population, now access a grass-roots, ad hoc broadband network, simply by turning on their wireless devices. Wireless bandwidth is the result of numerous devices that operate much like the Internet (each new wireless node, when connected, becomes an additional access point as well as a destination), seamlessly spreading the reach of free bandwidth.

Like the Internet, Open Communications began with a few technological pioneers—notably Brewster Kahle, chief executive officer of Web-navigation firm Alexa Internet, who wired up the north end of San Francisco's Presidio. Hard-core techies wanted more than a wireless connection; they wanted a high-speed wireless connection free of the long arm of the big telecommunications providers, and they built themselves a network.

The prototype network, SFLan, was a grass-roots project with both a technology base and a philosophy of sharing. In 1999, SFLan began with six radio repeaters that cost some $2,000 each and ran at megabits/second, covered only three miles, and used unlicensed and unregulated portions of the broadcast spectrum. In his SFLan Manifesto, Kahle wrote that he built the network in the hope that others would put up their own radio repeaters and usher in an era of widespread, low-cost, high-speed wireless access. "Imagine a citywide, wireless LAN that grows from anarchistic cooperation. From a laptop in any park, from a PC in any house, from any handheld device on the street, you can access the Internet at blazing speed. Imagine a phone that uses your base station when you are in your house and the net when you are out of range" (Kahle 2001). This crusade has been taken up primarily in geek-centric communities and in university towns across the country (for example Seattle, Boston, Silicon Valley, Austin, Ann Arbor). Although the numbers of consumers are not huge, their significance is very important, because they represent the groups that were the leading users of cell phone services, and their transition has destroyed the cellular service providers' business models.

What Kahle had not predicted early on was the concomitant generation of content that came about with the spread of bandwidth—leading-edge consumers create their own content, and spread it among their friends and onto the Internet. They use sophisticated tools from various software vendors (including Microsoft, Macromedia, Adobe and others), and video and audio hardware from consumer electronics companies (Sony, Matsushita, Hitachi, Toshiba, Samsung, and Philips).

Kahle's vision has benefited a number of commercial enterprises, including consumer-driven P2P enabling services and makers of wireless transceivers, and as a result has created a new breed of billionaire. The new business opportunities occurred because users quickly realized the value of investing a few hundred dollars to eliminate expensive monthly fees for wireless broadband. Consumers in geographic areas with less free wireless bandwidth still resort to commercial equipment, but this "bandwidth challenged" segment is also beginning to shift toward Open Communications deployments as the costs of entry decrease from rapidly increasing wireless network economies of scale. Free Voice over IP (VoIP) is a snap to set up, assuming enough repeaters are available, and a number of leading-edge consumers in major cities are stopping payment for most cellular phone services.

The development of Open Communications devices with wireless VoIP has stimulated a resurgence in consumer electronics, similar to the early days of personal computing, with a stream of new products and vendors. The philosophical underpinnings of the movement, with open sharing of code and designs among amateurs and an enthusiasm for new communications concepts, are similar to Silicon Valley's freewheeling Homebrew Computer Club of the 1970s, but with a large dose of commercial reality and an awareness of the greater potential of free universal communications. It is still unclear who the commercial winners will be among the vendors of repeaters and handheld devices, and already many of them are consolidating. But a viable, rapidly evolving group is there to sell basic equipment and provide support services to users, similar to the start-up corporations that founded business models under Open Source software in the late 1990s and early 2000s.

Involvement by consumers in content development is very significant. Consumers develop as much volume as is provided by the large brands. Online communities have grown dramatically beyond what existed in 2001, enabled by technology that is easier and cheaper to use, and a sense of renaissance and freedom from previous paradigms. New ways to develop and transmit electronic art are flourishing, starting from the grass-roots. Commercial vendors play a supporting role in this, with innovation coming from enlightened individuals and communities.

In retrospect, after only eight years, the telecom service and support providers are dramatically different from the telecom providers of 2001. Several telecom firms, of the ones that have survived, now provide equipment for users to create bandwidth for themselves, in addition to their traditional voice services and bandwidth for Internet. For those unwilling or unable to handle the maintenance and support, those telecoms also provide support services to assure the personal bandwidth is available. Since 2001, several firms have emerged from the highly entrepreneurial and chaotic marketplace and have never known regulation. In 2008, differentiation among these providers is by quality of service and cost-effectiveness, not geographic location.

Open Communications has brought a peaceful revolution. Its early visionaries and proponents have much to celebrate, while supporters of the regulated telecom businesses have had to transform, or are in the process of becoming irrelevant. The possibility of free bandwidth has resulted in a rise in the number of entrepreneurial activities, which now have much fewer restrictions in regards to location and bandwidth. It is almost as easy to communicate and do business with remote vendors and suppliers as with local ones. This supplier and distribution trend has created even further business for package delivery services, such as Federal Express, UPS, and the U.S. Postal Service, who often provide many of the logistical functions of the new entrepreneurs.

WORKSHOP MANAGEMENT PRACTICES FOR SCENARIO DEVELOPMENT

To achieve its goals in scenario development, the workshop approach requires organization, leadership, a recording mechanism, and ground rules. The basic issues in workshop management are:

- Define the objectives of the workshop.
- Identify the desired outcomes.
- Plan the workshop format.
- Involve proper participants.
- Maintain a creative atmosphere.
- Follow an agenda.
- Leverage the interaction.
- Prepare the participants beforehand.
- Leverage the power of visual aids.
- Create the appropriate physical setting.
- Hold everyone responsible for carrying out their assigned role.
- Encourage open minds.

Define the Objectives of the Workshop

The starting point is to determine the primary purpose for conducting the workshop(s). What are we trying to accomplish, and for whom? Without objectives, we have no basis for organizing the topics and the agenda steps to follow. In addition, if the participants do not consider the topics and agenda steps relevant to the scenario effort, they will not be fully responsive in the workshop(s) and success will be difficult to achieve.

Identify the Desired Outcomes

If all the workshop steps are effectively conducted, what specific results would be achieved? A clear definition of the expected outcomes and deliverables is needed to focus the energies of the group and to provide a basis for measuring success at the end of each workshop.

Plan the Workshop Format

A basic element in workshop design is the format of the workshop. What type of workshop activities will best achieve the objectives: Short presentations followed by discussion? Open discussion? Physical movements around the room by participants? Breakout groups for focused analysis? No single approach is necessarily correct, and typically several are used in workshops that last more than a couple of hours.

The criterion for selecting the format activities is whether they effectively channel the team's energy toward the issues, given the constraints of time, participants' backgrounds, and setting.

If a workshop lasts more than a few hours, it is generally necessary to use a variety of techniques to keep the team productive and interested. Those techniques include alternating among large groups, small groups, and individual thinking sessions, and giving participants means to express themselves in addition to the usual oral responses (e.g., flip charts, personal notes, PowerPoint slides).

Workshop participants will become tired quickly when they are engaged in "free-floating" or unstructured brainstorming sessions. Consequently, other types of exercises should be planned in addition to those unstructured sessions. Participants can often effectively generate ideas when their thinking is channeled by means of exercises such as direct associations, analogies, matrices, or other more structured techniques.

Given that scenario workshops involve a great deal of divergent, brainstorming-like thinking, workshop facilitators need to be very sensitive to participants "hitting the wall"—where their minds turn off and little productive work is possible. At this point, the leader should call a break or change the format to help get the participants engaged again.

Involve the Proper Participants

It is important to involve managers and decision makers in workshops to increase the likelihood that the results of the workshop will be implemented. Limiting involvement to those who may not be in a position of authority creates a situation in which the results must be sold to management. On the other hand, the results of a workshop attended by managers as well as business and technical people have already received an initial business and technical screening and have a head start toward implementation in the organization.

It is somewhat inhibiting for a workshop to include guests or observers who are there only to watch the proceedings. The intelligence of all guests should be used—regardless of whether they are experts in the subject at hand. Moreover, observers are invariably perceived as judges, and they cause participants to become more self-protective. Ideally, then, everyone who attends a workshop should be involved fully as a member of the group.

Maintain a Creative Atmosphere

It is important to establish a creative atmosphere for the scenario team in a workshop. Factors that help to create that atmosphere include holding the workshop in a relaxed physical setting; using visual aids; providing food and refreshments; and encouraging informal dress. The most important requirement, however, is establishing an appropriate psychological climate by avoiding "idea killers" and by deferring judgment on the ideas that are initially generated.

An effective method for breaking the ice in a workshop and getting everyone involved early is to ask all participants to introduce themselves. In addition, it is important for workshop leaders to know the participants' names and backgrounds well. That knowledge allows the leaders to give recognition to the participants that will help them to maintain a positive motivation; it can also help leaders to avoid potential problems.

Follow an Agenda

An agenda or schedule is required for any workshop. The agenda will help to keep the group moving toward a goal rather than floating aimlessly. However, the schedule should not be followed rigidly if the group is strongly engaged in a particularly productive activity. That involvement provides an opportunity to announce that the group is behind schedule because it has been generating results.

Once the agenda topics and times have been set, the facilitator needs to monitor the pace of the workshop against the plan and control the discussions so that they remain on the topic or activity and cover the necessary ground in approximately the time allotted. The facilitator needs to exercise control unobtrusively and with a reasonable degree of flexibility. Free and easy participation should be encouraged, and constant interruptions and reminders to keep moving should be avoided.

Controlling the content of the discussion is important for staying on schedule, as well as for ensuring that key topics are addressed. The facilitator must anticipate the topics that the participants are likely to discuss and prepare appropriate probes to draw out important issues. In addition, anticipating the points that should be covered will allow the facilitator to be aware when the discussion has been completed and the group should move on to the next agenda item. A good method for anticipating the content and potential problems of an upcoming workshop discussion is to hold a dry run of the workshop with one to three other persons. The dry run will give the facilitator practice in each step of the workshop process, and the comments from the small group will prepare the facilitator to deal with the issues that are most likely to concern the workshop participants.

If the group falls behind schedule, some options for increasing the pace include eliminating some of the activities to be conducted by the group; splitting up issues to be addressed by different teams; or conducting exercises in the large group, without breaking up into subgroups.

A key factor in staying on schedule is starting on time, so that you can end on time. In scheduling breaks for the group, the facilitator should give everyone a precise time to return. "Please be back at 10:35" is better than saying, "Let's take a 10-minute break."

Leverage the Interaction

In workshops, many of the best ideas will be generated bit-by-bit, in building block fashion, by many people, rather than by a single participant. To encourage contributions by many participants, facilitators and recorders should avoid labeling an idea as belonging to the first person who suggested it. Each idea that emerges should be publicly recorded in front of the group for all to see (and to relieve the group participants from the task of keeping notes to keep track of the ideas), but references to specific people should be omitted from the charts unless the recorder wishes to ask for further details at a later time.

Because the ideas will be judged eventually, the facilitator should announce a particular activity and time for sorting or screening the ideas at the start of the workshop. Knowing that they will have an opportunity to offer judgments later seems to help participants to avoid negative statements and idea killers in the idea-generating portions of the workshop.

The facilitator and the recorder should assume low-key roles, if possible, because they can inhibit or even antagonize a group by acting as lecturers, judges, or workshop leaders. The best results are likely when the group participants feel that the facilitators did not have to push to get the group to achieve the workshop's objective(s) and that they even appeared to be somewhat passive.

Prepare the Participants Beforehand

Some advance preparation for scenario-development workshops is highly desirable. Activities that help to put the participants in a good state of mind for an intense workshop discussion include learning and thinking about the workshop subject or objective(s) ahead of time, reading relevant articles and studies, conducting preliminary research efforts, or attending briefings about the workshop. In general, participants cannot walk into a workshop discussion "cold" and immediately begin to provide constructive responses to a problem or issue.

Leverage the Power of Visual Aids

Visual aids such as PowerPoint slides, flip charts, and wall recordings are an essential part of workshop management. The purpose of the aids is to facilitate the workshop process and reinforce issues related to the subjects being addressed. They set the stage for meaningful discussion and add important visual interest or impact.

A major benefit of visual aids is that they can demonstrate relationships that are not easily or quickly understandable through words alone. For example, an organization chart is a fast and easy way to show a complex set of reporting relationships that would otherwise require laborious text to cover the same ground. In addition, seeing the words after they have been spoken gives participants additional time to reflect on the content.

However, it is important to be selective in the use of visual aids. Workshop leaders should not present a visual for every single point to be made. If they do, the participants will drown in the information. Furthermore, not every word on each visual should be read.

PowerPoint slides are the one of most effective visual aids for facilitators and presenters. The facilitators can manipulate them directly, easily changing the sequence of the slides or returning to one that was previously shown. Because the room lights need not be dimmed, participants can remain engaged with one another, as well as with the visuals, and the facilitator can maintain continuous direct eye contact with the group. Finally, recorders can input new content directly onto a slide in much the same way they would with a flip chart.

Open walls or large white boards, on which 5" × 8" cards or Post-It notes can be posted or notes or figures can be directly recorded, are essential today in workshop management and often serve as the group memory of the discussion. The large spaces allow all workshop participants to be physically involved in building the public record. The spaces also support the use of graphical recorders, who are trained to work in real time to capture in words and pictures what participants are saying. The combination of words and visuals sparks people's imaginations and serves as a powerful record of the discussion. (See Figure B-1 for a graphical recording of a scenario-planning workshop discussion about future consumer needs.)

Flip charts or easel pads also have many uses in a workshop, and often are used to record the key points in the group discussions. Individual pages can be torn off and taped to the wall for continuing display. Flip charts are quite flexible and are often used to capture off-the-agenda issues or issues to be addressed later.

Create the Appropriate Physical Setting

The basic issues that need to be addressed in establishing the right physical setting are geographic location, facility, and workshop room. Convenience for the majority of the participants is usually the dominant factor in selecting the location. If most of the participants can commute in the same way that they normally would, a close location will be cost effective.

A number of different kinds of facilities might be used. The key factors in choosing one of them will be cost, travel convenience, and service. Typical facilities include company conference rooms, in-town hotels, conference centers, remote retreats, and resorts. Generally, a company's own multipurpose conference room has no equal in terms of cost and convenience. However, these benefits may be offset by real disadvantages. Some of the participants are likely to find that their regular offices are nearby and succumb to the powerful temptation to keep an eye on how things are going. The result is that they will be late in arriving at the workshops, late getting back from breaks, and exhausted from trying to do two things at once. Another disadvantage is the proximity of the participants' managers or colleagues. The participants may be called out for meetings or waylaid during breaks.

The features of the workshop room are more important than the geographic location and type of facility. The room must meet the physical and psychological needs of the group members. Important considerations include:

- Temperature
- Ventilation
- Lighting, lines of vision
- Acoustics

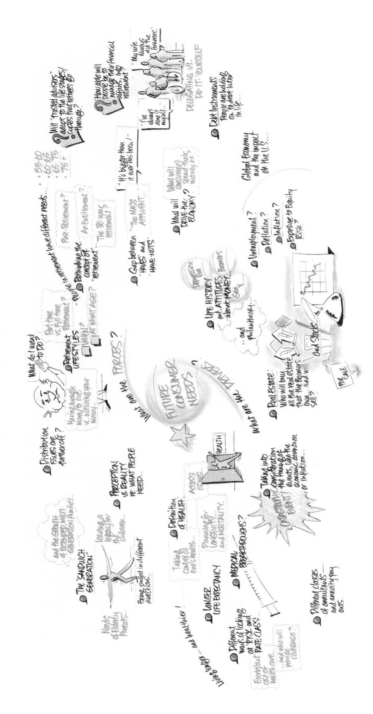

Figure B-1 Example of Graphical Recording from a Scenario-Planning Workshop

- Seating comfort (e.g., elbow room, knee room, and comfortable chairs)
- Psychological considerations such as space, noise, and visual distractions

Hold Everyone Responsible for Carrying Out Their Assigned Workshop Role

Successful workshop management requires that a number of people performing well-defined roles collectively contribute to the productivity of a group. Everyone has a stake in the outcome of the workshop, and all participants are equally responsible for the group's successes and failures.

The four key functions or roles in a workshop are: (1) the facilitator, who helps the group focus its energies on a task; (2) the recorder, who captures the ideas and results of the discussion and serves as the group memory; (3) the group members, who are active participants in the meeting; and (4) the leader, who sets the agenda and has the power to set constraints on the process. As long as all participants understand their roles and responsibilities, these four functions constitute a system of checks and balances that automatically corrects problems as they arise. If the facilitator dominates the discussion as an active participant, the others will object. If the recorder does not document the discussion accurately, the group members will point out the mistake. If the leader attacks a group member or vice versa, the facilitator will intercede. The responsibilities associated with these four functions are described below.

Facilitator. The facilitator helps the group to focus its energies on a task by setting the stage, suggesting methods and procedures, protecting members of the group from personal attack, and making sure everyone has an opportunity to participate. The facilitator serves as a combination of methodology guide, traffic officer, and meeting chauffeur. The facilitator also oversees all logistics.

It helps—indeed, we would say, it is virtually essential—if the facilitator has had prior scenario experience, knows where roadblocks most frequently occur, and is therefore better able to keep the discussion on track, stimulate discussion when it (inevitably, at times) flags, and meet the agenda objectives on time.

Some of the basic functions of the facilitator are to:

- **Set the group climate.** The facilitator has an important role in developing the climate of the group. Most often an informal approach works best in encouraging participation. The facilitator should also try to project a warm and friendly attitude toward all group members.

- **Define the task, process, deliverable, and time.** At the outset, the facilitator must let the members of the group know what is expected of them, and he or she should set a high standard of performance. Clear definitions of the task, process, deliverables, and time available are important in focusing the group's attention on its basic purpose. Clearly stated performance expectations also stimulate constructive and creative group participation. Later, during the workshop, the facilitator must keep the group informed about its performance, good or bad, against expectations. However, the facilitator should remain flexible and should even announce changes in expectations if the situation warrants.

- **Encourage group participation.** The facilitator can encourage group participation by:
  - Remaining aware of individuals' efforts to be heard and giving each person an opportunity to contribute
  - Pointing out the relationships between similar ideas offered by different group members
  - Conveying acceptance by exhibiting a noncritical attitude and by refraining from evaluating members' contributions
  - Refusing to allow anyone to take over and monopolize the workshop
  - Helping the group to identify errors in logic

  Techniques for obtaining participation from everyone include:
  - Asking silent members direct questions when you realize the person is fully capable of giving a knowledgeable response
  - When the size of the group permits, going around the table and soliciting a brief contribution from everyone
  - Talking with the silent persons privately and asking them to participate

- **Keep the discussion moving.** A brisk pace is desirable, but the facilitator must be careful not to move the group faster than it wants to go. Specific ways to keep the discussion moving include:
  - Preparing an agenda in advance.
  - Arriving early to the workshop.
  - Starting on time.
  - Keeping the discussion on the subject. Some diversions may be fruitful, but only if they can be related to the main subject within a reasonably short time. Things to say when the discussion is getting off track include: "Wait a second, we're jumping around . . . " and "Let's come back to that point later."

- **Discourage side discussions.** A group quickly stops working toward its common objective when side discussions are allowed. The facilitator should take quick and decisive action to discourage the side discussions. That can be accomplished by requesting at the outset that only one person talk at a time.

- **Test for consensus.** The facilitator can assist the group in developing concensus by periodically reviewing points developed during the discussion and by summaring what appears to be the group's conclusions. In addition, the facilitator should try to send issues back to the group by saying things like, "Let's check that out with the rest of the group," or "Oh, your perception is _____."

- **Avoid expressing strong opinions.** The facilitator is a neutral servant of the group. It is difficult to remain impartial, and at times the facilitator may feel the need to make a point about the subject being discussed. However, if facilitators become too involved in expressing and defending their own views, they cannot adequately perform the real functions of discussion leadership. If the facilitator feels a strong need to participate actively in the discussion of a particular subject (perhaps because the group has need of his or her special expertise in a given field), then he or she should pass the role of facilitator to someone else.

- **Avoid making decisions.** It is the group's job to make decisions, not the facilitator's. The facilitator should explain his or her role—and the group participants' role—carefully at the beginning of the workshop. The facilitator should answer those who try to force a decision by:
  - Throwing the question back to the group
  - Throwing the question back to the person who asked it
  - Explaining that it is the group's job to make decisions
  - Answering directly if the situation warrants, especially if the answer involves providing information that the group needs to evaluate the issue fully

Recorder. The responsibility of the recorder is to serve as the group memory by making a record of what is happening as it happens. Participants can relax and focus their energies on the discussion, secure in the knowledge that their contributions are being preserved. Often, the recorder writes down the participants' ideas on large sheets of paper in front of the group. The objective is not to record everything but to capture enough so that ideas can be preserved and recalled at any time. However, the recorder is a nonevaluating servant of the group and should not edit the words of the speaker.

The group's memory serves many functions. For example, it:

- Focuses the group on a task
- Provides an instant record of a workshop's contents and process
- Depersonalizes ideas
- Serves as a psychic release for participants who do not have to hold onto and defend their ideas
- Prevents repetition and wheel spinning
- Encourages participation because it respects individuals' ideas and reduces status differentiation
- Enables participants to check that their ideas have been recorded correctly
- Increases a group's sense of accomplishment
- Makes it easy for latecomers to catch up without interrupting the meeting
- Makes accountability easier because decisions are written down in clear view of the group—everyone knows who is going to do what, and when

Group Member. The group member is an active participant in the workshop and devotes most of his or her energy to the main task of the workshop. In addition, control of what happens in a meeting ultimately lies in the hands of the group members. They can make procedural suggestions, overrule the suggestions of the facilitator, and generally determine the course of the workshop. It is also the responsibility of the group members to ensure that the facilitator and recorder perform their duties and that ideas are recorded accurately.

To fulfill their basic roles and responsibilities, the group members must:

- Take responsibility for the success of the meeting.
- Focus their energy on the content of the problem.
- Respect and listen to other individuals.
- Ensure that their own ideas are recorded accurately.
- Ensure that the facilitator and recorder perform their functions.
- Try to keep an open mind.
- Refrain from making premature negative comments.
- Protect others' points of view.

Leader. Although the leader does not run the workshop, he or she retains the power to make the final decisions, to set constraints for the workshop, to set the agenda, and to regain control of the workshop if its progress is unsatisfactory. The leader also becomes a full participant in the group and argues actively for his or her points of view. Often, the leader represents the group in meetings with other groups.

Key duties and responsibilities of the leader are to:

- Assume responsibility for the group's performance of its duties.
- Be accountable to the larger organization for the quality of the decisions of the group.
- Give the group direction and assist the group in setting goals, procedures, and plans.
- Set up the workshop process and participate in setting the agenda for the group's meetings.
- Act as spokesperson or representative of the group to the larger organization.

Encourage Open Minds

Finally, to be successful, workshops require some clear and firm ground rules to govern the dialog among participants. If there is to be a free and open exchange among participants—sometimes about unconventional or controversial matters—the emphasis must be on the merits of the idea, and the strength of the evidence, not on the rank or forcefulness of the proponent (note our experience in the case of the domineering CEO in Chapter 10!). Achieving this openness may also require members of the team to "suspend disbelief" or be prepared to "think the unthinkable." This does not mean they should suspend their critical faculties—these will come into play later in the process. It does mean that they should not reject an idea about the future out of hand simply because it is a departure from the past or challenges conventional wisdom. How far a team is prepared to depart from conventional thinking and deal with sensitive issues in developing its scenarios is a measure both of the team's flexibility and the facilitator's and leader's persuasiveness. Perhaps the greatest challenge facing the scenario team leader is achieving this balance between openness and imagination in stretching the boundaries of the team's thinking, and maintaining discipline and logic in structuring the team's scenarios of possible futures.

APPENDIX C

FUTURE IMPACTS OF INFORMATION TECHNOLOGY ON THE SCENARIO-PLANNING METHODOLOGY

The complicated scenario-planning process—the intricate steps of the scenario-planning methodology, the need to integrate so much information about the external forces and drivers, and the importance of collaboration in the process—opens up many possibilities for information technology to improve the methodology and align the results better with strategy decision making. In this appendix we describe potential opportunities to change the process, their pros and cons, and how we think the methodology will be advanced in the next few years.

Computer Models of the External Environment

We can see the potential of computer models for scenario planning from the rapid development of computer games for all age levels for entertainment, training, and business planning. The representations of the game worlds are in effect scenario descriptions. Computer models are created for the interrelationships among the forces and for projecting possible story lines.

But while it's clearly possible to create computer models of external-environment dynamics, to date they have not been useful in strategic decision making, because senior executives for the most part are not involved in their development and because the models take too much time and resources to build and get right. In scenario planning using workshop teams that include senior executives, it takes three months of calendar time and maybe five to eight days of each team member's time to create tailored written scenarios. To build a computer model capable of generating potential scenarios for the decision, it would likely require six months to a year, a large contract costing $1 million or more for a specialist to build the model, and still a fair amount of time required of company personnel to provide and validate the content. And the model would likely still be a black box to senior executives, hard to maintain, and potentially difficult to use.

The models today can be, however, valuable learning tools. There's no timetable involved for making a decision and the model doesn't have to be tailored to a specific situation. Having constructed the model, managers and executives can "play" with it in varying circumstances, alter strategic assumptions, and experiment with different strategies.

The signpost to indicate that computer modeling or game building is reaching the stage where it will have an impact on strategic decision making is the time and resources required to build a tailored model. If the time can be reduced to one month or less and the cost of creating the model, outside of the internal executives and experts' involvement for the content, can be $100,000 or less, then it's time to begin experimenting with the computer models.

Expanding the Number of Participants Involved in the Process

Scenario planning, as practiced in strategy development, usually involves the participation of only a small group of participants in all steps of the methodology. With every input, analysis, and decision-making activity being performed, each participant in the group becomes immersed in the methodology, thereby benefiting the most from the knowledge and insights gained from active participation. Perhaps the biggest potential impact of IT in the future will therefore come from the increasing the number of participants involved in the development process. This might occur by "outsourcing" some of the process activities to more internal and external experts, by using virtual teams or remote participants, or by expanding the numbers of persons participating in the workshops.

Increasing the Productivity of Workshops

One of the major strengths of the scenario-planning methodology is that it brings together many different perspectives on the external environment and then weaves those perspectives together into a common view of the range of possible futures. In this sense, the methodology is fundamentally collaborative, depending on consensus building and inclusion to develop the scenarios. Given an honest disagreement about any relevant force, whether it is about its content, dynamics, influences, or possible outcomes, it is more useful to record the disagreement, and view it as establishing a range of possibilities, than to choose the "most likely" or "best" alternative. The technologies that could have a big impact on the process in the future therefore are those that advance idea generation, collaboration, and consensus building. Those could include new means for:

- Stimulating structured brainstorming
- Recording audio and written inputs from participants

- Allowing workshop participants and facilitators to write and draw on whiteboards or walls that record the information digitally
- Displaying stored digital information on whiteboards or walls
- Selecting scenario-planning methodology templates from a library, displaying them, and allowing them to be filled in

An important challenge to computerizing the development process relates to the need for a facilitator. The facilitator must constantly flesh out the steps of the methodology to ensure the scenario team does a good job. A skilled facilitator has a deep understanding of the purpose and requirements of each step of the methodology and can effectively judge when the team has appropriately completed a step. In addition, he or she applies workshop management techniques to address the different ways that a team can fall short of its goals for a step. Making this experience and knowledge explicit and applying it when appropriate using information technology will be a difficult challenge in the foreseeable future.

Improving the Communication of Scenarios

While a paragraph of words can be extremely effective in describing a set of dynamics, for scenarios to be useful in decision making, they require a number of paragraphs, linked, to build a picture of the future that executives will believe is possible and useful in their decision making. To immerse oneself in the scenarios, it takes careful reading of the many pages of the scenarios. For many, that's a chore and not particularly entertaining, particularly if they weren't involved in the development.

The development of videos from scenario scripts is likely to occur more and more because video production costs have come down so much and because it's so much easier to see and understand the scenarios and their differences when seen as videos. In addition, it's much easier to extend the scenarios to other users by getting them to watch the video.

Environmental Analysis System

Perhaps the greatest impact of IT so far has been in environmental analysis, and this is where we also expect significant developments in the future. The amount of information that we're able to acquire almost instantaneously using the Internet and Web search engines has expanded exponentially over the last 10 years. And we can certainly expect to see improvements in this in the future. But the big improvements in the next 10 years are going to come on the analytical side of the system, after information has been gathered and stored. Today, we rely exclusively on humans to make sense of all the data that is being acquired. No tools can replicate the pattern-recognition capabilities of the human brain and the ability to deal with such widely disparate data. We're beginning already to see new tools to assist analysts and decision makers in making sense of the data (see the discussion below about a promising tool being used by the U.S. government), and further out, maybe 10 years, we're going to see tools that spot the patterns and signals like humans.

Structured Evidential Argumentation System (SEAS™)

Successful strategic decision making requires dealing not only with identifying and assessing new signals on a timely basis but also with channeling the signal issues into appropriate response modes such as options initiation, crisis management, and ongoing monitoring. To address the needs for ongoing monitoring in the government-intelligence community, the U.S. Defense Advanced Research Projects Agency (DARPA) sponsored SRI International to develop the Web-based tool SEAS for monitoring of important intelligence topics. SEAS records an analyst's thinking about new intelligence in structured arguments, so that results are easier to understand and compare. SEAS is especially useful for facilitating decisions that must rely on results from complex collaborative-environmental analysis efforts.

SRI developed the initial design of SEAS in 1990 for an oil company to provide early alerts relative to project-management plans for complex oil and gas facilities. SRI later generalized SEAS for DARPA to support crisis warning for national security.

By providing transparent, credible, early alerts to decision makers, SEAS allows effective response to changing situations. In this way, SEAS can enhance environmental monitoring and scenario-planning efforts by leveraging its automated evidence-based reasoning system to integrate large amounts of data and provide clear early conclusions about potential opportunities or risks facing an organization. Because SEAS is Web based, it allows simultaneous access to a broad number of users, thus promoting essential collaboration and peer review. The Web server approach also supports a corporate "knowledge base" from which users can retrieve past analyses and learnings.

How SEAS Works

SEAS is an evidence-based reasoning system, which means that it uses structured arguments or specific lines of reasoning that relate evidence to conclusions. Argument templates provide the structure in the form of a hierarchy of questions for monitoring a topic and developing conclusions. The answers to upper-level questions in the hierarchy derive automatically from the answers to lower-level supporting questions. The questions at the lowest, base level are answered directly by an analyst. The role of the analyst who is building an argument (that is, monitoring a topic) is to answer as many questions as possible and to attach supporting evidence together with a description of rationales for the way the questions were answered (see Figure C-1). SEAS acknowledges that desired information or evidence on a topic is often unavailable and thus does not require all answers before it develops a conclusion. Instead, SEAS continuously updates the current beliefs of the analyst, given the supplied information.

A key feature of the tool is that it presents the answers and conclusions of the argument graphically using a traffic-light metaphor, with a red light indicating a major development, a yellow light indicating some warning signs, and a green light indicating that no problems are evident. Results are readily understandable and are transparent in that warning signals are easy to trace to key evidence.

Another key feature is that SEAS allows representation of numerous inputs and opinions. The evidence used by an analyst to support answers may come from a variety of information sources—such as published articles, Web pages, e-mails, interviews, observations, and another SEAS argument—and can be changing or uncertain. Analysts assess and record the relevance and quality of the data. They may flag newly created evidence to alert other users to new information.

An analyst wanting to share results or collaborate with others uses SEAS access-control features to allow others to alter or just view the argument. When satisfied with an argument and its conclusions, the analyst or group of analysts can publish it to an audience and to the corporate memory. Publishing is an element of control over the argument and guarantees that an argument is always available in an unaltered form.

Advantages of SEAS

One strength of the SEAS tool is that it encourages disciplined, thoughtful, and timely analysis of disparate information by introducing a structure. In addition, SEAS implementation as a Web server enables easy collaboration across the company and leverage of past results and methods. The structured-argumentation methodology stimulates the analyst to consider and monitor the full spectrum of indicators. It also supports the analyst in doing his or her main task: analyzing the evidence and developing conclusions from that

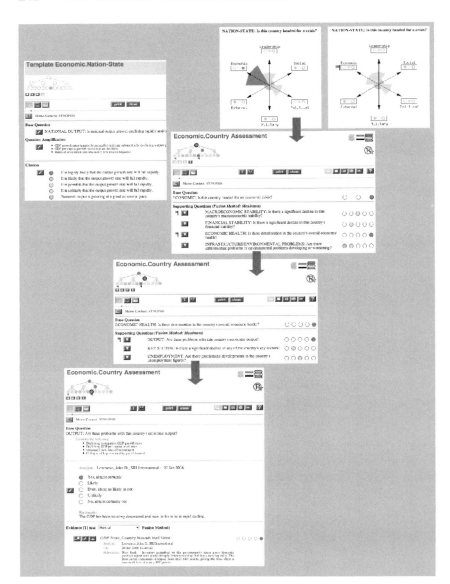

Figure C-1   Example of SEAS Design: Structured Arguments, Templates, and Graphical Depictions of Conclusions

Source: SRI International

evidence. By providing transparent, credible early alerts to decision makers, SEAS allows effective responses to changing situations.

SEAS can also foster strategic alignment. The key to success is for the template architect to spend sufficient time at the beginning to frame the problem correctly and to ask the right questions. The architect needs to break the problem down into a hierarchically structured set of interrelated questions, with the highest-level questions representing the company's strategic focus. The base-level questions to be answered by the analyst should be quantitative and phrased in such a way that two analysts sharing a common understanding of a situation would choose the same answers.

Scan™: Radar for Signals of Change

Successful Process

Probably the best place to start in creating a scanning process is with a successful example, given that scanning is not a traditional and well-established activity for most organizations. One particularly difficult challenge is building a process that can sustain itself for more than one year. As we noted in Chapter 23, Developing a Comprehensive Environmental Analysis Capability, a scanning process by design lacks a focus: It does not know in advance what exactly it is looking for. Consequently, there is no guarantee it will generate results that will influence strategic decision making, although it has the potential of bringing something to the table at any moment that will alter the course of the organization.

SRI Consulting Business Intelligence has been managing a scanning process continuously for over 25 years. Every month it produces over 100 reports of possible discontinuities, innovations, new trends, or things just out of the ordinary in the external environment, analyzes them, and then publishes from four to eight new signals of change that should be of interest to the companies and government organizations that subscribe to SRIC-BI's program.

The Scan™ program did something clever from the beginning. It identified individuals throughout the parent organization who were naturally curious about changes in the external environment and already active in the United States, Europe, and Asia in watching and studying business, technology, social, and political-economic issues and coaxed them to volunteer new and interesting items they came across as part of their work. The program set up a template for describing the new and interesting items and a strong leader who actively recruited inputs from the volunteer network and helped make sense of all the signals each month. Those two elements have been in place ever since and have contributed significantly to the development of a very rich flow of information that has stimulated and influenced individuals and organizations for over 25 years.

What Scan Is Trying to Accomplish

Globalization, privatization, deregulation, competition, and an acceleration of the advances in science and technology all are creating increasingly complex, interdependent, organic systems that demonstrate nonequilibrium dynamics typical of complex ecological systems. Such systems are susceptible to non-linear perturbations that can have far-reaching or even catastrophic effects. The commercial environment is constantly emerging from the interactions of thousands of variables—from market-driven pricing processes to government regulations, from consumer opinion to market competition, from international trade flows to the development of new materials—that defy comprehension, let alone quantitative analysis and prediction. Mark Buchanan, writing in *strategy+business* ("Power Laws & the New Science of Complexity Management"), refers to these new types and levels of risk as interdependent risks. Interdependent risks constitute a form of risk that requires adjustment on the part of managers and planners accustomed to more direct cause-and-effect chains of events.

As complexity increases, successful businesses will be those that turn themselves into adaptive systems that work in an organic manner to find, capture, interpret, and act on cues from an ever-changing environment. Stephan Haeckel, author of *Adaptive Enterprise,* notes, "Where organizations choose to place their sensory probes and how they distinguish signals from random noise determine whether they will be sufficiently aware of what is happening 'out there.'" The marketplace is an ever-changing, turbulent confluence of commercial, societal, and technological factors. The most important tools for remaining afloat in the turbulence are a constant awareness of the changes going on around your organization and the ability to sense, make sense of, and adapt to these changes.

SRIC-BI's Scan process depends heavily on human cognition and pattern-recognition capabilities, group discussion, brainstorming, creativity, ideation, and humor. As Ray Kurzweil points out in his book *The Age of Spiritual Machines,* the bulk of human neural circuitry excels at pattern-recognition functions. The human mind has an enviable capacity to scan the thousands of variables operating in the turbulent marketplace, sort the results, and extract patterns on which to base decisions for future actions. The Scan process provides a framework with which we can regularly and systematically marshal the pattern-recognition capabilities of a group of professionals to identify important changes in the business environment.

The organizations that survive today's marketplace turbulence will be those that can adapt rapidly to change. The organizations that thrive in today's turbulence will be those that live for change, are constantly aware of developments emerging beyond their own particular domain, and recognize oncoming threats in time to turn them into opportunities.

The management literature is replete with admonitions to pay attention not only to competitors but also to external factors, discontinuities, and signals of change. The very title of Andy Grove's (former chairman and CEO of Intel) management book *Only the Paranoid Survive* trumpets the premise that a necessary practice of successful managers is the constant, furtive glance over the shoulder to avoid being blindsided by circumstances or competitors. Dorothy Leonard-Barton, in her book *Wellsprings of Knowledge,* maintains that the most important streams of knowledge for any company are not internal but rather those that flow in from outside the company.

Simple awareness of signals of change is insufficient in and of itself to provide an organization with a competitive edge. A futures orientation among decision makers is necessary to take advantage of foreknowledge of change. Eric D. Beinhocker and Sarah Kaplan talk of creating "prepared minds ... so that executives have a strong grasp of the strategic context they operate in before the unpredictable but inevitable twists and turns of their business push them to make ... critical decisions in real time" ("Tired of Strategic Planning?" *McKinsey Quarterly*).

David Snowden, director of IBM's Cynefin Centre for Organisational Complexity in Cardiff, Wales, advocates a form of what he calls "immunization" against the shocks of a constantly changing business environment. He believes that organizations should regularly expose employees to chaos. The procedure avoids *entrainment of thinking,* a condition in which successful approaches and ideas from the past discourage employees from innovating. The Scan process can provide a quick splash of chaos to employees and managers on a regular basis.

The management literature is short on practical solutions for methodically gleaning early signals of change from the surroundings or for cultivating a futures orientation in employees and managers. The companies that currently incorporate externalities well usually depend on a leader at the top of the corporation who performs the scanning function on a continual basis, has an inherent futures orientation, and imports the knowledge that he or she develops into the decision-making process intuitively. The Scan process is a tool for collecting early signals of change and for nurturing a futures orientation more broadly in an organization.

The Process

The Scan process is, in fact, a continuous loop that repeats endlessly—or certainly has done so for the past 25 years. This description describes a beginning and an endpoint of the process, but the process is in fact continuous, with many parts going on simultaneously and in concert. The constant surveillance on the part of scanners, the rhythm of monthly Scan abstract meetings, and the deadlines of client deliverables (in which Scan findings appear) are part of the normal, continuous cycles of working at SRIC-BI. The process has created an awareness on the part of SRIC-BI employees of the constancy and importance of change in the business environment and the world at large. SRIC-BI employees come to expect the appearance of discontinuities and become familiar with how they play out in a variety of industries and domains. The analysts and researchers learn that change rather than stability is the coin of the commercial realm, and metamorphosis is the common currency.

Key Elements of Scan Process

An overview of the process is shown in Figure D-1. The beginning point to describe the Scan process is the collection of a set of data points from the business, cultural, and technological environments. The data points can be events, developments, opinions, findings, or products that our researchers and analysts believe to be early signals that portend significant changes. Other ways of describing what we're looking for include:

- Signals of change
- Discontinuities

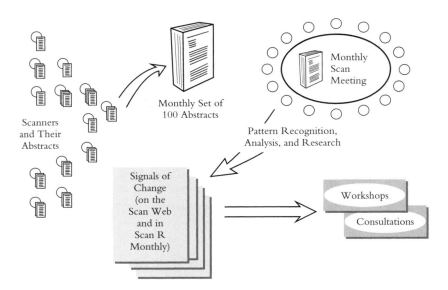

Figure D-1   The Process of Scanning
Source: SRI Consulting Business Intelligence (SRIC-BI)

- Outliers (events or developments that are off the current trend line)
- Items that defy conventional wisdom
- Inflection points
- Disruptive developments or technologies

Our scanners cast their nets broadly to bring in signals of change from various domains, including:

- Politics
- Regulation
- Culture
- Consumer behavior
- Public opinion
- Business processes
- Science
- Technology

The breadth of scope inherent in the diversity of the categories represents one of the most important strengths of the Scan process. The turbulence of the marketplace consists of the confluence of factors from all these categories. And foreseeing the fate of particular products, services, or innovations in the marketplace depends on reading the early signs from and interactions among all these categories (see Figure D-2). Organizations that focus on their own industry and areas of expertise will miss important signs from the broader business, cultural, and technological environments.

Each month SRIC-BI employees enter more than 100 abstracts describing signals of change into an online Scan database. The Web-based entry form

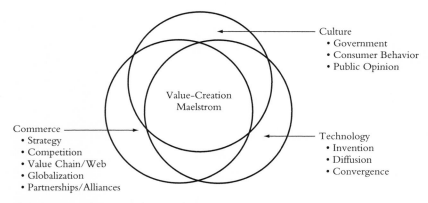

Figure D-2   The Complex Market Environment
Source: SRIC-BI

includes fields to cite the source of the signal, to summarize whatever the abstractor believes is important about the article or event (which may have nothing to do with the original author's premise), and to suggest implications for the business environment. The computer system assigns each abstract a reference number. The database is text searchable, and users can collect individual abstracts from any month into sets of any number of abstracts by date, topic, scanner, or source. At the beginning of each month, the database administrator finalizes the current month's set of abstracts and directs the continuing stream of incoming abstracts to begin the next month's set.

What makes a good Scan abstract? New employees at SRIC-BI generally participate in Scan for six months before managing to submit consistently good Scan abstracts. Developing an intuitive appreciation for unusual patterns and learning to distinguish between truly innovative developments and those simply repackaged by promoters can take a considerable amount of time and discipline. An employee's first submission might concern a new microchip from Intel that is twice as fast as and half the size of its predecessor. But that microchip is directly on the projected development curve of microprocessors. Moore's law predicted that chip 20 years ago—not quite what we're looking for. After six months, the same employee might submit an abstract on the development of a microchip that contains all the software necessary to run a minimal Web server—a much more interesting development in terms of potentially enabling small or portable devices to serve as Web servers.

One recent Scan abstract described how Tetsuya Tada, chief engineer for the development of one of Toyota's recent concept cars, complains that young people today pay more attention to cell phones than to cars. The abstract's implication is that cars compete in the marketplace with cell phones, an apparently absurd assumption given that the prices and functions of the two items are so dramatically different. But if we, just for the moment, entertain the assumption as a possibility, we become aware of the possibility that products in today's highly competitive environment are increasingly competing with products outside their category for the attention of the consumer. In an attention economy, products compete with every other product on the market. If a company wants to attain mind share in a large segment of the consumer market, concentrating on flash instead of function when making technology decisions may be an appropriate strategy. The abstract is valuable because it questions conventional wisdom and broadens the reader's concept of competition beyond the traditional bounds.

Each month's set of 100-plus abstracts serves as the starting point for an open-ended discussion and brainstorming session by analysts, researchers, managers, sales and marketing staff, and consultants. Half of the meetings each year are open to client observation or participation. SRIC-BI's staff in Croydon, England, hold a bimonthly Scan meeting in addition to the monthly meeting at company headquarters in Menlo Park, California.

The meetings consist of two parts. The first part is facilitated rather than led and takes the form of a free-floating discussion of any of the Scan abstracts that participants find provocative, interesting, disturbing, or important. The facilitator discourages judgmental, idea-killing behavior and steers the discussion clear of extended exchanges of opinion or philosophical discussions. Politics and philosophy are definitely fair game, but arguments simply waste the group's time. Frequent calls for new clusters of abstracts or discussion topics are necessary to mine the month's abstracts as thoroughly as possible for signals of change. The facilitator makes certain that the discussion stays reasonably close to the abstract data points in order to make sure that the meeting doesn't degenerate into a discussion unrelated to the marketplace and client needs.

The Scan meeting facilitator urges participants to identify clusters of abstracts. We describe here just two of the countless ways Scan can lead to valuable insights. In the first method, a cluster of several abstracts can characterize a conceptual overlay that a client organization can lift off the Scan data and apply to its own processes, products, or services. This type of clustering allows companies to gain ideas from other industries or product domains. Figure D-3

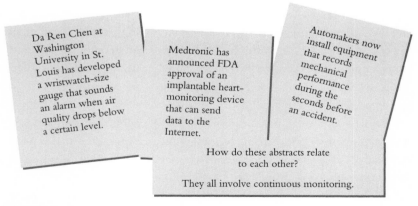

Figure D-3   Conceptual Overlays
Source: SRIC-BI

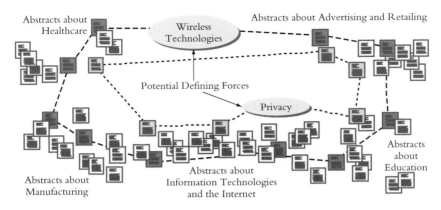

Figure D-4   Defining Forces
Source: SRIC-BI

demonstrates this type of overlay or conceptual pattern. Three abstracts from different areas—air-quality assessment, healthcare, and the auto industry—demonstrate new applications of continuous monitoring. Continuous monitoring, as a concept, is not new of course—thermostats use the basic principle to control the temperature of rooms. But the three abstracts demonstrate how new networking, computing, and sensing technologies are dramatically expanding the capabilities of and domains in which continuous-monitoring concepts can operate. An awareness of such new capabilities will serve as a jumping off point for generating ideas for new technology-based products and services.

The second method operates in a cross-category manner to help Scan researchers identify the defining forces that are operating in the business environment. When abstracts on particular topics (such as wireless technologies or privacy concerns) constitute clusters that cross industry-domain categories (such as health, education, information technology, retailing, and government), the analysts know that the technology or topic will have widespread impact (see Figure D-4).

The second part of the meeting consists of identifying the topics and clusters from among the results of the brainstorming session that bear further analysis and research for potential presentation to client organizations. Participants place the topics on a very rough ranking spectrum between "actionable" and "speculative" simply as a means of preserving a perspective on a time frame for a projected impact.

Clients observing or participating in the Scan meetings for the first time frequently comment on the fact that the meetings are dramatically different from meetings that they typically experience in a corporate setting. The meetings are nonhierarchical because participants know the process works best if everyone values each other's contributions regardless of rank in the organization. The meetings are relatively self-regulating because the participants have sufficient experience to know what kind and what level of discussion and participation are most productive. The meetings include a wide variety of expertise and backgrounds, from technology to specialties in consumer behavior, from engineering to anthropology, and from management to marketing.

Following the Scan meetings, the filtering process that identifies valuable ideas and knowledge for client organizations begins in earnest. The Scan researchers and analysts carefully examine the clusters of abstracts and potential topics that surfaced during the meeting. The analysts compare the new topics and ideas to ones the Scan process has previously identified, and they probe and test the ideas and topics for their substance, plausibility, and potential implications. The analysts finally conduct some quick research to gather more evidence. Particularly time-sensitive topics immediately become Signals-of-Change documents that see circulation to clients within the month. Topics requiring further research or analysis and longer explications become topics for Scan's white papers, which the program calls Insights and which have a longer development and publishing schedule. The program's *Scan™ Monthly* presents six new Signals of Change each month and two in-depth Insights each month.

The Players

Because the program is interested in a wide variety of perspectives in the abstract-collection process and the Scan meeting, it solicits participation from

- Researchers and analysts
- Technology monitors
- Strategy consultants
- Principal consultants
- Marketing and sales staff

SRIC-BI hires from a wide variety of academic and professional backgrounds, including anthropology, business, economics, international affairs, communication arts, marketing, information technology, life sciences, and chemical and electrical engineering. Employees from all levels of the organization, from CEO on down, participate in the process of submitting abstracts and attending Scan abstract meetings. The Scan abstract sets include abstracts from SRIC-BI staff in SRIC-BI's Tokyo, Japan, and Croydon, England, offices, providing a global perspective.

Employees participate primarily on a voluntary basis because creative or proactive thinking is difficult if not impossible to mandate. The Scan program is interested to have people participate who are interested in participating.

Scan experience on the part of participants is highly valuable for the Scan process. Learning what constitutes a good Scan abstract can take six months to a year of attending Scan meetings. Learning to identify truly unique clusters of abstracts can take a year or more. Experience on the part of Scan meeting participants also makes for a smooth meeting, with participants pacing the introduction of new topics themselves rather than depending on the facilitator to set the pace. A consistent set of attendees at Scan meetings also establishes a memory for the meetings so that topics and ideas don't appear repeatedly unless new developments merit a resurfacing of the topic.

The Product

The most important product of the Scan process, either through subscription to Scan or through customized implementation within a company, is an increased awareness on the part of planners, employees, and managers of the importance of a heads-up attitude about the external environment. The likelihood of strategic plans being blindsided by external developments increases every year with the increasing complexity and competition in the business environment. The Scan process provides a language, infrastructure, and mind-set for cultivating a future orientation in any organization. The process also provides a tonic against the entrainment of thinking that we talked of earlier.

In order to "distribute" a future orientation throughout client companies, Scan offers clients both push and pull distribution mechanisms. A pull mechanism, in which employees in the client company can pull content from the Scan Web site as the need arises, is a necessity in today's fast-paced environment. To meet this need, the searchable Scan archive is available 24-7 to researchers and clients. A push mechanism, in which the Scan program pushes content into distribution within the client company, is necessary because the topics and questions that Scan regularly surfaces are not typically on the radar screen or agenda of client companies. The *Scan™ Monthly* serves the push function by highlighting six new Signals of Change each month that have come out of the latest Scan meeting and announcing the availability of two new Insight documents that further explore the implications of previous signals of change. Each month's Signals of Change are also available to subscribing clients in HTML format on the Scan Web site. Recent Signals of Change include:

- Creativity Services
- The Body Electric
- Sensation-al Design
- A New Species in Telecom
- The Malleability of Aging
- Biotech Ontologies and the Semantic Web
- The Irrational Consumer
- The Art and Science of Sound
- The Emerging Digital-Media Landscape
- Petsumerism
- The Instant Economy
- The Human Environome
- Emotions, Faces, and Robots
- Integral Medicine
- Automating Research
- The United States of Asia
- Elderly Assumptions
- E-Commerce Ecosystems

Hurdles to Success

Part of SRIC-BI's experience consists of an awareness of the hurdles companies typically face in attempting to implement the Scan process internally. Hurdles include:

- *Hierarchical meetings.* The presence of a senior manager can inhibit the discussion and stifle innovative ideas and input. Junior employees don't want to risk looking bad. Senior managers must understand their role (refraining from normal decision making, judgmental behavior patterns), and junior staff must feel comfortable in expressing themselves.
- *Accountantitis.* Given the opportunity, the accountants will want immediate documentation of a return on investment for the cost of the meetings.
- *Premature evaluation.* The Scan process benefits from experienced participants, so the early meetings can seem ambiguous, unfocused, and unproductive.

- *Naysayers.* The Scan process is particularly susceptible to tunnel-visioned naysayers who focus on this quarter's earnings. One naysayer can deflate an entire room of energized, creative, innovators. Selection of appropriate personality types for participation in the process is the most important success factor in implementing a Scan process.
- *Low priority.* To sustain the process beyond six months requires a strong commitment from the organization to make the process work and to use the results in planning and decision making.

Benefits to Clients

Although the Scan process serves most effectively as an early warning system, clients have found it helpful in other ways. Among the uses are as a form of peripheral vision (to avoid being blindsided by events outside one's industry), as an input to innovation processes, as a strategic stimulant, as a strategic irritant, and as a means of questioning the conventional wisdom or complacency within an organization.

Through the years, Scan has played an essential role in our clients' foresight capabilities by providing a systematic means for surveying the broad external environment for change vectors. Traditional monitoring processes in most organizations are largely arbitrary, depending on what concerned individuals in the organization are reading, thinking about, and sharing informally with each other. But in today's world, *arbitrary* is insufficient. No foresight function can operate with confidence without a disciplined process for spotting new patterns of change and bringing those issues into the organization for early consideration and action.

BIBLIOGRAPHY

Allison, Graham, and Philip Zelikow. *Essence of Decision: Explaining the Cuban Missile Crisis.* 2d. ed. New York: Longman, 1999.

Beinhocker, Eric D. "Strategy at the Edge of Chaos." *The McKinsey Quarterly,* 1997 Number 1: 24–39.

Bonabeau, Eric. "Don't Trust Your Gut." *Harvard Business Review* (May 2003): 116–123.

Brassard, Michael. *The Memory Jogger Plus+.* Revised edition. Methuen, MA: GOAL/QPC, 1996.

Brown, Shona L., and Kathleen M. Eisenhardt. *Competing on the Edge: Strategy as Structured Chaos.* Boston, MA: Harvard Business School Press, 1998.

Courtney, Hugh. *20/20 Foresight: Crafting Strategy in an Uncertain World.* Boston, MA: Harvard Business School Press, 2001.

Coutu, Diane L. "Sense and Reliability: A Conversation with Celebrated Psychologist Karl E. Weick." *Harvard Business Review* (April 2003): 85–90.

Cross, Robert L., and Susan E. Brodt. "How Assumptions of Consensus Undermine Decision Making." *MIT Sloan Management Review* (Winter 2001): 86–94.

Davis, Ged. "Scenarios as a Tool for the 21st Century." Paper prepared for the Probing the Future Conference, Strathclyde University, July 2002.

De Geus, Arie. *The Living Company.* Boston, MA: Harvard Business School Press, 1997.

Fahey, Liam, and Robert M. Randall, eds. *Learning from the Future: Competitive Foresight Scenarios.* New York: John Wiley & Sons, 1998.

Godet, Michel. *Scenarios and Strategic Management.* London, UK: Buttersworth Scientific, 1987.

Haeckel, Stephan H. *Adaptive Enterprise: Creating and Leading Sense-and-Respond Organizations.* Boston, MA: Harvard Business School Press, 1999.

Heuer, Richards J., Jr. *Psychology of Intelligence Analysis.* Washington, D.C.: Central Intelligence Agency, 1999.

Kleiner, Art. *The Age of Heretics: Heroes, Outlaws, and the Forerunners of Corporate Change.* New York: Doubleday, 1996.

Liedtka, Jeanne M. "Linking Strategic Thinking with Strategic Planning." *Strategy & Leadership* (September/October 1998): 30–35.

Mandel, Thomas F. "Scenarios and Corporate Strategy: Planning in Uncertain Times." First published by the Business Intelligence Program, SRI International, Menlo Park, CA, November, 1982.

Mandel, Thomas F., Bruce H. MacEvoy, and Ian H. Wilson. "Trends and Uncertainties in the American Consumer Environment: Values and Lifestyles Scenarios in the Year 2000." Published by the VALS™ Program of SRI International, Menlo Park, CA, October 1989.

Miller, William C. *The Creative Edge: Fostering Innovation Where You Work.* Reading, MA: Addison-Wesley Publishing, 1987.

Pearson, Andrall E. "Tough-Minded Ways to Get Innovative." *Harvard Business Review* (August 2002): 117–124.

Randall, Robert M., ed. "Decision-Driven Scenarios of the Near Future." Strategy & Leadership Volume 31, Number 1 (2003).

Randall, Robert M., ed. "Integrating Scenario Learning with Decision Making." Strategy & Leadership Volume 31, Number 2 (2003).

Ringland, Gill. *Scenario Planning: Managing for the Future*. Chichester, UK: John Wiley & Sons, 1998.

Roberts, John. *The Modern Firm*. New York: Oxford University Press, 2004.

Schoemaker, Paul J. H. *Profiting from Uncertainty: Strategies for Succeeding No Matter What the Future Brings*. New York: The Free Press, 2002.

Schwartz, Peter. *The Art of the Long View: Planning for the Future in an Uncertain World*. New York: Currency Doubleday, 1991.

Smith, Douglas K. *Taking Charge of Change: 10 Principles for Managing People and Performance*. Reading, MA: Addison-Wesley Publishing, 1996.

Stokke, Per R., Thomas A. Boyce, William K. Ralston, and Ian H. Wilson. "Scenario Planning for Norwegian Oil and Gas." *Long Range Planning* 23 (1990): 17–26.

————. "Visioning (and Preparing for) the Future: The Introduction of Scenarios-Based Planning into Statoil." *Technological Forecasting and Social Change* 40 (1991): 73–86.

"Storytelling that Moves People: A Conversation with Screenwriting Coach Robert McKee." *Harvard Business Review* (June 2003): 5–8.

Strategy & Leadership has traced the evolution of the use of scenarios in planning, including two consecutive issues devoted exclusively to this subject: "Decision-Driven Scenarios of the Near Future," Volume 31, Number 1, 2003; and "Integrating Scenario Learning with Decision Making," Volume 31, Number 2, 2003.

Sullivan, Gordon R., and Michael V. Harper. *Hope Is Not a Method: What Business Leaders Can Learn from America's Army*. New York: Times Books, 1996.

Sutcliffe, Kathleen M., and Klaus Weber. "The High Cost of Accurate Knowledge." *Harvard Business Review* (May 2003): 74–82.

Van der Heijden, Kees. *Scenarios: The Art of Strategic Conversation*. Chichester, UK: John Wiley & Sons: 1996.

————, Ron Bradfield, George Burt, George Cairns, and George Wright. *The Sixth Sense: Accelerating Organizational Learning with Scenarios*. Chichester, UK: John Wiley & Sons, 2002.

Wack, Pierre A. "Scenarios: The Gentle Art of Re-Perceiving: One Thing or Two Learned While Developing Planning Scenarios for Royal Dutch/Shell" Working Paper, Division of Research, Harvard Business School, 1984.

————. "Scenarios: Uncharted Waters Ahead." *Harvard Business Review* 63, No. 5 (1985): 72–79.

————. "Scenarios: Shooting the Rapids." *Harvard Business Review* 63, No. 6 (1985): 139–150.

INDEX

Note: Page numbers in *italic* type indicate figures or boxes.

V

Van der Veer, Jeroen, 179
Videos of scenarios, 133, 202

W

Wack, Pierre, 6, 17, 42, 47, 109, 111,
    119–120, 201, 205
War room approach, 201–202
Weick, Karl E., 142
Welch, Jack, 203
"What if . . . " thinking. *See* Contingency
    planning
Wild cards, 112
Workshops
    axes of uncertainty development in,
        114–115

as communication tool, 201
facilitators for, 65–68
focused research presentation
    in, 100
initial, 81
management of, 60–62
modeling external environment in,
    90–92
off-site location of, 62
for rehearsals of future, 143–148
scenario selection in, 123–124
value of, 59
Writing scenarios. *See* Scenario
    composition
Written case for scenario
    planning, 43

Library of Congress Cataloging-in-Publication Data

Ralston, Bill.
    The scenario-planning handbook : a practitioner's guide to developing
and using scenarios to direct strategy in today's uncertain times / Bill Ralston
and Ian Wilson.
        p. cm.
    ISBN 0-324-31285-7
    1. Strategic planning.   2. Business planning.   3. Organizational change—
Management.   I. Wilson, Ian, 1925 June 16- II. Title.
    HD30.28.R348 2006
    658.4'012—dc22
                                                                        2006016453